D1213286

WHY WAR?

PHILIP SMITH

WHY WAR?

THE CULTURAL LOGIC OF IRAQ, THE GULF WAR, AND SUEZ

THE UNIVERSITY OF CHICAGO PRESS · CHICAGO AND LONDON

Philip Smith is assistant professor of sociology and deputy director of the Yale Center for Cultural Sociology. He is the author or coauthor of several books, including the widely praised *Cultural Theory: An Introduction*.

The University of Chicago Press, Chicago 60637
The University of Chicago Press, Ltd., London
© 2005 by The University of Chicago
All rights reserved. Published 2005

Printed in the United States of America

14 13 12 11 10 09 08 07 06 05   1 2 3 4 5

ISBN: 0-226-76388-9 (cloth)

Library of Congress Cataloging-in-Publication Data

Smith, Philip (Philip Daniel), 1964–
    Why war? : the cultural logic of Iraq, the Gulf War, and Suez / Philip Smith.
        p.   cm.
    Includes bibliographical references and index.
    ISBN 0-226-76388-9 (cloth : alk. paper)
    1. War and society. 2. War (Philosophy). 3. Political aspects. 4. Culture conflict.
    5. Iraw War, 2003—Social aspects. 6. Persian Gulf War, 1991—Social aspects.
    7. Egypt—History—Intervention, 1956. I. Title.

    HM554.S64   2006
    303.6'6—dc22   2005011958

♾ The paper used in this publication meets the minimum requirements of the American National Standard for Information Sciences—Permanence of Paper for Printed Library Materials, ANSI Z39.48-1992.

This book is dedicated to my parents, Raymond and Valerie Smith. I have often heard their own, more personal stories of "the war" and learned in this way something of the meanings of both war and peace.

CONTENTS

ACKNOWLEDGMENTS

This book was written and researched while I had institutional affiliations at various locations: the sociology department at the University of California, Los Angeles; the Juan March Institute in Madrid; the School of Social Science at the University of Queensland, Australia; and the Department of Sociology at Yale. Sections of this work were enabled by fellowship support from the Del Amo Foundation and the University of California. A good deal of time was spent collecting and analyzing data in the microform reading room at UCLA, the Sterling Memorial Library at Yale, and the library of the British Consulate in Madrid. Along the way comments, challenges, and other feedback on written material were received from John Heritage, Ron Jacobs, Elizabeth Long, Michael Mann, Jeff Prager, Bess Rothenberg, Ivan Szelenyi, Eugene Weber, Michael Wood, and the various members of the UCLA Culture Club. There have also been more diffuse inputs en route from diverse friends and colleagues too numerous to name individually. The entire manuscript was read by Jeff Alexander, Wendy Griswold, Barry Schwartz, and Steve Sherwood. I am especially grateful to Barry for his long and eloquent challenges that forced clarifications and intensifications of my arguments even if we could not come to any final agreement on the limits to constructivism. Many enjoyable conversations with Edmond Wright assisted my understandings of the relationship between perception, knowledge, and storytelling and have shaped this book in subtle ways. Particular recognition is due to Doug Mitchell as a consummate editor and for demonstrating that the leap of faith is not simply a metaphysical concept. Dawn Hall assisted the metamorphosis from typescript to book with efficiency and an eye to detail. My thanks are expressed to all the above.

A major intellectual debt needs to be acknowledged to Jeff Alexander and Steve Sherwood. The analytic frame used in this book originated with Jeff's neo-Durkheimian work of the mid-1980s. It was then systematically elaborated and extended in a narrative direction by the three of us in the period from 1988 to 1993 at UCLA. This was very much a collective exercise in theory construction. Ron Jacobs and Agnes Ku added valuable refinements to the model that I have drawn upon (see endnote 1, chapter one). Jeff Alexander should be further thanked not only for his ongoing intellectual generosity but also for his relentless and insistent motivational inputs on this project. At various points my partner Philippa Smith provided financial, logistical, and emotional support, research assistance (especially for chapter five), and expert editorial labor.

It is in conducting the affairs of civil society, that mankind find the exercise of their best talents, as well as the object of their best affections. It is in being grafted on the advantages of civil society, that the art of war is brought to perfection; that the resources of armies, and the complicated springs to be touched in their conduct are best understood. ADAM FERGUSON

ONE

WHY WAR?

Theorizing the Role of Culture and Civil Discourse

"Why War?" was the question that launched a celebrated correspondence between Albert Einstein and Sigmund Freud (1939). Although those two great thinkers could not agree on a definitive answer, today there does seem to be a broad consensus. Popular beliefs and academic theories alike point overwhelmingly to the machinations and interests of elites and the struggle for power and security within and among nations. If not exactly false in any simple way, such a vision is nevertheless narrow and misleading. This book sketches out an alternative answer to the "Why War?" query—one that illuminates the role of culture and deliberative democracy. In a series of matched case studies it will show that codes defining the sacred and profane in social life and a limited pool of narrative structures within a civil discourse form the cultural bedrock upon which military policy is made legitimate and thinkable. Working in combination with material forces and instrumental actions these allow for violent interventions to be made and for human lives to be acceptably risked and sacrificed. Contingent and negotiated in the cut and thrust of debates but also robust and determining in their effects, such cultural structures persist over time and transcend national boundaries. By decoding their elementary grammar we can come to understand why we get that feeling of déjà vu as the same hands are dealt time and time again in the cultural politics of debate over war, why some wars are seen as deeply problematic and others as broadly legitimate, how heroes are made and heads roll. We will see that military and political policy is constrained by ideal determinants and that decision makers can be held accountable to the myths that they themselves have spun. By the end we will understand that war is not just about culture, but it is all about culture.

THE REDUCTION OF THE REALISMS

Within the social sciences there is a general tendency to understand any violent conflict as the product and process of struggles for dominance. We are told that actors and agents, be they individuals beating their spouses, classes engaged in revolution, or states invading their neighbors, are all looking to maximize their power. No matter that passions are apparently involved or justifications repeatedly—some would say ritualistically—invoked. This is just talk. Fights are "really" all about something else, such as capturing scarce resources, controlling the bureaucratic apparatus, or establishing imperial dominion. People want to be in control of others and to be free of the control of others. This is the logic of so-called conflict sociology with its dismissive orientation toward cultural explanation and its crabs-in-a-bucket view of social life. It is a tradition that can be traced from Karl Marx through Max Weber and on to their contemporary acolytes such as Michael Mann and Charles Tilly. Such influential figures understand culture largely as a form of "ideological power" (Mann 1986) that at best has the ability to mobilize an underlying constituency sharing some common structural location and consequent agenda.

The vision of an endless, strategic, self-interested quest to dominate, of a grim world where there are weak or dependent cultural constraints upon and motivations for violent and power-seeking activity seems to be deeply entrenched in Western culture. It can be traced like a Roman road cutting straight and true through the heart of political science theorizing on war over the centuries. In his *History of the Peloponnesian War,* the ancient Greek writer Thucydides depicted a brutal, anarchic struggle for power and survival in which the strong did as much as they could to subjugate and exploit those who were weaker. Nearly two millennia later, Thomas Hobbes was to famously speak in *Leviathan* of a "warre as is of every man, against every man" as the original human condition in which domination through force and efforts to avoid the power of others were the prime drivers of social life. From Machiavelli and Karl von Clausewitz and on to twentieth-century scholars like Hans Morgenthau (1985) and Kenneth Waltz (1979), from the "classical realist" and "realist" and "neorealist" and "structural realist" paradigms and the more recent mathematical contributions of game theory, through all these we can map the genealogy of the idea of the rational, selfish war. The entire disciplines of international relations and security studies are founded on this tradition and its imagery of agents (usually but not always sovereign states) in an anarchic system looking for power and control in situations of uncertainty by violently pursuing their interests, constrained only by their resources and the relative strength of others in the field. Put simply, the story they tell is that wars happen when states calculate that the likely net profits to combat will exceed the likely net loss. The rest is just detail.

The more influential recent work on conflict in the international relations field can be understood in just this way. It has tinkered in innovative ways with the detail while retaining core beliefs. Consider the much-vaunted "corrective" to realism from neoliberal institutionalism (e.g., Axelrod and Keohane 1985; Keohane 1984). It accepts the proposition that states and other agents are conscious, goal directed, maximizing actors, but places more faith in the ability of international and cross-national institutions to ameliorate and contain the strains associated with anarchy. This is not a warm and cheery invocation of the brotherhood of man and the emergence of a global human solidarity. The point is that legal and institutional agreements between states can subtly shift the distribution of rewards and costs toward cooperation and so head off war. They can do this by making cheating harder (e.g., arms inspections); allowing or threatening defensive coalition formation; generating iterative transaction environments where current gains to violence need to be offset against potentially greater future gains to peace and where players can be rewarded for good faith; and by allowing information sharing about the relative strength and relative gains of other states to head off the poisonous effects of the prisoner's dilemma. So here again is a theory that places power and a narrow calculative reason center stage and pushes the normative drivers of action into the wings. Likewise, efforts to argue that we should look for the origins of war *within* rather than between states fail to get us very far in our search for cultural explanation. The quest for lebensraum of a growing population, the death of a king, the desire of a leader to garner popular approval or paper over domestic divisions, the need for the military to justify its budget and so forth—on close inspection these are yet more environmental conditions that can tip the actuarial balance as the costs and benefits of a war are weighed by decision makers inside and outside a given nation (see Blainey 1988).

If dominant understandings of the *causes* of war in sociology and political science can be summed up in sentences containing various combinations of words like threat, gain, power, strategy, security, or ingenious permutations of the mathematical ciphers that stand in their place, it is hardly surprising to find that models of the *conduct* of war and military life are similarly bereft of a cultural moment. Military action is taken as a paradigm exemplar of what efficient, goal directed but ultimately meaningless collective social action looks like under the condition of modernity. Clausewitz (1968) acknowledged the role of feelings in war, but believed these to be subordinated to "the importance and duration of the interests involved" and to have been replaced over history by a cooler 'understanding' among civilized people (1968, 4). He famously likened war to a duel or combat between two wrestlers wherein "each strives by physical force to compel the other to submit to his will" (1968, 1). Whereas Roland Barthes (1973) helpfully interpreted wrestling as a communicative semiotic system involving stylized characters and demonstrative gestures directed toward an overlooking audience of noncombatants, Clausewitz's vision is of a one-dimensional struggle for supremacy. Hence the majority of his text is taken up with a discussion of the tactics, strategies, and logistics of war—in effect with the instrumental means to material domination over the opposing hostile party. In a related spirit Michel Foucault (1975) saw the military as a lead institution in the emergence of a "disciplinary" society. It has helped blaze the trail from a medieval order characterized by colorful symbolism and eruptions of the sacred, toward a world where institutions, bodies, and technologies are tied together in a passionless structure of coordination and control. Likewise, within the academically routinized field of "conflict sociology" in our era, a pervasive belief in the rationalization and bureaucratization of society described by Weber has been fused to the image of war today as the ugly child of realpolitik and industrial society. Now the playing out of violence becomes a question of coordination, mobilization, and production accountable only to the gods of organizational efficiency, not an activity that has a performative dimension or that is answerable to deeply meaningful symbolic codes. Discipline, mass production, and war are not only linked to each other but also explicitly opposed to earlier, more spiritually motivated forms of social life (Weber 1978, 1148–55). The result is a bleak vision.

> War in our time is a war of machines and this makes centralized provisioning technically necessary, just as the dominance of the machine in industry promotes the concentration of the means of production and management. . . . Only the bureaucratic army structure allows for the development of the professional standing armies which are necessary for the constant pacification of large territories as well as for warfare against distant enemies, especially enemies overseas. Further, military discipline and technical training can normally be fully developed, at least to its modern high level, only in the bureaucratic army. (Weber 1978, 981)

For all its dominance the account of war's origins and conduct given in this rationalist über-paradigm is seriously flawed. The "state" tends to be reified and hypostasized. Yet if concrete decision making is introduced as a variable, this autonomy of action seems to be confined to political and military elites—those who have their hands on the diplomatic bags and the keys to the war room in their pockets (Salmon 1992, 9). There is little or no understanding of the complexity of policy formation, the fact that within democracies wars are intensely debated and scrutinized by audiences and that the state and its political leaders need continuously to seek support from an often-skeptical civil society. Issues of perception are also curiously neglected. Threats in the anarchic interstate system, for example, are generally treated as if they could speak for themselves plus or minus an error term for information reliability. Their quality and quantity is seemingly so self-evident that it is assumed they can be fed raw into the calculative machinery of the Babbage Difference Engines of rational policy formation. There is little effort to theorize how cultural bias might influence evaluations of "risk" or "anarchy" (Wendt 1992, 1999), and no sustained attempt to interpret wars as patterned meaningful activity, to understand how their legitimacy in contemporary democracy hinges on more than simply fidelity to the national interest or to the black letter strictures of domestic constitutions and international laws.

In opposition to this hegemonic position the argument of this book is that we need to decode the ways in which constituencies and players make sense of wars and the situations that might lead to them. This entails investigating how culture frames "right" and "wrong," risk perceptions, and divergent determinations of every "national interest." Yet when we look to the scattered alternative, more meaning-centered theories of war that are currently available, these do not help us a great deal in our task. It seems that one reason for the dominance of rationalist theoretical positions has been the relatively unattractive and implausible quality of opposing proposals that ground their interpretive challenge in theories of mind rather than symbolically mediated communicative activity. The most developed tradition, originating with ancient Greek ideas about the passions as drivers of action, subsequently reflected in Christian doctrines about innate evil and finding a more recent home in the search for a "moral equivalent to war" of William James (1910), is one that points to the pivotal role of inescapable psychological forces and primal emotions in the urge to fight. Specifications of this position have frequently evoked evolutionary codes or subconscious drives, such as Freud's musings on the "death instinct," in an effort to explain overtly affect-laden responses to threats and violence. The problems with such formulations are endemic to studies in the area of collective psychology. If wars are all about our simian rage, gonad-driven hatred, and unchecked or desperately rechanneled instincts, then how are we to account for the relatively disciplined and methodical nature of military conduct? What exactly are the mechanisms that translate diffuse prejudices, drives, and emotions into more precise institutional realities and policies? Why is there such a huge disconnect between the feverish workings of the irrational mind and the more refined language games through which orthodox political debate, diplomacy, and public deliberation are conducted?

What we might recognize as less psychologically reductive efforts to show that war is meaningful have fared little better. When Margaret Mead (1964) suggested that war was a "human invention" and Bronislaw Malinowski (1964) that it arose from a clash of cultures in a context of diffusion and expansion, the anthropological bent of such thinkers led them to see culture as an entire way of life, rather than as a code or text. The result was an approach that could only take us away from meaning. Hence, subsequent efforts were made to explain wars in terms of comparative civilization—a turn that led explanation toward discussions of institutional complexity, stratification, and morphology and which inevitably linked up with understandings of war as a cause and consequence of human (Storr 1968) or societal (Andreski 1971) evolution. The anticultural momentum in such perspectives reached an early apotheosis in Quincy Wright's (1942) somewhat deterministic models correlating wars with disequilibrium in social development, and in sociobiological accounts. The latter seized upon the idea that evolution and struggle were inextricably linked and so came to exhibit a striking resemblance to realist political science, insisting that wars were all about territory, dominance, and competition (Tiger 1984). Here is a path that has only brought us back to our point of departure, with war now described as a "rational" evolutionary strategy.

Perhaps more successful for thinking about meaning systems and wars have been efforts from within the peace studies field to uncover the cultural foundations of conflict through the analysis of media reporting, cartoon imagery, and political language as well as the investigation of popular attitudes toward violence and the Other (e.g., Aubrey 1982; Dennis et al. 1991; Dower 1986; Medhurst 1990). These have had the benefit of contemporary cultural theory and often make sophisticated interpretations of cultural frames and packages. The cumulative effect has been to unmask ideological complexes such as militarism, racism, imperialism, technocratic outlooks, Orientalism, and xenophobia that make war possible. Such work is important because it has laid down a formidable challenge to the idea that war is simply a question of machines and rationality.

And yet a raft of problems remains. The first can be seen in the manner in which the peace studies literature combines normative and evaluative criteria too tightly with the analytic. It has close historical ties to the Wilsonian idealism that emerged at the end of the Great War, the antinuclearism of the cold war and more recently the agendas of NGOs (nongovernmental organizations) and new social movements. It has been further knotted to the practical themes of peace building, conflict resolution, and social justice. The result has been a discourse of advocacy from which there is no clear pathway to value-neutral social science. The second problem we find in this culturally sensitive strand of the peace studies literature is that it tends to focus on documenting and denouncing longstanding structures of meaning that we might think of as predisposing factors to war: Britain is imperialist, France racist, the United States has a militarized popular culture, and so forth. This leads to a conundrum in explaining why nations can switch into and out of wars or why they might fight some countries and not others at a given point in time. Persistent ideologies can best explain consistent national behaviors, not the nitty-gritty of policy formation and policy flexibility at more contingent levels. If America has always been racist, imperialist, or Orientalist, how come it was hostile to Iran and not Iraq as well during the 1980s? In the American imaginary are not both Iraq and Iran full of untrustworthy, anti-American fanatics? Within the framework of peace studies, answers to such questions of contingent policy usually involve recourse of other, noncultural factors, such as national interests and realpolitik. For example, it has been said that during the 1980s America needed a strong Iraq in the Middle East. Now we are back where we started with the noncultural trumping the symbolic. A third limitation of this field is that it works toward the decoding or interpretation of particulars rather than pushing for a general theory. By looking to the peace studies literature we can learn a good deal about the negative imagery of the Soviet Union in Reagan's America or the media briefing strategies of the Gulf War, but it is far from clear whether such scattered, ideographic insights into culturally encoded information—or "frames"—can mount a sustained campaign against the big-picture rationalist explanation of military conflict. Attacks on this or that intellectual target in the name of meaning have nuisance value but do not amount to a full frontal assault. The fragmentary nature of frame analysis permits only guerrilla warfare against the dominant paradigm. For cultural explanation to have an impact, what is required is some heavy artillery, not yet more scattered sniping. We require a systematic and universally applicable model of culture and war—one that can be connected more easily to positivistic ideologies and the ambitions of general theory.

Even if such a model were at hand for peace studies there would remain the problem of cultural autonomy. Because the critical cultural theory that it draws upon tends to anchor cultural forms in institutional or political interests, we end up with a close coupling of ideal systems to social structures. Once ideas about imperialism, militarism, and so forth are tied to hegemonic process or political ambition it is difficult to theorize how these idea-bundles might be independent from power or exert a constraint on their own masters. We have turned to the realm of ideology and false consciousness and away from a strong cultural explanation. A final question mark hanging over this literature relates to the limited fit between the language games of legitimate public discourse about war and the nasty ideological complexes of the kind usually identified by peace studies scholars such as racism, imperialism, and militarism. Martin Shaw (1991) has identified contemporary Western societies as increasingly "post-military." They are a realm in which war has become justifiable only as a last resort, in which militarism is viewed with a certain measure of suspicion, and where military activity is often subject to close scrutiny in the media and popular opinion. True enough, in the nineteenth-century epoch of high militarism even blatantly expansionist conflicts could be justified with cheery reference to imperial grandeur and the white man's burden. In the aftermath of World War I it required considerably greater effort to mobilize opinion in support of war—and it still does today (Fussell 1975). The old justifications have become tarnished and are illegitimate coin in public discourse.

No doubt we still live in a society that is in many ways racist and imperialist. It is important for interpretative work to continue to focus on what is present but not spoken, on the lies and half-truths, and on the furtive backgrounds of prejudice that form a powerful part of the cultural landscape of international relations. But at the same time we need to recognize that these cultural traits can no longer be so easily and openly assimilated into the more universalistic language games of contemporary public discourse and opinion formation. War today is relentlessly scrutinized, debated, and motivated with reference to the universalistic yardstick themes of justice, freedom, and democracy. We have equal need to understand this "foreground" of culture during war, looking to the said as to the unsaid. This means taking seriously the speech acts through which legitimating public discourses and claims are structured—both for and against war—rather than dismissing these as window dressing. This is not being naive and taking people at their word. It is, rather, about working through the cultural logic behind their utterances and reconstructing the cultural systems through which their claims make sense to others. This is the explication not of an underlying ideological complex, but rather of visible public codes.

There is a pressing need to understand the cultural foundations for war as entrenched, not only in atavistic prejudice and false consciousness but also in an arena of open public debate oriented toward norms of rationality and universalism. This discursive activity involves both claims-making activity revolving around the presentation of "good reasons" and the scrutiny of these claims by others. It is an inherently dialogic process mobilizing and deploying symbol systems that provide cognitive and moral guidance in the interpretation of complex and unfolding crisis situations. The legitimacy of wars, political actors, and policies comes up for grabs in such a process of opinion formation through public intercourse, critique, and efforts at persuasion. By conferring or withdrawing legitimacy, public discourse operates to make the option of war more or less attractive for administrations. Alignments with cultural systems open up and shut down lines of policy as viable options, garner support for some initiatives, and make others hard to sell. In this way we can think of culture as a contributory if not sufficient cause for war. Fighting without the correct cultural systems in place is like driving with the parking brake on. It can be done but it is rarely a good idea. Sooner or later there are clouds of smoke and then wheels fall off. Likewise a war without a cultural mandate is hard work: It drains morale, sometimes secrecy is required that limits effectiveness, there is dissent, parliaments become noisy and editorials shrill, budgets are hard to justify, and deaths even more so. These kinds of wars almost invariably lead to a change of government. Our political leaders know this. That is why they work so relentlessly to establish cultural foundations for conflict before the bullets start flying.

THE ROLE OF CIVIL SOCIETY AND CIVIL DISCOURSE IN WAR

How might we connect a public discourse about war to the social structure in such a way that all this front stage talk can be seen to be more than hot air and well-chosen rhetoric? To answer this question we need to start by moving away from the state-centered model of realist political science toward an understanding of society as comprised of multiple, differentiated, reciprocally influencing arenas of activity (Luhmann 1982; Parsons 1964). Civil society is one such sphere, and indeed in modern social structures it provides the critical venue in which issues of public legitimacy are played out and leverage exerted (Cohen and Arato 1992; Keane 1988). More precisely it can be conceptualized as an autonomous realm of institutions, sentiments, and public debate and discourse directed toward the "moral regulation of social life" (Alexander and Smith 1993, 161). This regulatory activity is facilitated by cultural resources. The codes and narratives of civil discourse are the symbolic media through which the myriad details, complexities, and uncertainties of real world events are simplified and converted into useable information with a normative and programmatic valence (Luhmann 1982, 166ff.). This information shapes public opinions and generates action consequences such as voting behavior, acquiescence or dissent, consent or its withdrawal, trust or suspicion, the exertion of influence and good will, political lobbying and public demonstrations. Civil society, then, is a kind of dialogical hydraulics squeezing together events, meanings, and evaluative criteria, such that intense pressures eventuate on those who are perceived as violating normative prescriptions. It is thanks in part to the power of this collective interpretive system that we have seen institutions, roles, discourse spaces, and activities emerge over the past two or three centuries dedicated to both the reading of events and the attempt to shape fungible opinions. Specialization among politicians, journalists, and intellectuals has taken place with some becoming the virtuosi who elucidate the world for others. Speech genres like the op-ed and the parliamentary question, the letters page, reportage, the presidential address to the nation, and the street march can be understood as adaptive responses to and expressions of the emergence of a civil sphere and its increasing political influence. This is the discourse of persons speaking not so much to each other in the concrete but rather to a generalized, overhearing Other who accumulates and assesses not only "good reasons" but also as we will see "good interpretations."

Our model of a policy regulating civil discourse that is much to be feared by powerful and powerless alike needs to be insulated from the charge of idealism. So let us back-peddle a little and insert here the usual disclaimers. The outputs of civil society should, of course, be understood as aggregate responses that are influenced by factors such as resources and interests as well as by more authentic phenomenological and cultural inputs relating to moral and cognitive universes. Those who control the means of communication or who represent dominant constituencies, for example, are likely to be relatively advantaged. Differing groups within and outside civil society can sometimes have deeply incompatible perspectives, aims, and ambitions such that civil debate more closely resembles a cultural battleground than a solidaristic sphere. Individuals and interests may act for cynical reasons in advancing their claims and promoting their particularistic ambitions. Sincerity, however, is not the issue because—and this is a crucial point—in order for claims to be effective they must be couched in terms of the shared codes of civil society. Regardless of intent there is a need to present to others a compelling interpretation of events. Civil society is the location of struggles over meaning, not a shared moral and affective community in any *gemeinschaftlich* sense. Yet it has given birth not to Babel but to an agonistic politics with a center of discursive gravity. Agents relentlessly struggle for the moral and interpretive high ground, and they cannot achieve this objective by speaking in their own, more particularistic terms or by using their own veiled cultural codes and local idioms. To take this strategy is to risk being ignored by others, or perhaps worse, to be incomprehensible to them even if this option brings the easy gratifications of preaching to the converted. Efforts at a more active persuasion, justification, and proselytism require social actors to fix meanings for multiple audiences by using the lingua franca of the public sphere. When it comes to building a cultural platform for or against any given war this is the common arena, the institutional sand pit in which all must play, no matter how strong their material interests and instrumentally driven motivations, no matter how strong their personal beliefs and convictions.

THE STRUCTURE OF CIVIL DISCOURSE: TOWARD A SYSTEMATIC MODEL

Understanding *in abstracto* the centrality of civil discourse to political life and its constraining influence on policy is one thing, figuring out what it looks like is quite another. Semiotic theory in anthropology, folklorics, and literary criticism provides the basis for our reconstruction over the next few pages.[1] Semiotics, or the science of signs, conceptualizes meaning as arising from more or less coherent systems that are internally structured by patterns of opposition and resemblance between constituent elements. Understanding culture as *organized* in this manner enables us to untangle complex dimensions of meaning in systematic ways and arrive at an underlying architecture that is often of surprising simplicity. Semioticians have differed, however, on whether we should focus our attention in this task on the paradigmatic (or synchronic, or cross-sectional) or the syntagmatic (or diachronic, or sequential) arrangements of signs within a system. This analytical distinction, originally formulated by Ferdinand de Saussure (1960), was institutionalized in the debates and projects of succeeding scholars. On the one hand thinkers such as Claude Lévi-Strauss (1968), Roland Barthes (1970), and Marshall Sahlins (1976) stressed the importance of cultural codes and discourses that arranged symbols and concepts in patterns of binary opposition. On the other, Vladimir Propp (1968), Algirdas Greimas (1990), and Paul Ricoeur (1967) asserted that narrative structures—in effect stories and story architectures—are pivotal as the bearers of meaning. Notwithstanding polemics to the contrary these perspectives can be thought of as potentially complementary, each being concerned with a specific but not hegemonic axis of meaning. In the paradigmatic dimension binary codes are responsible for classifying the world and so doing according to moral criteria, detailing the qualities and attributes of the sacred and profane, polluted and pure. Along the syntagmatic axis, however, narrative structures place actors and events into plots, allocate moral responsibility, causality, and agency, shape outcome expectations and in some cases provide exemplary models for action. Binary codes provide building blocks, but narratives add subtlety to our understandings of the world and convert situations into scenarios. These two axes are the foundations of the cultural systems through which what Émile Durkheim (1965) called the "collective conscience" comes to engage with the more concrete realm of events and things, in effect making them into nonmaterial social facts.[2]

Anthropological research has repeatedly demonstrated how members of so-called primitive societies use binary codes and the storylike myths that are built from them to construct collective representations of the world. These are the basis of the shared understandings that define for a community ontological and epistemological realities and moral boundaries, and provide mythical charters for activities. They operate as a pragmatic template for organizing existing information and for the assimilation of new experiences to possible ways of seeing and acting. It is a premise of the present work that albeit more technologically mediated, institutionally differentiated, and arguably more reflexive, exactly the same process takes place within contemporary civil society. We make sense of the world, including world events, using astoundingly simple cultural resources. Over recent years a number of studies have repeatedly demonstrated the presence of a remarkably durable set of binary oppositions structuring the discourses of Western civil society (Alexander and Smith 1993; Edles 1998; Jacobs 2000; Ku 1999; P. Smith 1991, 1994, 1998, 2000). Empirical investigations in settings as diverse as Britain, the United States, Hong Kong, and Spain, which have examined both political centers and margins, as well as comparative treatments of fascism and communism, have allowed a reasonable inference to be made that these are universal within the public sphere in liberal democratic contexts.[3] The codes have been shown to crop up time and time again at the very center of civil controversies where inclusion and exclusion, legitimacy and illegitimacy, rewards and sanctions are at stake. Wars we will see are no exception.

With a little license we can think of the binary codes of civil society as if they were a kind of cultural DNA. They are a set of basic and shared structures from which myriad individuated complexities of debate and interpretation emerge and reproduce themselves over time. An emergent product of the evolution of the Western tradition, the codes draw upon and weave together a secularized residue of the Judeo-Christian heritage, the remainders of civic republicanism and various strands of liberal enlightenment thought. We can trace their genetic fingerprint in sources as distinct as ancient Greek philosophy, Shakespeare, John Locke, Adam Smith, Voltaire, and the Bible. The accreted product of centuries of symbolic bricolage, this discourse of civil society papers over abstruse and analytical lucubrations involving contending philosophical definitions of the good and bad society in the Western canon. It pulls these themes of diverse valence together into a package that is seamless for all practical purposes. The resulting binary codes mark out and classify the world, defining and evaluating in terms of the sacred and the profane the motivations, relationships, and institutions that are to be sought out, or avoided.

It is worth explicating the three codes of what we will call the "discourse of civil society" in a little detail, as they will play a central role in our empirical treatments of talk on war. Turning to the first of these, on motivations, we find that actors are valued and trusted only if they are autonomous rational subjects. Those who lack reason or are emotive are devalued and excluded from full participation in society. Hence, struggles for inclusion and legitimacy involve efforts to claim rational status, and efforts to discredit and debunk others depend upon the application of labels from a negatively coded list of psychological attributes. Movement from one status to another can have real consequences. It was eventually realized that Hitler was a dangerous madman who had to be destroyed. Women and other minorities, long excluded as not fully rational or capable of true understanding, pitched their claim for political equality around claims to reason and eventually won—albeit an incomplete and still contested victory.

The civil discourse of motives

Active	Passive
Rational	Irrational
Reasonable	Hysterical
Calm	Excitable
Controlled	Emotive
Realistic	Unrealistic
Sane	Mad

Much the same pattern holds for the discourses when they specify desirable and dangerous social relationships. Valued relationships are open and trusting, and involve the free and fair exchange of ideas. Relationships that are unduly deceitful and calculating (Iago to Othello), involve secretive conspiracies (witches, spies, Watergate) or demand passive dependence (totalitarianism) are devalued in this discourse. Legitimacy can only accord to those relationships that are seen to align with the left side of the binary, and to administrative policies that foster these.

The civil discourse of social relationships

Open	Secret
Trusting	Suspicious
Critical	Deferential
Truthful	Deceitful
Straightforward	Calculating
Autonomous	Dependent

Social institutions outside the private sphere are charged by civil society with responsibility for implementing and sustaining the good society, making possible the autonomy of actors and the profit of honest relationships. The guiding spirit here is one of universalism. Institutions should be subject to the impersonal rule of law and contract, not subject to the vagaries of fear and favor. For example the rule of power, arbitrary decisions, ascriptive office holding, and unpredictable personalities were attributes used by the French revolutionaries to denounce the *Ancien Régime,* the American revolutionaries to condemn the British, and President Nixon's critics to attack his administration.

The civil discourse of social institutions

Rule regulated	Arbitrary
Law	Power
Equality	Hierarchy
Inclusive	Exclusive
Impersonal	Personal
Contractual	Ascriptive
Groups	Factions
Office	Personality

Powerful cultural logics determine the process through which these three codes are zippered together to build up a unified discourse. There are relations of presumed contiguity linking concepts on any one side of the code. Sacred qualities key to each other within the discourses. Likewise profane code elements are assumed to go together as it were "naturally." At the same time relationships of binary contrast keep the codes and their component signifiers apart. Thanks to this internal structure of positive and negative ties, the discourses become remarkably stable. It is difficult to imagine someone as trusting and realistic in their vision and yet at the same time mad, deceitful, and deferential. It seems unlikely that a rule-regulated and inclusive institution will be associated with an irrational political party or that the rule of law will be endorsed by a secretive organization. If we perceive a group as hysterical we have a strong expectation that their relationships and institutions will turn out to be excessively hierarchical. The discourses of civil society are a cultural filter and classification system that operate as a dominant but necessary moral and cognitive frame. They are the "common sense" we use for thinking about and talking about social and political life, including wars. It is a common sense that we can boil down to two contending codes extending over the three domains: A Discourse of Liberty that marks out the sacred and valued (the combined left columns) and a Discourse of Repression (the combined right columns) that denotes the profane, polluted, evil, and dangerous. Some identification of the enemy with the Discourse of Repression is a minimal requirement for war. We do not attack the good guys.

These binary codes mop up a good deal of the variance when it comes to explaining how civil discourse is structured in disputes over policy, inclusion, and exclusion. They fare particularly well in accounting for moral boundaries, classifications, and labeling. Yet they also have liabilities for cultural analysis. Their exegesis and application can obfuscate or reduce complexities of meaning, flattening out the interpretative field, stamping out nuances of tone, and squeezing cultural messages into sterile boxes, thereby ignoring culture's potentials for engendering creativity, imagination, fantasy, and the projection of ethical possibility and responsibility. More importantly, an analysis of codes will not take us very far in understanding how lines of action are constructed. We might think of lots of countries as acting in ways that are consistent with the Discourse of Repression, yet we rarely declare war. Binaries help us make sense of the world but do not offer an instruction manual for what to do next. Unless we are to default to explanations derived from realpolitik to account for the move to war in this situation but not that situation, something else is needed for our model of civil discourse. This is narrative.

We can understand narratives as the stories we construct and exchange in the effort to make sense of the world. The French philosopher Paul Ricoeur has perhaps the most instructive lessons on this point. He insists that narratives, in contrast to binary codes, order through sequencing rather than through assertions of resemblance and difference. They display actions arrayed in chronological time and allow us to answer the journalist's questions: Who? What? When? Where? And How? Importantly, narratives open up the subjunctive by accounting not only for what is but also for what could be or could have been in worlds both actual and possible (Ricoeur 1984, 45). The result is a comprehension of the universe that includes both phenomenological reason and ethical modes of being (Ricoeur 1970, 480). For Ricoeur (1967) narratives are a way we can align our actions with ultimate questions and purposes, such as those of salvation or simply the quest for the morally right thing to do and in this sense his message is deeply consonant with the model of civil society as moral regulator we have just presented.

Although couched in the language of normative hermeneutics, Ricoeur's insistence on the centrality of narrative as a sense-making cultural form that links actions to cognitive, ethical, and value systems is one that has received support from empirical studies in sociology and social linguistics. These have demonstrated that stories are important in structuring perception and moral accountability in ways that have consequence from the level of everyday life (Garfinkel 1967, 130–31; Scott and Lyman 1968; D. Smith 1978) to massive social transformations (Bloch 1985; Cohn 1961; Slotkin 1973; Walzer 1985). From these we may distill the following essentials: narratives allocate causal responsibility for action, define actors and give them motivation, indicate the trajectory of past episodes and predict consequences of future choices, suggest courses of action, confer and withdraw legitimacy, and provide social approval by aligning events with normative cultural codes. Social action can be seen as deeply embedded in a narrative framework. People make sense of the world with stories and act accordingly.

For all its promise of linking culture to agency, narrative theory as conventionally applied in the social sciences is not without its disappointments if we are looking for a generalizable, empirically applicable cultural theory. Elaborations on hermeneutic and existential themes such as Ricoeur's show that narrative has intersections with moral regulation, but they tilt us away from the systematic consideration of how this might play out on the ground in favor of a kind of abstract normative philosophy. It is a subjunctive and imperative discourse of "shoulds" and "cans" and "maybes" and "musts" that explores the potential of narrative for enabling ethical being. As for social science on narrative, it is largely idiographic and inductive. All too often the application of narrative theory in social science becomes an invitation for the exploration of the particular—perhaps as an investigation of the sense making activity of people as they reflect on their own experiences whether as individuals (Riessman 1993) or as groups (Eyerman 2001), or as a mode of representing historically embedded mythical charters and ideological prompts (Somers 1992). There is no developed understanding here of the structural properties of narrative—the robust cultural architectures and the resistances that forms can impose upon event understandings as they push contingencies into systematic alignments, or the fact that narratives must be understood relationally as determined nodes and combinations within a semiotic field rather than as idiosyncratic expressions in concrete situations. More promising for such an agenda has been the structuralist narrative analysis of texts in social science and history. Here narrative theory is proposed as a way of engaging in a kind of ironic metacommentary on intellectual production. The point that authors like Hayden White (1987) make, and it is an important one, is to insist that academics are involved in storytelling and are constrained in this telling by a relatively fixed repertoire of genres and tropes. The way scholars write about, say, the French Revolution is not shaped simply by what happened but also by the narrative templates that are at hand for the act of writing. In pulling events together into coherent sets and patterns authors make use of these molds, pouring the cascading and infinite detritus of history into generic forms that offer fixity and explanatory perspective. The limitation with this approach, of course, is that it looks at academic work rather than at the deployment of narratives in the "real world" by "ordinary" people in their responses to an unfolding event sequence.

Imagine these three approaches to narrative as three intersecting circles on a plane. Cultural sociology needs to work with the cell that is at the center of our Venn diagram. We should think about the role of narratives in real social life (the social science approach) and how these will have implications for the ethical or normative regulation of social action (the moral philosophy approach), and do this through a generalizable theory of culture (the structuralist understanding) that takes narratives as a canteen of cultural tropes and genres and not as a smörgåsbord of infinite variety.

A start can be made on this task by returning first to the tradition established by Aristotle's (1987) *Poetics* and continued in the work of scholars such as Vladimir Propp (1968), Algirdas Greimas (1990), Etienne Souriau (1950), and Northrop Frye (1957). This is the track of what is sometimes thought of as structuralist poetics or archetypal criticism, with its insistence that dramatic and narrative forms are limited in number and constructed from a pool of familiar and finite elements. Just as Saussure insisted on the distinction between language (*langue*) as a rule-governed system and speech (*parole*) as what is said and devoted his time to explicating the procedures and rules of the former, so does structuralist poetics ignore the surface detail of this story or that drama in digging for the patterned relationships and regularities that unite particular genres of storytelling activity as a "social fact and mode of communication" (Frye 1957, 99). Souriau (1950), for example, argued that all dramatic plots have agents, actions, and outcomes. These are (re)arranged into sequences that have proven remarkably invariant over history. He points in particular to the structural core of all narrative as the interrelationship between competing actors over *un bien désiré* (1950, 86)—an object, goal, or good that can be material (a thing), embodied (a person), or abstract (a value or ideal). The way that this competition is resolved determines the generic form. In our interpretation of civil discourse, then, we might begin by working out who the agents are said to be and over what they are understood to be struggling.

The part of Frye's rather more substantial contribution that is of interest to us here is his formalization of narrative genres into an ordered hierarchy in his systematic *Anatomy of Criticism*. Drawing on Aristotle's (1987) *Poetics*, Frye (1957) astutely observes that as we move from irony and low mimesis through comedy, romance, tragedy, and on to heroic and mythical genres, the power of the hero as agent to transform his or her environment increases. In myth, agents have powers that are different in kind from ours, in the high mimetic genres they are superior in degree to our own but not of a different order; in low mimesis people have powers rather like our own and in ironic and comedic tellings the agents have abilities inferior to our own. Perceptions about these powers assist the formation of an emotional register, generating feelings as diverse as ridicule, sympathy, or awe. These can be understood as the structure of feeling that attaches to genre.

Frye was talking here about properties of myth and fiction. Yet I believe his observations can be equally applied to the ways that we narrate and read current affairs. In other words the formal properties of narrative might have "real world" implications as important events are narrated in the public sphere. For example, we might look to a politician with respect, empathy, or contempt depending upon the genre through which we perceive them. Our expectations about the scope of their action possibilities and the likely outcomes of these at any given moment are equally likely to be shaped through the genre conventions that are at play. The lower mimetic modes confer limited powers of action and reduce expectations. Heroic and romantic understandings encourage the belief that radical changes and great deeds are possible and for this reason are often implicated in the allocation of charismatic status on notable individuals (P. Smith 2000). The consequent standards of accountability and judgment are tuned to our modes of representation, and not the contrary.

In Frye's *Anatomy of Criticism*, then, we glimpse some characteristics of narration that might have implications for public sphere discourse. I believe his model can and should be made more complex by introducing a further range of simple characteristics that line up with generic forms. (1) The motivations attributed to actors vary between narrative genres much as powers do. As a rule of thumb, as the powers and freedom of the actor increase in a process that we will call "narrative inflation," so do motivations become more ideal and abstract and less material and base. In Weberian terms action motivations become less *zweckrational* and more *wertrational*. When we are in the low mimetic genres of understanding we find actors motivated by mundane concerns and everyday emotions. At the more mythological end of the scale we encounter drives to action that are more closely tied to moral impulses of a transcendent nature. When characters are enacting the good or bad, sacred and evil, they are not worried about marrying the girl next door or balancing their checkbook. (2) While Frye talks for the most part of heroes, Souriau draws our attention to the fact that this protagonist needs to have an opponent. We should think, then, about how this rival or enemy is represented and what powers are attributed to them. As we will see later in this book, depictions of "evil" seem to have greater implications for war politics than images of our own "good" leaders. They generate strong moral emotions and a less cool and detached reading of events. Thus Adam Smith (1976, 34) noted long ago in speaking of the "unsocial passions" of hatred and resentment, "the villain, in a tragedy or romance, is as much the object of our indignation, as the hero is that of our sympathy and affection. We detest Iago as much as we esteem Othello." The process of narrative inflation is marked by an increasing polarization of this kind between the protagonist and their opponent. The extent of this polarization depends on the intensity and lack of ambiguity with which binary codes of the sacred and the profane are applied to the characters. In the low mimetic forms, agents who oppose and confront one another are broadly similar and each has a share of vices and virtues. As Frye puts it there is some fidelity to the cannons of probability. In the inflated forms, such as myth, their moral worth is more highly differentiated. The shades of gray that mark personalities in realist fiction, for example, are replaced by iconic, stylized character qualities that are emblematic of overarching moral positions. (3) With narrative inflation we see the issue at stake, what Souriau (1950) identified as the object of conflict or desire, becoming increasingly portentous. In the lower mimetic forms conflict may be over a small incident like a stolen bicycle or perhaps the fate of an individual in the

Bildungsroman. In the more inflated narrative genres, the future of kingdoms and even the world may be at stake and transcendental themes relating to the need for salvation and redemption become increasingly significant.

The discussion that I have given so far is limited in that it maps out relationships between narrative genres in terms of static character and object attributes and conjunctions. Yet the essential dramatic tension of narratives comes from change and conflict over time within a plot. In the course of a story both characters and the environment over which they are in competition are transformed from one state to another. It is this progress that gives narratives their retrospective-prospective quality and enables them to be both accounts of the past and predictions of the future, not only reporting but also shaping human actions through anticipating outcomes. Such a realization is central to Souriau's work, with its understanding that struggles are always resolved in particular ways in the course of a telling. Frye's developed thematization of this issue can be found in his Harvard lectures. Published as *The Secular Scripture* and delivered some twenty years after *The Anatomy of Criticism*, this lesser known work constitutes a major elaboration of his position (Frye 1976). In this late study Frye notes that from a starting point in a given plot the protagonist can only "go" in a limited number of directions. Simplifying even more radically than Souriau he arrives at the following set of possibilities: "First, the descent from a higher world; second, the descent to a lower world; third, the ascent from a lower world; and fourth, the ascent to a higher world. All stories in literature are complications of, or metaphorical derivations from, these four narrative radicals" (Frye 1976, 97). While Frye sees this movement as partly spatial, it is clear that he also considers moral and social status to correlate with these geographical movements. Through descending to a labyrinth or ascending a mountain the hero typically changes and grows in moral stature.

Frye's portrayal of this movement is, however, rather one-sided. Because *The Secular Scripture* is mostly concerned with the genre of romance, Frye focuses for the most part on the upward conversion of the individual hero to an improved condition of moral and physical well-being. Once again we need to acknowledge options for more profane or polluting alternatives and those that encompass the potential for the disintegration of the social. One might think of the possibility for a downward movement for the hero or the social world or, in terms of narration in civil discourse, their shift from a consonance with the Discourse of Liberty toward one with the Discourse of Repression. Much of the compelling dramatic force of the narratives through which we understand the world of current events emerges from the real or imagined shifts of character and object outcomes relative to these codes. This is a key reason why we watch the television news or read the papers. Crises, scandals, and controversies, for example, often involve the dangers of descent and we hope for the rescue of individuals, institutions, or nations. Although redemption is usually a possibility, in some situations narrative inflation has taken hold to the extent that there is very strong polarization of the principal characters. This makes their reconciliation and convergence in one civil discourse code or another increasingly unlikely. In more inflated representations of current affairs the hero and the villain rarely change their moral status. It is only the environment or object over which they are fighting that can take on a new moral valence as it is pulled toward congruence with either the sacred or profane. Because this fixed polarization makes the reform of personal attributes impossible, evil must be either permanently excluded from society or else destroyed.

So particular narratives cannot just take any form we wish. They cluster in genres with defined attributes. As figure 1 shows, these are characterized by conventional but also systematic relationships concerning: protagonists and antagonists in terms of their relative polarization and potential for moral transformation; powers of action in terms of their world-ordering potential; patterns of motivation as mundane or extraordinary; and objects of struggle as trivial or world-historical. These hold true not only for myth, folktales, and fictions but also for the stories that are told about real world events.

Having introduced these analytic criteria for identifying and classifying narrative forms, we are in a position to take to a more detailed and nuanced look at the four narrative genres that will be central to the interpretations made in this book.[4] The purpose of this discussion is to familiarize the reader with the indicators and tell-tale signs that indicate a particular genre is at play in structuring collective representations of the world and thereby to establish shared, public criteria for the interpretative activity that will follow in later chapters.

Our first genre is the rather unappealingly named *low mimesis*, a term deriving from the ancient Greek root for copying or imitation. The German thinker Max Weber spoke of the disenchantment of society. By this he meant that transcendental, religious, and magical motivations in social life had slowly disappeared over the centuries to be replaced by a bureaucratic logic and with a society marked by narrow, instrumentally rational actions. This thesis can be restated as an argument for the increasing primacy of low mimetic narratives within social life as an organizing cultural frame. Indeed Weber's own output can be understood as a study in this genre, albeit with a tragic and fatalistic twist. In a sense Weber reproduces what he purports to describe. Low mimesis is the least obviously plot driven of all narrative genres—in fact this

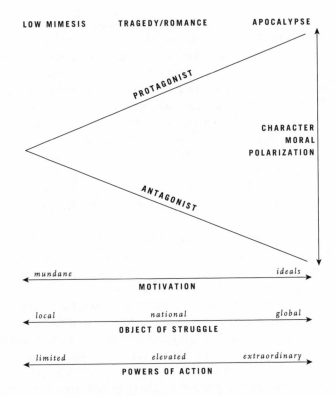

Figure 1. The Structural Model of Genre

is the genre of the antistory and the kitchen sink novel or of Weber's low key, detail-obsessed account of the origins of modernity. Actors are understood to be complex in their motivations and they are essentially "just like us" in terms of their ambitions and powers of action. Characters are not strongly polarized in terms of their moral worth and nothing much is at stake. In this genre there is no clear trajectory to events, which can potentially take weakly developed romantic or tragic lines. Money, power, and diffuse value commitments alike guide actions in a world that is all about the mundane and business as usual. Life as represented in this genre is drab and routinized and characters are reliable and stoic. Actions are held to be pragmatic and constrained.

The low mimetic mode is the predominant narrative for our understanding of everyday politics. It is the mode in which newspapers report on the potato crop in Idaho, debates are conducted on the new EPA negotiations concerning fuel emissions, and CNN relays the election results of distant countries few particularly care about. In short, all those events that do not seem to have a lot of drama to them—at least for us, the distant and emotionally detached audience. Although some typification in terms of the binary codes of civil society is often latent in low mimetic discourse, talk is usually about mundane themes such as efficiency and price, routines and procedures. When civil narrative is located in this mode, legitimacy is usually dependent upon political action attaining measurable success and demonstrating the prudent use of resources. Proponents of low mimetic discourses often claim that their understanding is somehow more "real" or less "exaggerated" than that of others. We see attacks on positions that have been couched in more inflated narrative genres as "mere rhetoric." Weak character polarization sees low mimesis result in efforts to talk down war and to understand crises as fixable through prudence, routine diplomacy, compensation, and sanctions. It is a genre that sits very uncomfortably with military action because it does not provide a convincing and legitimate justification for blood sacrifice.

By contrast to low mimesis, which is emotionally flat, Aristotle wrote of *tragedy* as a genre that evokes powerful sentiments of moral empathy, pity, and terror (Aristotle 1987, 16; also Frye 1957, 36–37). The tragic genre is marked by a strong sense of character movement and plot development that can be described in terms of themes of descent, along with motivations for action that can be more clearly defined by the parameters of good and evil than by routines, petty emotions, and bank balances. The essence of tragedy is the futility of human striving, the fall from grace, the missed opportunity and the horror of suffering, the disintegration of society, and the movement from social integration to social isolation and atomization. In effect things go horribly wrong. Sentiments of pathos are developed toward the fallen, failed hero (Othello) and/or the object of struggle (Desdemona, Romanian orphans, or the Amazonian rain forest). The object of struggle is often an innocent and largely passive victim who has been sadly let down by the poor decisions, bad luck, and the evil doing of others. Tragedy is particularly effective in generating sentiments of identification with the suffering innocent in part because things could have been otherwise if some error had not been made (Aristotle 1987, 16). At the same time fatalism is often a theme, with actors somehow "star crossed" despite their considerable powers of action. Consequently, the tragic genre can lead to paralysis in political life rather than demands for intervention even though things are perceived to be going from bad to worse—indeed this is a common rebuke from those advocating alternative genre positions. Where tragic frames exist the corresponding structure of feeling is not one that sustains activism or violent struggle. There is an amplified awareness of suffering, an atmosphere of pathos, and a belief that human motivations are misguided and can lead only to poor outcomes.

If tragedy involves a futile struggle against the fates, the ubiquity of bad choices, the inevitable failure of heroic actions, and the horror of consequent suffering, the essence of *romance* is the triumph of the hero over adversity. Not necessarily about love, this is a fundamentally optimistic genre marked by the belief that actions can make a difference and that change for the better is in the air. In romance the hero is motivated by high ideals and overcomes a series of obstacles, challenges, and enemies associated with powers deemed evil. Hence, we find a "polarized characterization . . . a tendency to split into heroes and villains" (Frye 1976, 50). Romance sees an upward movement of the hero, and the environment of struggle, and sometimes the conversion for the better of the forces of evil, too. In the secularized forms of romance the hero has no supernatural powers, but rather uses human ones to great effect perhaps as an activist or political leader often blessed with the luck, guile, wisdom, *froda*, that lets them succeed time and time again (Frye 1976, 68). There is an emphasis on the transformative power of the human agent and on "themes of ascent" (Frye 1976, 129ff.) that lead to social improvement and integration—to a better world or the recovery of a lost Eden (Jameson 1981, 110). Romantic narratives can be highly effective in generating collective action, support for ambitious political programs, and solidaristic collective effervescence in Durkheim's sense (Jacobs and Smith 1996). For this reason charismatic authority, legitimacy, trust, and good will often emerge in conjunction with romantic narratives. For all its virtues such a genre cannot sustain a war even if it often inspires social movements. It carries with it a feel-good factor and a sense that crises can be resolved without recourse to large-scale and systematic violence. There might be character polarization, but this tends to be moderate and the antagonist is potentially capable of upward conversion toward reason. Romantic narratives tend to be highly unstable. They are vulnerable to deflationary attacks from advocates of realist and tragic visions. These might point to the hyperbolic and Pollyanna qualities of the romantic vision of the world, or suggest that efforts at action will be futile and lead to unintended outcomes (see Hirschman 1991).

And what of war? The narrative foundations for war lie in the *apocalyptic* mode of narration. This most powerful of all narrative genres enables the cultural constraints on violence to be overcome and for support to eventuate for the sacrifice of priceless human lives. The tragic and romantic genres we have reviewed both might exhibit the morality play characteristic of good confronting evil, but only in a modest sense. Apocalyptic narratives also display this attribute, but do so in a peculiarly stylized way because they involve the most intense character polarization that invokes the highest and lowest of human motivations. Stories such as J. R. R. Tolkein's *Lord of the Rings* trilogy or the final pages of the Bible depict events as a struggle between radical evil and the forces of fundamental good in a supernatural setting. Secularized equivalents where our very salvation is at stake can be found from time to time in civil discourse (Lincoln 2002). When radical evil is afoot in the world there can be no compromise, no negotiated solution, no prudent efforts to effect sanctions or to maintain a balance of power. This evil is so absolute that there is no possibility for trust or for upward conversion of the bad through reason or happenstance as there may be in romance; in consequence that evil must be destroyed. In such apocalyptic narratives events are seen as unequivocally world-historical, and as in need of heroic interventions, for the object of struggle is the future destiny of the planet or civilization. This is typically represented as being in the balance with outcomes dependent on faith, decisiveness, and resolve. Now the usual bureaucratic and legal constraints on action can be thrown out of the window with internalized motivational fidelity to higher ideals a more important criterion for evaluating action than budgets and established procedure.

Apocalyptic narratives are the most effective at generating and legitimating massive society-wide sacrifice and are today the only narrative form that can sustain war as culturally acceptable. Yet because they have raised the stakes so high they are exposed to risks of deflation. Those encoded as pure and those encoded as polluted, must act in ways that sustain this imagined scripting. If the gap starts to close between the good and the evil or events start to look less apocalyptic we can negotiate. If the object of struggle turns out to be simply some local issue then the future of the world is no longer at stake and we need not send troops to die for it. Efforts to de-legitimate war typically involve these kinds of attempts to prick the balloon of apocalypticism through redescription of objects, actors, and motivations and thereby move our cultural frame of reference back down the genre hierarchy.

GENRE WARS AND THE GENRE GUESS

A knowledge of narrative genres allows readers to understand and interpret texts such as novels and poems (Hirsch 1967). This is because, as Frye (1957, 88) puts it, archetypes are conventions that underpin communication; they are a "communicable symbol" (Durkheim would have said "collective representation") that is in public circulation as a cultural resource for writers and their audiences. In an analogous way the narrative genres we have just reviewed provide agents within civil society with conventionalized paths to understanding current affairs and for transferring these understandings to others. They allow events such as emergent crises to be "storied" and comprehended. An intuitive knowledge of roles, trajectories, powers, and event evaluation criteria comes into play in the effort to make or impose a sense of what is going on. Visions of who protagonists really are, what they are struggling over and where that struggle looks to be headed guide our activity in the interpretation of world politics. It is in this way that culture operates as a tool for understanding, a tool for predicting, a tool for evaluating, and also as a brake or constraint on action because action is held accountable to narrative. Aware in a practical way of the power of narratives, actors struggle in sometimes self-interested and sometimes disinterested ways to align genres with events and also to perform in ways that are consistent with prevailing or legitimating narratives. As has become apparent in the era of political spin management, even the most purely reflexive and rational of political agents has to take account of the cultural environment within which policies are taken up for public debate. Where policy cannot be aligned with an appropriate genre it begins to look shaky, wrongheaded, sly, or morally bankrupt. For this reason agents, both individual and collective, engage in struggles over the "real meanings" of events. These can be understood in many cases not as contests over "facts," or even as efforts to uncover new facts, but rather as contests over interpretative frames, the encompassing systems that enable us to make sense of all those details. We can think of this agonistic struggle as a *genre war* in which interested parties try to impose their version of reality by providing not simply generic statements of position, but rather by attempting to institutionalize and disseminate a broader, more diffuse and therefore more powerful genre of interpretation through the public sphere.

A genre war might break out over the correct way to interpret a scandal, an election result, or a social policy. No doubt each of these has its own particular motifs. In this book, however, our concern is with wars and so we find that issues of risk evaluation are central. Within the various branches of realist political science that we introduced at the outset of the chapter, threats and risks to security are understood to contain their own interpretation and to dictate policy accordingly once filtered through decision-making systems of greater or lesser efficiency and rationality. Here we take issue with such a perspective and indicate more strongly the culturally constructed qualities of risk. When events happen they are not treated in an isolated way, but rather are inserted into a broader narrative matrix that tells us what they mean— what their wider future implications might be in ethical and action spheres. Harold Garfinkel (1967), drawing on Karl Mannheim, spoke of the "documentary method of interpretation" and alluded to the human agency that is required in the construction of coherent scenarios from scattered fragments of information. Accordingly, we can think of risks being talked up or talked down according to this creative identification of broader patterns for isolates of data. The narrative genre that is applied might work to amplify or diminish the apparent threat to which a nation is exposed, select some facts as relevant and not others, adjust the valence and spin of particular items of information.

Narrative inflation and deflation through the genre gamut is pivotal to the cultural process through which this ramping up or talking down of threats is achieved. Aristotle's *Poetics* has been called a cookbook for writing drama. Figure 1 and the accompanying discussion can be thought of in an analogous way. For practitioners they provide instructions and rules for narrating events in a particular genre ("increase the moral polarization," "shrink the object of struggle") and a set of "how to" pointers for challenging the interpretation of others ("contest the moral polarization," "claim this is not just a local issue") in debates over the "true" reading of any particular threat or crisis. Methodologically they offer us the signs and tells with which we can identify such positions, and the tools for understandings of genre that in Fredric Jameson's (1981, 106ff.) terms are both syntactic (how genre works, its architecture) and semantic (what it means, the structure of feeling that is evoked).[5]

Recognizing the existence of this process of cultural filtering and processing and acknowledging the pragmatics of talking up or talking down threats does not mean endorsing the kind of radical postmodern constructivist position in which it is held that everything is described into being or in which nothing is real or has worldly impacts but what is thought to be real. Let us be clear: Wars involve real threat statements from real leaders, involve real armies and real bombs and real deaths. Yet these brute facts cannot tell us what threats mean or what we should do. They do not tell us whether we should fight or flee or negotiate or impose sanctions or look for diplomatic solutions. Even when we agree on the low level empirical details, as we often do, we might disagree on their broader implications. This situation brings to mind the distinction between meaning and significance (Hirsch 1967, 1976), between the interpretation of the words on the page and the more general reading of the novel as a whole. E. D. Hirsch Jr. (1967, 98) remarks, "every disagreement about an interpretation is usually a disagreement about genre" (significance) not about petty issues of a more factual nature such as the empirical referents of a single line of poetry (a red rose, the moon). Consider the cold war in this light. All could agree that nuclear bombs could kill millions of people, and that the Soviet Union had many of these as well as a large standing army and considerable industrial capacity and that from time to time Soviet leaders said nasty things about the West. There was hardly any dispute about factual details—the number and size of the Soviet nuclear arsenal or the location and size of its army or the words of a speech to the Communist Party.

Yet there was vigorous argument about the implications of all this, namely the "real" danger of the Soviet threat and what to do about it. Some argued for a hard line response to every flare-up and spoke of the domino effect. Others called for cultural exchanges and even unilateral disarmament as the best way to secure peace. Recommendations for action and consequent policy decisions depended on the stories we told about the Soviets—were they the kind of people who were more or less rational and could be trusted (in other words describable in terms of the Discourse of Liberty as Gorbachev was toward the end of the cold war) or were they fanatics of icy disposition, hell bent on world domination? Was this an apocalyptic scenario where a final showdown was sooner or later inevitable, so we should get our retaliation in first? Or could a romantic narrative fall into place in which mutual understanding and peaceful coexistence could be expected to grow slowly and in which democratic reforms would eventually and spontaneously take place in the Soviet Union? Perhaps we should look at events in a low mimetic, Henry Kissinger kind of way and use treaties and diplomacy and theories of détente to keep things from boiling over? Events and 'facts', like those thrown out by each crisis in the cold war, should be thought of as clues to the reality of the Soviet threat. Like lumps of Play-Doh they have some ontological weight. They are real and sticky but they are also a little malleable, and are capable of being conjoined with others in diverse imaginative combinations. They are not directly epistemic, but acquire this property post facto from the bigger stories we tell. And this telling is constrained by the cultural logic of genre.[6]

I am suggesting that to some extent genre wars in civil society are analogous to disputations among literary critics as they argue furiously over the correct classification of a poem or work of fiction—but only "to some extent." Most obviously the stakes are higher when the understanding of events such as crises, revolutions, wars, and scandals is at hand than when we are trying to figure out in which theoretical pigeonhole we should place a *New York Times* bestseller. Elections can be won or lost, presidents impeached, lives spared. There is also a more subtle reason why the analogy has its limits. Coming to terms with this is absolutely fundamental to seeing how genre wars unfold and for comprehending the argument of this book. When looking at a text such as . . . well, *War and Peace* seems appropriate, we have the advantage of finitude. There it is in black and white, with covers, on the table in front of us as a shared empirical referent. The object for debate is complete and completed. It has defined boundaries marked by the first and last pages. Having read it we know how the story events unfold from the first page to the last. We can agree on this narrative sequence even if we do not concur on its wider significance as a literary artifact. We also know about contexts external to the text such as the character of its long dead author, Tolstoy, his unconventional beliefs and lifestyle, and the qualities of his other writings. Once up to speed on all this we can enter into the academic debate on how best to interpret *War and Peace*. Within civil society, by contrast, we are making sense of events that are unfolding in real time before our very eyes, in the present tense, with a heavy twist of the subjunctive and with information of sometimes doubtful validity. In short we are in an ill-defined and information poor, high contingency context, not an information rich, closed one. It is an unstable situation for interpretation because the rug might be pulled from under our feet at any moment by a new revelation or twist in emergent circumstances: A Middle Eastern dictator that we previously liked and to whom we sold arms will invade the country next to him and threaten our oil supply; terrorists whom we previously wrote off as ignorable minor players will crash airplanes into the World Trade Center towers. It may be that we got our earlier readings wrong. Some retrospective accounting is called for: We look back to the past, think about old clues in new ways, construct revised narratives, and contemplate changing our genre.

Such revisions are a possibility because although genres can be remarkably robust in determining expectations and shaping interpretation, they are not information-proof in some hermetic way. Practical efforts at validation are ongoing, involving the incessant collection and dialogical scrutiny of details and their marshalling into a bigger frame. This activity is particularly relentless because crises are not situations in which we can sit back in our seminar rooms and congratulate one another on the artful construction of plausible interpretations. The important question is not who has the most clever or creative interpretation, but rather which one is *the right one*. In some cases enough discrepant facts might be collected and reasoned through in public deliberation to tip the balance, even if the tipping point might differ for each of us. In others there will be a single knockout punch—the item of information or event that for the vast majority most will categorically refute a genre choice. So reality matters—albeit not in an unmediated way. This being the case the challenge of ongoing world interpretation is closer to that which we experience when we pick up pick a new book for the first time—a book about which, as it happens, we have no prior information for the covers and title are missing—and turn the initial couple of pages. In that context we make our genre guess, then move back and forth between this and the details subsequently unfolding, all the time looking for signs of validity in our reading (Hirsch 1967). Crisis situations involve a *genre guess* made from a few events and then ongoing efforts to check this as things develop. Citizens, journalists, commentators, and politicians take prior knowledge and the bits and pieces of information at hand and then, to put them together into a meaningful whole, each makes their genre guess. Further lines of fact, supposition, and rumor are next pressed into these familiar cultural templates and a dialogue about validity starts up. This draws in an implicit way upon the genre characteristics we have already outlined. Object of struggle: Is this really all about world domination or is it just some tin pot dictator's ego trip? Character motivation: Is this about the price of oil or the survival of democracy? Trajectory: Are things going to get better by themselves? And so forth. Superficially concerning hard facts, these kinds of questions are really all about who has got the story right and about whether we should be engaged in genre inflation or deflation. When we see actors, objects, motivations, and trajectories being debated in this way we know that a genre war is at hand.

But even the analogy we have just made to the genre guess at the outset of the unknown novel by a previously unknown author has its problems. At least we know that the opening pages of our book belong together. With the exception of the most avant-garde works such as stochastic, computer-generated writing, we can have very strong confidence that our pages are a *set* glued literally together in the material artifact and metaphorically by conventions relating to intellectual production and authorial intent. Reading world politics in real time involves attributing sets to events that may or may not be discrete. Decisions need to be made as to what belongs with what, which episodes and actors are linked, where the boundaries of the set lie, in short to identify the "thing" at hand in the shifting continuum of world politics. How big is the conspiracy? How far back in time does this pattern extend? Should we think of this third or fourth country or terrorist group as in or out of the frame of relevance of the matter in hand? These are questions that require estimates and judgments. The situation here is closer to that of the reader on a desert island who finds scraps of waterlogged paper washed up on shore every day, of which a few scattered lines are still legible. Are these even from the same book? In such a context we do not read simply from text to genre guess, but rather use the guess to tell us what the boundaries of the relevant story might be—to define the text itself by deciding which of the lines belong to one story and which, perhaps, to others. Consequently, genre driven expectations about actors, plots, objects, and trajectories are a resource used to manufacture and mark out relevant story-sets from scraps of information.

There is further and final point of contrast to be raised here between reading books and reading the world. When critics debate the significance of a work their thoughts might influence the way we understand a book, but do not change the ontological reality of the text itself, the words on the page. You might think that Marcel Proust's *Remembrance of Things Past* is best understood as autobiography, and I might claim it has unexpected virtues as a low mimetic contribution to social theory (P. Smith 2004). You might argue it has a tragic sensibility relating to loss and I that it can be more profitably be read as an analytical tract on social status, time, and self. We could have an interesting discussion but for all that the three thousand or so pages and the print on them would remain the same. The genre guess made within civil society is different. Readings of events that become influential or institutionalized can change the course of events as they unfold. Possibilities arise for self-fulfilling prophecies or the failure of prophecy as alliances are formed, diplomatic responses made, protest marches organized . . . history is written as it is read.

In his Eleventh Thesis on Feuerbach, Karl Marx famously wrote the aphorism that although philosophers had only interpreted the world in various ways, the point was to change it. It is regrettable that such an intuitively appealing and crisp dictum should be predicated on a false distinction between interpretation and action. The genre politics of civil society can be thought of as a practical philosophical activity not as disinterested speculation, a form of engagement in which efforts are made to change history by means of interpretation and dialogue over interpretation. Readings of events and actors are thrown out into the public sphere as speech acts with the hope that there will be some illocutionary force or performative impact. There is anticipation that these will confer legitimacy or withdraw it, change opinion, lead to political pressure. Hence this book is more than a formalist study of genres of political discourse, it is a demonstration of genre wars as a mode of human praxis.

Lacking a god's eye perspective we cannot make easy rulings on who has gotten this practical, world-transforming activity of ongoing interpretation right or wrong. Because events do not contain their own interpretations, and because readings interfere with the unfolding of subsequent events in multiplayer environments, and because our own political opinions cloud our understandings, even the benefit of hindsight does not allow us to say: "That was the way it should have been seen. That was the right genre guess." In some cases we can make a pretty good estimate. From our liberal democratic perspective, for example, it seems reasonably clear that the danger that Hitler objectively represented during the 1930s was not adequately recognized by Britain or America. An earlier move to apocalypticism might have served better than a policy of appeasement grounded in low mimesis (see final chapter). In contrast, the threat to civilization posed by domestic American communists during the 1950s seems to have been massively overestimated, and lead to pointless witch-hunts and counter-democratic policies of surveillance and exclusion. In many cases, however, we have few clues precisely because readings can propel events down one track and not another. Was the suspicion of the Soviet Union during the cold war overdone? We will never know because the cold war was itself in part a product of forty-five years of genre guessing. Interpretations led to military and political actions, these actions to "clues." These clues were fed back into interpretation. As for the wars that are the subject of this book, their genre politics is still contested. For the most part we will be unable to say who made the better interpretation of the initial precipitating crisis. We will, however, be able to identify the basic structures of the genre war and trace their implications as events unfolded. Mapping rather than arbitrating is task enough for the present volume.

INVESTIGATING CULTURE IN WAR

Methodology, Causality, Case Studies, and Data

Thus far we have critiqued the noncultural models of war that are currently dominant and sketched out a robust alternative that gives an autonomous role to cultural inputs as these are expressed in civil discourse and debate. We have also provided some indication of the structures of such civil discourses and suggested how they might operate. Observe that our alternative was precise and predictive. I did not argue that wars take place when some never-to-be-repeated, event-specific contingency of framing or imagery falls into place. Rather, the claim was made that we will find empirical regularities in war-generating discourses. These arise from the structural properties of culture. We will see identical discursive positions, with the same interpretive moves and plays at genre politics coming up time and time again. Efforts are made to understand crises and to legitimate or de-legitimate war by moving players around inside the same old plots and by differentially applying familiar cultural codes to events and actors. Civil societies do not develop interpretive schemas de novo each time a crisis eventuates.

Realizing that war talk is always a case of new wine in old bottles takes us a step away from relativism, subjectivism, and the fetishization of the unique-ness of each setting toward a deductive and generalizable theory of what culture might look like and how it works in crisis situations. Accordingly, we need a methodological approach that engages with interpretation but does so in a way that is consistent with norms of what we might think of as hypothesis testing. The conduct of social scientific research has traditionally entailed tradeoffs between these poles. There are long-acknowledged tensions between specificity and generality of focus, between the refinements of interpretative sensibilities as they grapple with the quiddity of the particular and the brisk satisfactions of closure and accountability that can come from the embrace of the science model. This chapter maps out an approach that can respect each of these contending paths to understanding. It also exercises some of the other old war horses from the battle lines of the *Methodenstreit:* the problematic dualism separating structural and agentic models of culture, the sterile distinction between accounts of action that focus on meanings and those that look to interests, the perspective holding that actors believe what they say and that which sees words as a cloak for the will to power. By the end we will be armed with an understanding of how culture works that does more than split the difference between each and all of these.

RECONCILING HERMENEUTICS AND THE COMPARATIVE METHOD

Because wars are understood here as a form of meaningful human activity we need to start with the claims of hermeneutics. Put simply this is the position that cultural analysis is all about interpretation (Dilthey 1989) and that social life can be treated like a text. Not *as* a text, but *as if it were* a kind of text—at least for the purposes at hand in order to make some kind of provisional sense of what is going on (Ricoeur 1981). Accordingly, the invisible symbol systems and structures of feeling that motivate action can be read, translated and then reconstructed again in a process of writing that the anthropologist Clifford Geertz (1973) famously talks of as the provision of a "thick description." In effect this can be imagined as a bouillabaisse of observations, evocative text, analogies, and nuggets of tentative theory that showcases the flavors of social life in particular settings. Such interpretative action relating parts to wholes and showing their interdependence was traditionally thought of as the closing of the hermeneutic circle. As Geertz himself points out, we should no longer think in terms of this metaphor. Cultural life is itself always plural, proliferating, hybrid. There is no "Balinese mind" or culture or worldview just as there is no single view on any given war within any given country. So our task of analysis is better likened to that of the archaeologist sifting through the debris of a vanished civilization. We locate meaningful fragments and then systematically relate these to each other as best we can. There will be gaps and overlaps in the resulting mosaic. There will be no "whole," but we can create a number of individuated pictures of sometimes better, sometimes weaker resolution. The sifting and sorting and ordering are enterprises requiring the exertion of sensibilities, but for all that they are far from an exercise in helpless and hopeless relativism. We stand on the shoulders of giants when we make our claims. The traditions established by previous theoretical work discipline and contour the process of reading and give guidance as to the culture structures that we might expect to find. In the case of this study we have the benefit of an established tradition and theory in genre analysis that tells us where to look and what we are looking for and how to relate each item to other items of data. This provides not only clues on how to proceed with the act of hermeneutic reconstruction but also a repertoire of publicly available criteria for interpretation and evaluation. Genre theory sets up analytic goalposts and offers templates that can be invoked to yardstick any given reading.

If a generalizable cultural theory such as structural hermeneutics is our best defense against relativism, solipsism, or wild interpretation, then respect for evidence is next in line. The process of constructing a thick description involves the marshalling of multiple strands of data into a patterned order (Hirsch 1976). In isolation each of these is weak, but when we align direct quotations from interventions in the public sphere as varied as speeches, editorials, and letters, with opinion poll data, and actions such as demonstrations or objective political stances, we can construct more than just plausible claims about the culture-structures at play in a given field. The subsequent presentation of just a small sample of this material in the act of writing enables readers to see for themselves how the interpretation was made, how invisible structures can be inferred from parts, and then permits them to join in the process by imaginatively recreating this in the act of reading. When bolstered by citation to and invocation of the secondary literature, much of it by historians but also contemporaneous reflexive commentaries and cultural diagnoses by organic intellectuals themselves engaged in genre wars, a robust case can be made for each reading.

Hermeneutic analysis, then, is the way in which this book engages in readings of the culture patterns in each crisis and war. Yet the hermeneutic approach is not without problems. In the social sciences it has traditionally been deployed in support of arguments against general theory. Its advocates tend to point to the role of the geographically local and historically specific as contexts within which meanings and actions are determined and determinable, and consequently to the need for endogenous accounts of outcomes and process. Geertz himself, for example, insists that societies contain their own interpretations and apparently sincerely believes that understanding involves excavating and communicating these indigenous templates of culture rather than imposing our own etic frameworks. Regrettably, hermeneutics has been further damaged for social science by a nineteenth-century normative philosophical baggage. This connects to romanticism with its arguments against determinism and makes problematic claims for the somewhat metaphysical triumphs of the human spirit. For noted critics such as the historical sociologist Theda Skocpol (1979) such characteristics of hermeneutics can be generalized into an indictment of cultural arguments more generally: they are fatally subjectivist and cannot be reconciled with a more predictive social science that generates core knowledge in any cumulative way. Or putting it in W. G. Runciman's (1983) terms, cultural sociology does description and reportage better than true causal explanation. Hence, in her noted analysis of the causes of revolution, Skocpol (1979) pointedly excluded ideologies altogether and paid homage to more material variables such as weak states, lagging economies, and military defeats. Applying an analytic logic derived from John Stuart Mill (1967) and looking at a pool of successful, failed, and nonemergent revolutions, she indicated that the presence or absence of these critical factors correlated with historical outcomes. The result was a powerful demonstration of how social science can develop strong causal claims and generalizable theories from the analysis of comparable event sequences.

Cultural sociology must learn from such critics, but without compromising its commitment to the meaningfulness of social life. This means sharpening Occam's razor and engaging in what John R. Hall (1999, 180) thinks of as "generalizing practices of inquiry" that test hypotheses by comparison and apply theory to cases in order to make sense of them. Rather than abandoning interpretation altogether as Skocpol tries to do or, conversely, engaging in philosophical arguments that however brilliant will pass unobserved by skeptics like meteors over the beds of the sleeping, we are better served by meeting objectors on their own turf. Hence, this study should be understood as very much in the social scientific tradition that intends to make broadly predictive, but not crudely deterministic, claims about causalities and empirical regularities. Yet it also wishes to engage in deep readings of culture. The way we can have this cake and eat it—to interpret and also to search for what some might think of as "laws"—is to clone Skocpol's own method and engage in a systematic comparative study that looks for uniformities in cultural conditions and aligns these with outcomes. In short, we are to engage in the "parallel demonstration of theory" over multiple cases (Skocpol and Somers 1980). This becomes a possibility when we move toward what I have called elsewhere a "strong program" in the sociology of culture (Alexander and Smith 2001) characterized by belief in cultural autonomy, a structuralist hermeneutics, and an understanding of the causal paths through which culture exerts its influence. This is a cultural sociology where we have a robust and predictive theory of culture that enables us to speak of repeated instantiations of particular culture structures rather than of unique conjunctions and unrepeatable, locally situated meanings; to pay homage but not obeisance to the specific and situational; to contest the belief that the nonmaterial is somehow more "real" than the ideal; to replace a sociology of culture with a cultural sociology where it is the collective representations themselves that do the explaining and drive history onward.

And so it is that the following chapters provide an account of the genre guess and the genre wars in civil discourse in four Western countries as each responded to three crisis events with broadly similar magnitudes, durations, and qualities. Perhaps we might like to think of these narrative forms as our "independent variable." In some cases the countries went to war and in others they did not. This is our crudest "dependent variable." A more refined one is identifiable as the relative legitimacy or enthusiasm for each war. The countries to be looked at are the United States, Britain, France, and Spain and the events are the Suez Crisis of 1956, the Gulf War of 1991, and the War in Iraq of 2003. In sum we have twelve aggregate state/event cells, with more outcomes available if we consider divisions and constituencies within each state.

Where Millian logic is at hand there is a need for sufficient resemblance—what Arthur Stinchcombe (1978) has referred to as "deep analogies"—among the cases to permit the instructive comparison and repeated demonstration of key propositions. Yet at the same time we need to have some variability in historical outcomes so that there are contrasts to be explained notwithstanding these similarities between cases. The logic of concomitant variation, after all, needs to be challenged to explain why things turn out differently. Our three selected conflicts manage this tension of sameness and difference effectively. The Suez Crisis of 1956, the Gulf War of 1991, and the War in Iraq of 2003 are broadly similar in that they are recent wars between developed and less-developed nations. They were also highly contested and controversial, with opinion divided within and between our four Western nations. Both Nasser's Egypt and Saddam Hussein's Iraq were militaristic, populist dictatorships with charismatic leaders who espoused ideologies that combined themes from socialism, militarism, and pan-Arab philosophy. Each had explicitly expansionist policies. Both engaged in actions that were deemed by many to threaten the stability of the Middle East and endanger the West's vital interests, including its oil supply. While history never repeats itself, this is a pretty strong set of family resemblances that allows us to hold various factors constant as we explore cultural variability and correlate this with outcomes. As for the countries central to our investigation of civil discourse, these are also analogous. Britain, France, and the United States had large and well-developed civil societies, parliamentary democracies, and powerful industrial economies in all the wars. All might be considered players in global geopolitics. Spain was starting to become an operator during the more recent two conflicts but was a backward and conservative dictatorship at the time of Suez. With this exception we find here the broadly similar structural and event characteristics that will enable pointed comparisons to be made between countries and sequences over twelve cases. Regardless of the specifics of the positions and issues at hand, and with the possible exception of Spain in the 1950s, these structural similarities allow discourses and outcomes in any one of these countries to be cautiously weighed against those in any other.

Millian logic is a powerful tool, but also a rather clumsy one that can all too easily enrage critics with its sledgehammer finesse. Like all applications of routinized social scientific positivism it is stalked by the dangers of a shallow determinism that denies agency and a synchronic bias that flattens out the more subtle causal processes of an unfolding of history (Abbott 2001; Hall 1999). For this reason I would like to insert a hairpin bend into our methodological track and urge that the case study material can be understood not only as allowing us to deploy and test a crude model but also as offering a space for the refinement of argumentation and the tempering of generalizing abstraction with some reference to the idiographic and concrete, contingent and sequential. The sequence accounts further provide a heuristic through which more general theoretical concepts can be investigated and elaborated rather than simply demonstrated (Eckstein 1975). In other words, engagements with empirical materials afford a locus for the clarification and talking through of our culture-structure models as well as their testing. Each relatively short historical sequence opens possibilities for undertaking deeper interpretative activity and for explaining outcomes in terms of local and sequential factors within and between each national context: disputes, turning points, political and cultural cross-pressures, images of the nation itself, and perceptions of its place in history. Comparisons within nations can refute essentialized visions of a unified national response to events and can be used to great effect to demonstrate the autonomy of code from event, ideology or "national interest" and to flag the radical contingency of interpretation by situated actors. Counterfactuals are implicit when we look to signals and clues that are identified but not taken up, which are adopted in this country but not that country, which are noticed and then forgotten, which are read one way by one group and differently by another. With the counterfactual comes the flowering of a vision of history as the realization of the possible. Hence we get to see the genre guess opening up the plane of the subjunctive, and the piquant vocabularies of choice and chance become as central to our telling as those of structure and cause. These emerge from the ironies of a methodological approach that works by juxtaposing contrasting accounts of

events and invoking stillborn possibilities. The ensuing complexities generate a Rashomon effect in which we come to comprehend that realities open
themselves up to multiple narrations rather than dictating the terms of their
own representation. Culture is made free, history a making. Yet at the same
time, and without violence to such a processual understanding, we can step
back from the trees and see the forest in its entirety. By systematically comparing our four nations over the three wars and ignoring detail we can identify
twelve broad outcomes—a sufficient number to mobilize those seductively
tannic concepts of "concomitant variation" and "hypothesis testing."

And so we arrive at a fusion of the comparative method with structuralist
hermeneutics that does not make determinism the cellmate of explanation
because it recognizes the possibilities for layered planes of understanding.
Attention to detail and irony allow us to appreciate the extent to which contingency, struggle, good and bad luck, and persuasive interpretative efforts
by real world actors produce those big picture, aggregate outcomes at the national level. Civil discourses are built from the bottom up. Yet it is precisely
because agents in so doing draw upon archetypal resources within determinate cultural structures that the cumulative outcomes of such activity cluster
in nonrandom patterns. They can accordingly be classified and analyzed in
ways that allow for generalizing knowledge to be formed about culture, policy,
and legitimacy in times of war. This provides possibilities for the leverage of
the comparative method. Over our multiple cases we can see, for example,
whether prowar positions are associated time and time again with particular
culture structures, whether these differ in patterned ways from those held by
those opposing the war, and whether these cultural structures have invariant relationships among their constituent elements as predicted by our theory. We need not reduce such a comparative sociology to a formulaic activity
that eliminates complexity and renders diversity consistent with tick and flick
summary charts (although I will provide one of these in the final chapter). The
challenge, rather, is to embrace creative possibilities for what Neil Smelser
calls "systematic comparative illustration" (1976, 157). This mobilizes an implicit use of Mill's (1967) methods of agreement and difference, but does so
in a dialogical way. The subtleties and contingencies of diverse situations can
be used to qualify and split generalities as much as to confirm their causal
power or to make blunt comparisons over cases. The theoretical model of
history at play can be one that emphasizes the shifting, dynamic, and contingent; in consequence the thrust of comparison over cases illuminates the
ideographic and particular in each case (Bendix 1964) as well as that which is
common across them. With this credo as a guide the studies in this book can
be thought of as exploring the interrelationship between cultural forces and

the life history of issues. They are written in a narrative manner with comparative and contrastive illustration undertaken as a kind of headlining activity that drums home key empirical and theoretical regularities. For these reasons too, the American and British cases are treated in more depth than the French and particularly Spanish ones. This uneven treatment provides space for thickening discussion, focusing attention on proliferations of details as these collide with broader genres, opening up the door to contingency.

Earlier we had recourse to the rather tiresome metaphor of the archaeologist with their shards in explaining our methodology of hermeneutic reconstruction. Here is a rather better one that is not altogether unrelated, applying not so much to the reconstruction of particular meaning systems but rather to our use of these once their hermeneutic has been realized. In moving the level of understanding back and forth through varying analytic planes, from explicating the symbolic structure of this or that speech, or letter, or opinion poll through to talking about concomitant variation in aggregate national narratives, our explanatory and expository strategy takes on something of the characteristic of a David Hockney photomontage. His picture of, say, a building, will consist of images of the façade, doors, windows, the letterbox and gutters, and the surroundings taken at different levels of resolution and magnification. Curiously enough, when assembled these better capture the idea of what the property might be like—its complexity and spirit—than a traditional house photo, such as we might find in the window of a realtor or a copy of *Better Homes and Gardens*. To make sense of the assemblage we can and should look at each component image, with its particular depth of focus and magnification and historical determinations. Yet there is also an imperative to explore how each fragment, albeit complete in itself, articulates in a relational sense with adjacent others. And eventually we can step back to take in the gestalt and see what the big picture lesson might be for social scientific explanation of the most macro intent. To attend to one plane of analysis does not mean to disrespect another so long as we shuttle back and forth, and then back again, then forward between detail and generality as isolates and aggregates confer multiplying and reciprocating insights. This is the ticket to a hermeneutics that acknowledges but also reduces complexity.

CULTURE, ACTION, AND CAUSALITY

The case that culture makes a difference or is a necessary cause of concrete outcomes in social life, such as wars, can be supported through theoretical armature as well as the methodology of comparative social science. As sketched in the previous chapter, there are several ways in which we can think of ties between systems of signs and ideas, and material; concrete actions and outcomes. Reviewing these here a little more systematically will permit a firmer anchoring of the claims of this book by elucidating the variety of ways in which culture structures must have some kind of determinate impact. Or to put it bluntly, to show that these are more than simply stories and labels. This activity is regrettably necessary because much of the most influential work in cultural theorizing has been disappointingly vague in its understanding of the relationship of culture to action and outcomes (e.g., Geertz 1973; Hunt 1986), preferring instead to reconstruct systems of meaning and then simply insist on their ubiquity and necessity for collective life. Structuralist cultural theorizing, which is the *point de départ* for our analysis, shares this flaw. Its greatest strength is in understanding culture as a relational system with its own logics and grammars. This linguistic analogy is the foundation for claims of analytic autonomy for culture (Kane 1991). Just how this magnificent and elegant and self-sustaining culture-structure connects with what happens on the ground has never been satisfactorily resolved, but the structuralist vision has been generally considered antithetical to an actor-oriented approach to social science. In the canonical writings at least sign systems seemingly propel social choices and social action in a more or less one-sided manner, following their own perverse logics. Claude Lévi-Strauss (1964, 20), the founder of anthropological structuralism, famously understood myths as "speaking themselves through men and without their knowing." Here we see glimpses of a determinism that needs to be avoided every bit as assiduously as that sometimes unintentionally generated by Millian logic.

One way we can counter this agency-free determinist move is to suggest that culture-structures provide the moral horizons and schemas of value that afford internalized motivations for action. Put simply, people strive to attain that which is good or ideal and to regulate and control that which is bad. In the political sphere we try to build democracy, bring down dictators, construct an open society, and so forth because these seem like the right things to do. By defining the sacred and profane, vice and virtue, the binary codes of civil society introduced in the last chapter provide normative fuel of this kind. Such a vision of culture has the merit of simplicity but remains vulnerable to accusations of idealism and so it has become increasingly fashionable to talk of culture in more cognitive and pragmatic terms as a provider of ways of seeing and as a resource or "tool kit" through which paths of action can be assembled (Swidler 1986). And so this book equally relies on a second argument for how culture-structures impact upon action. Agents are conceptualized in this scenario as employing established genre resources to construct stories that helpfully interpret their world. These might exert a subsequent power over their actions, for as the journalist and cultural commentator Walter Lippmann put it years ago and with astounding insight, "it is clear enough that under certain conditions men [sic] respond as powerfully to fictions as they do to realities . . . by fictions I do not mean lies. I mean representations of the environment which are in lesser or greater degree made by man [sic] himself" (Lippmann 1934, 14–15). This second position, which sees culture as a sense-making resource *for* action is not incompatible with our first position that holds culture to be a sphere of motivation and value *driving* action. As Émile Durkheim and Marcel Mauss (1963) indicated around a hundred years ago in their work on *Primitive Classification,* collective representations are ways of sorting information that are at once cognitive and evaluative. Again Lippmann got it right when he stated that "public opinion is primarily a moralized and codified version of the facts" (Lippmann 1934, 25). The discourses and narratives of civil society encode both normative directions and environment-simplifying knowledge simultaneously. We do not make sense of the world and then act in terms of our values for these operations are simultaneous and conjoined. When filtered through the discourse and story codes of civil society facts are always already moralized facts, actions sacred or profane, events full of heroes and villains.

    In confronting both determinism and idealism it is essential to remember that ceaseless, ongoing action and interpretative effort are what enables such classifications to work at the coalface of history. Geertz (1973, 5) speaks of humans as "suspended in webs of significance" that we ourselves have spun. This is an unfortunate image because it suggests that once we have made our culture, we are held fast by it. We become flies and not spiders and a kind of determinism returns. A rather better understanding—and one that Geertz was probably striving for—is to see culture as a nonmaterial internal environment of action that is continually worked and reworked by actors in an effort to endow their world with meaning and provide them with guidance toward lines of action (Alexander 1988). For the cultural system to pattern social life real people can, and indeed must, typify from contingency to culture-structure, from events to the code of this internal environment for "to traverse the world men must have maps" (Lippmann 1934, 16). In interpreting with cultural structures, we build up not only a cognitive understanding but also a moral universe and derive compass bearings for action out of what William James called the "blooming, buzzing confusion" that surrounds us. The "effort" (Alexander 1988) that individuals put into this process, both in isolation and as members of dialogic communities, is a source of indeterminacy, contingency, and creativity. Actors face choices in allocating events to sacred and profane codes and in selecting and fitting a genre from the pool of contenders that, they believe, best explains the passage of events. Expressing this issue in system-theoretic terms we can assert that codes and narratives provide resources for reducing the infernal complexity of the environment. Moreover, they operate cybernetically to thereafter generate system outputs through information processing and consequent signaling. However, the cumulative product such as we measure as opinion or legitimacy is not wholly predictable from any given environmental input. In other words both the individual human being and the collective discourse engine of civil society are nontrivial machines. So between actors and culture structures there is a felicitous reciprocity; if it is the presence of extrinsic codes and narratives that enables individuals exposed to the dialogical activity of civil society to do the work of interpreting their world, bringing contingency back into a consideration of the dynamics of legitimation, it is their effort at understanding and speaking that enables codes and narratives to make a difference.

In a rather enigmatic but often-invoked passage the German thinker Max Weber (1991, 64) famously wrote that, "Not ideas, but material and ideal interests directly govern man's conduct. Yet very frequently the 'world images' that have been created by 'ideas' have, like switchmen, determined the tracks along which action has been pushed by the dynamic of interest" (1991, 64). Often cut short and selectively quoted by conflict sociologists as proof of Weber's anticultural credentials, this statement in fact allows a strong case to be made for cultural causality. It is an insight that permits us to conceptualize culture as a steering medium that shapes action orientations. Interests provide proximate motivations for action. They are the engine of history churning out a certain kind of energy and desire. However, they need to be concretized and steered in particular directions, in part because they are frequently too general to allow us to formulate decisions about just what to do in particular situations. By influencing the perception of events, collective representations (roughly analogous to Weber's "world images") work to channel diffuse, arguably contending, interests into specific pathways of choice and enterprise. Our interests in building democracy, wealth, power, or simply "security," for example, cannot dictate our lines of action because these are mute. To understand how interests become converted into lines of policy that actually direct historical sequences we require some kind of middle level intervening variable, the cultural pointsman who defines the situation and so signals which action path should be followed.

A theoretical clue to this process can be found in what Antonio Gramsci (1992) referred to as the "conjunctural." This concept captures the ways that particular complexes and accretions of ideas shape beliefs and actions in defined concrete situations. Such conjunctural specifications of culture determine how more general interests are played out in any given here and now and converted into specific policies, strategies, and injunctions. Stuart Hall (1983), for example, has written usefully about Thatcherism as an articulation of various conservative interests and ideologies. Decoding this particular middle range ideology enables us to understand what went on in 1980s Britain. Reference to Thatcherism provides a better explanation of why Margaret Thatcher, the prime minister, and her supporters decided to go to war against Argentina, break the miner's strike, and drum up law and order politics than do generic citations to, say, the abstracted interests of capitalists or the dominant class or indeed a reified British "national interest." Although it rejects such a neo-Marxist vision of culture as (in the last instance) insufficiently attentive to cultural autonomy, this book endorses the broader vision of situated cultural formations as the filter through which more general and diffuse ideologies, beliefs, and material interests are translated into real world opinions, decisions, and actions. In the previous chapter I suggested that this pointsman task becomes particularly salient in crisis situations. Where there is imperfect information, where future outcomes and political moves have to be guessed and where intentions and bluffs have to be read, where the fog of war abounds, culture-structures offer the moral and cognitive resources that we need. In such moments of uncertainty and complexity, where it is hard to rationally calculate the right thing to do, culture steps up to the plate even more so than at other times. Once we have made our genre guess it provides an ordering and simplifying technology through which environmental cues, better thought of as "clues," are aligned first with each other to form a coherent pattern and then with prevailing material and ideal interests and so, at last, we know how to respond.

In confronting idealism it must also be emphasized that such sense-making, opinion-forming activity does not take place only inside isolated brains. A danger of the vocabulary of tool-kits and metaphorical extensions of the idea of the genre-guessing readers is that these seemingly represent cultural pragmatics as little more than the problem-solving actions of individuals. Reducing pragmatism to individualism in this way neglects the dialogic and collaborative ways in which cultural templates are deployed and sustained within civil discourse. We do not live in a society of hermits who read their newspapers, think for a little while during their evening stroll, and then consolidate their world interpretations over a pipe after supper. Interpretations are collective, emergent, and negotiated. The civil sphere is one of unfolding, dialogic, argumentative, shared activity, even if much of this is subsequently reprised and reviewed in the mental deliberations and internal, imagined conversations of each subject. Each new reading that is proposed is given over to discursive testing and challenge, to revision, and to modification and adaptation in the light of new "facts" and contending explanations. Public discourse is a place where we find a constant movement back and forth of ideas and actions, struggles to consolidate and fix meanings, adjustments of tone and narrative in wars of discursive position that involve not simply accommodations to the object world but also to the world of representations as these are made by and received by others. The Russian linguist Mikhail Bakhtin (1981) well captured this dynamic with his notion of heteroglossia, a concept that refers to the proliferation of unintended meanings and the shuttling of idea-emblems between centers and peripheries. Meaning formation and message reception is always open, incomplete, partly frustrated, and subject to efforts at renewal and repair. For this reason culture can be thought of as a "cause" in a surprisingly public and social sense. Cultural causation is not only about the invisible processes of reasoning within the mind, but rather about the witnessable public activity of sense making and persuasion. Analysis becomes a question of mapping this life history of ideas, issues, and interpretations as these unfold in multiple and intersecting ways through real-time historical sequences and leave behind their visible traces.

SOMETHING FOR CULTURE SKEPTICS

We have looked to culture as a provider of motivations and classifications, and as a resource that enables interests to be translated into actions within the broader, supraindividual context of dialogical activity within a public sphere. Those who believe in the power of cultural explanation will not need to be further convinced of these arguments. Regrettably, many do not believe and so we now need to consider and fold into our cultural explanation a third position, one that can accommodate a radical challenge to the claims of this book. There is a Machiavellian stance that insists discourse positions are agonistic strategies and are part of the wider dissimulation that cloaks more instrumental paths of action. It has long been asserted on the basis of the need for allegedly greater "realism" that ideal forms have no determinate relationship to action, with principles, morals, and beliefs invoked as a post-hoc justification for decisions that are driven by ulterior motives (Namier 1930). In social theory these alternative, "true" motivations are predictably seen as rational, strategic, and self-interested quests for money and power, and the false motives invoked by the actors as simply a cynical bid for legitimacy.

Let us play the devil's advocate and suppose that speech acts are indeed shaped solely by the rational calculus of actors in search of power. These sneaky individuals and groups refer to cultural codes and narratives in order to justify their selfish actions and choices and to give them the sheen of respectability. Let us further assume that these rather implausibly clever and sociopathic Iagos are somehow able to determine their mean-spirited best interests in uncertain, multiplayer environments in a way that is not filtered by complexity reducing cultural codes. Does that mean this book should be thrown away? Of course not: There would remain at a minimum the intellectual merit of mapping out the language games and forms of legitimate discourse through which this bogus talk about war is conducted. This, however, is a seemingly formalist endeavor even if it gives us the cheap satisfaction of epistemological advantage that comes from decoding a dominant ideology. To escape from such formalism we need to show that culture makes a difference even if we grant such adverse assumptions. It is indeed possible to go further and reconstruct a causal role for culture that cynics might find appealing and to show how discourse can still constrain action even in the presence of bad faith and the absence of internalized moral commitments. We might point first to the strand of social theorizing that emphasizes the performative aspects of social interaction (Goffman 1963, 1967), ethnomethodological studies on the problem of "accountability" to others (Garfinkel 1967), and scattered texts in the social and political sciences (Bourdieu 1977, 30–71; Mills 1978; Skinner 1988, 97–118). These works have in common the assertion that normative community standards, institutionalized speech genres, and situational frames compel actors to behave in certain ways regardless of whether they themselves (perhaps even anyone else) subscribe to these. Humpty Dumpty was wrong when he said that words meant whatever he wanted them to mean. There are limits to which the ideologies invoked by actors can be stretched to legitimize their actions—linguistic and cultural systems are, after all, collective, conventional, constraining, and supraindividual (Saussure 1960). Thus, actors are not able to perform any action they wish with the expectation that their rhetorics of legitimation will be always accepted or believed.

Even the most cynical and strategic of actors must be careful to tailor their behavior so that it appears that they sincerely hold to the rhetoric they invoke. In Alexander's (2004b) sense this minimal congruence of action and utterance is pivotal to meeting the challenge of "refusion" in public performance and demonstrating apparent good faith. In Garfinkel's alternative but surprisingly congruent formulation, actors must be witnessably in conformity with the prevalent standards of accountability, even and especially those that that they themselves have set in place. Rhetorical utterances issued in a spirit of highest cynicism will often bind the speaker to perform in certain ways regardless of their will. The critical sociologist C. Wright Mills speaks with great insight of the ways that a businessman upon joining the Rotary Club is constrained by its "public-spirited vocabulary" when he has to act out his business conduct. Consequently, the "vocabulary of motives is an important factor in his behavior" (Mills 1978, 304). Likewise the political philosopher and historian Quentin Skinner remarks that "the courses of action open to any rational agent . . . must in part be determined by the range of principles which he can profess with plausibility" and that as "any course of action is inhibited from occurring if it cannot be legitimated. It follows that any principle which helps to legitimate a course of action must also be amongst the enabling conditions of its occurrence" (Skinner 1988, 116–17).

So culture-structures, including those at work in civil discourse, shape environments of moral accountability even if they do not motivate action for all people at all times. Even cynical leaders in times of war will experience performative pressures to comply with the codes and narratives that are current within their civil society, and even more so there will be expectations of fidelity to stories that they have spun themselves. The penalties for failing to coordinate action to a prevalent or legitimate cultural charter are diverse. They might include the loss of support among elites, electoral sanction by the voting public, scratches to political Teflon, shit hitting the fan and mud that tends to stick, poor press coverage, and a tarnished image in posterity. It is precisely because our Machiavellian agents are not free to create any discourse they wish that critical social science needs to uncover Skinner's "range of principles" that are at hand in a setting and investigate their constraining properties. There is a requirement to unpack the cultural repertoires—in our case civil codes and structured narratives—through which even the most instrumental political leaders and elites attempt to legitimate their activities by rhetorical means. Speech acts directed to publics must make sense to publics, they need to appeal to accepted standards and conventional codes. Even the most propagandistic activity is constrained to work by means of these cultural structures, for it is only to the extent that they package new messages in old formats that are institutionalized and carry established resonance that propagandistic activities become successful as forms of political entrepreneurship.

With the separation of intent from utterance in this way, a new set of ironies opens up for empirical investigation. When political leaders are successful in manipulating codes and narratives in order to drum up support for dubious and self-interested policies, they may often have to live, like the overly ambitious Dr Frankenstein, with the monster they have created. Not only are they obliged to act concretely and immediately in ways that are broadly consistent with the motives and analyses they proclaim, but they may also have to do so at their own inconvenience at a later date. If agents and cultural entrepreneurs control discourse at one point in time, they might find themselves subsequently tied by their very discursive success and thereby illustrating quite nicely the claim that the force of an utterance is something that needs to be understood independently of the motivations of its speaker (Skinner 1988, 83–96). Knowledge of the formal mechanics and semantics of narratives and codes will enable us to better understand these illocutionary dynamics.

Human beings are complex in their motivations. My best guess is that actors have both normative and symbolic, and rational and strategic reasons for actions. These can be both a passion, motivated by deep internal symbolic commitments, and also a performance, oriented more instrumentally toward persuading others to see the world in a certain way. Such a multidimensional conception of strategic action, morality, and sense-making typification working simultaneously in complex situations provides a hermeneutically sensitive and yet surprisingly tough-minded model of the processes whereby action and cultural forms interact in concrete political struggles. If actors attempt to disseminate beliefs through the community with varying degrees of reflexivity, commitment, and bad-faith, disentangling the relative strength of these components is perhaps impossible. Although we can assemble evidence that sometimes supports one and sometimes another perspective, closure remains an impossibility. Nevertheless, as we have seen, positions can be developed making the case for culture ubiquitous, for talk counts perhaps more than thought.

DATA SOURCES

Issues of epistemology, method, and social theory dealt with, we can turn now to the more specific problem of data. If narratives and codes in civil society make a difference we need to find them. But just where do we look? The key to answering this question is to follow a clue from Jürgen Habermas (1989), reject his pessimistic conclusions about modernity, and realize that the mass media today function as our public sphere (Jacobs 2000). Justifications for policy are launched into this public sphere, as are critiques and commentaries on the state of the world. The mass media is the realm where remarks are directed and reproduced that are intended for an overhearing public. It is the pivotal arena where claims-making and sense-making activity takes place and where dialogical combats over ideas, struggles over cultural codings, and interpretative genre wars take place. This claim perhaps requires some explanation in the light of common theories, which hold that the content of the mass media reflects little more than hegemonic interests (usually those of advertisers and owners), or else that it arises from organizational and practical imperatives of news organizations or from the demands of the communications technology itself (usually journalistic deadlines, editorial hierarchies, and format conventions; see Gans 1979, 78–79). Consequently, in what follows I elaborate the pluralist conception of the media and explicate its relationship to civil society.

Civil society is by its nature and very definition public rather than private, and can be understood as an associative sphere of communicative activity (Walzer 1991) oriented toward the moral regulation of society (Alexander and Smith 1993) that thrives on and demands the relatively unrestricted interchange of information and opinion. In starting the Reformation, Martin Luther had to nail his theses to the church door to make his point. Today he would have an easier time of it locating a dispersed audience, making use of newspapers, television, the Internet, and radio to get his critique across. These make possible the exchange of symbols and circulation of collective representations by operating as a "functional substitute for concrete group contact" (Alexander 1988, 108) and allowing the flow of information between separate societal spheres (McCormack 1986). It is through the mass media that constituencies and interests engage in dialogue and make their case to the unseen generalized others of public opinion. Hence, the mass media in liberal democracies are to be understood not only in economistic terms as "the outcome of an adjustment between demand and supply for information and cultural services" (McQuail 1985, 96) but also in a more constitutive way as the ideas forum and narrative engine of our time. In Herbert Gans's (1979, 297–98) terms the media are the "managers of the symbolic area" who reinforce and construct the collectivities of nation and society. They "narrate the social" (Sherwood 1994) and in so doing contribute to the collective effort of weaving those webs of meaning of which Geertz (1973) spoke.

Power, it should go without saying, plays a role in the formation and distribution of these meanings. There are real inequalities of access and influence. Yet the media are not "completely subservient to the state or political institutions" (Negrine 1989, 18)—a reality we see when presidential scandals are uncovered, politicians hounded, and corporations denounced for running sweatshops. There is feedback and symbiosis between the divergent concerns of civil society itself, including those of dissident pressure groups, and the content of the media (De Fleur and Ball-Rokeach 1966, esp. 20ff., 233ff.; Negrine 1989, 19; Newcomb and Hirsch 1984). Such a pluralist theoretical stance has been long supported by a body of research from the days of Paul Lazarsfeld onward demonstrating the very real power that the audience has in shaping messages in the mass media (e.g., Becker 1982; Billings 1986; Griswold 1983; Lazarsfeld, Berelson, and Gaudet 1944). This understanding rejects the degrading stereotype provided by critical theory of the audience as an undifferentiated, uncritical and passive "mass of powerless individuals" who are "bombarded with hegemonic values" (Billings 1986, 200; cf. Horkheimer and Adorno 1972; Marcuse 1964), replacing it with an understanding of the media as a forum for both shaping and expressing popular concerns—albeit an imperfect one.

There are several ways in which this producer-audience reciprocity is reproduced and through which the media come to provide an indirect index of public opinions rather than simply elite or professional worldviews. In the first place, journalists and commentators are living and breathing members of society and they share the same world with everyone else. They take kids to school, watch TV, and sometimes even eat junk food. They do not have a Martian habitus. In point of fact research shows they share many of the cultural orientations, reality judgments, and biases of their readers (see Gans 1979, 39–55, 201–2), notwithstanding the existence of a distinctive journalistic culture that is variously characterized as liberal and conservative depending on the origin of the critique. Secondly, editors and writers select and write stories with the abilities, interests, and preferences of their intended audience in mind (Cantor and Cantor 1986; Gans 1979, 89–90). The act of cultural production is oriented toward consumption. The fit may be imperfect but it is a nonrandom approximation. Thirdly, strange as it may seem, there is feedback to this approximation through the armatures of the capitalist economy. One hates to sound like a record stuck in a groove, but our friend Walter Lippmann (1934, 321ff.) got it right yet again when he pointed out long ago that consumers have a remarkable degree of freedom as to which media they will purchase, and as to whether or not they will purchase. Moreover, people tend to buy newspapers and magazines in which they have trust and confidence, that reflect their interests, and with which they are in moral agreement. Economic forces thereby compel the printed mass media to continually adapt to the tastes of their readership for a newspaper that angers its consumers "is a bad medium for an advertiser" (Lippmann 1934, 323–24; see also Gans 1979, 214).

One problem with turning to the media to retrieve culture patterns is that there is a surfeit of information. Can we narrow the search for civil discourse a little more closely and efficiently? Restricting the focus becomes possible and the research effort thereby practicable when we apply some criteria. The sources need to: (1) be available over each war and country to allow for cross-national and trans-historical comparability; (2) be of seriousness and centrality to civil discourse rather than peripheral or primarily entertaining; (3) contain the extended and elaborated discourses through which complex narrations are articulated. These requirements lead to a focus on printed information in the enduring, widely distributed broadsheets and quality magazines of each country. Whereas in Enlightenment salons, political tracts and essays were eagerly digested (Speier 1980), so today informed and concerned members of civil society read the serious-minded press— Schumpeter's (1950) model citizen is an avid consumer of the mass news media. This view is perhaps elitist. This does not mean that it is wrong. Conflict sociology itself has long asserted that we need look for the most part to elites and higher-status groups in order to understand the issue of legitimacy (Campbell 1987). Short of interview studies the quality print media provides the best window we have into the cultural frames held by those who are closer to the centers of civic life and what Shils (1975) has called the sacred centers of institutional power in our societies. Regardless of private opinions, this is still the place where serious *public* accounting and *public* world-ordering activity takes place.

Notwithstanding its current ubiquity the electronic media is of less use to our project than we might suppose. Television was in its infancy at the time of our first event, the 1956 Suez Crisis and the Internet only really got cracking in the mid-1990s, raising methodological issues of comparability over the cases.[1] There is also the matter of data availability. In America, for example, the archiving of television programs only really began with the establishment of the Vanderbilt Television Archive in 1968. Problems arising from state ownership and control dog historical research on early television in Europe where it was often the carrier of the voice of the nation. In any case television can be sidestepped because research has long suggested that the print media—and in particular organs such as the *New York Times, The Times, Le Monde*—continue to set the agenda for serious current affairs coverage. Such sources are "virtually mandatory reading for the political, intellectual and journalistic elite" and have "a tremendous influence over the network television news broadcasts" (Jacobs 2000, 8; also Gitlin 1980). The latter tend to be parasitic on the quality print media's decisions as to what is important. Additionally, it should be noted that the content of radio and television is typically fragmentary. Their news and current affairs programming usually involves factual adumbration and reportage rather than extended discourse oriented toward justification or critique. The print media, by contrast, is more dialogic, with debate and advocacy often structured into its activity as a normative component of cultural production. It is the technological format whose economic and semiotic systems permit extended, reasoned expositions in editorial, op-ed, and feature review writing. These are the places where cultural codings and narratives are formed and justifications made most explicit in

our society. The print media, in short, are the strategic research site for un-
covering the complex structures of civil discourse.

Consequently, my primary research activity involved more than a thousand
of hours of reading in library newspaper and microform rooms, although, in
the case of the War in Iraq, I also used online versions of regular newspapers.
In subsequent hermeneutic reconstructions patterns were identified, genres
attributed to utterances, and efforts made to understand the narrative universes of both advocates and critics of each war. The presentation of data
in the empirical chapters of this book broadly reflects the analytic priority
that saw most attention given over to the core, agenda-setting print media
of each nation. We are talking here about the central, must-read sources of
serious information and debate that have national importance. For example,
The Times, The Guardian, the *New York Times, El País, Time, Newsweek, Cambio
16, Le Monde, Le Figaro.* In many cases I read every single edition of these publications for the most intense months of each crisis. Some further sampling
effort was made to ensure that views across the Left/Right spectrum were
captured for each country and that the reproduction of these views in the
dominant print media was representative. This sometimes led to peripheral
media targeted at particular constituencies, or to newspapers and magazines
with national circulations but with less pretence to neutrality.

Although items of extended textual data through which the media narrates
the social, such as editorials, op-ed, and in-depth evaluative reportage and
commentary are pivotal to the project of this book we are not solely dependent on such material. Other sources of information can be used to thicken
our account. Parliamentary debates and political speeches provide a fruitful
source of data when it comes to unpacking the structure of civil discourse and
its distribution over the ideological spectrum. Arguments between politicians
that are conducted in public forums are not simply the political language
of the state but rather speech acts directed toward a public sphere of generalized others. Frequently consisting of justifications of particular forms of
controversial action, they provide an unusually explicit resource with which
to reconstruct the relationship between cultural logics and event interpretations in underpinning particular policy positions. Autobiographies by political players and secondary texts by historians and journalists often contain
"backstage" information about what people were thinking or saying. Official
reports from state bureaucracies often include carefully coded critique and
advocacy couched in a neutral bureaucratic language. Letters to the editors
of newspapers are, of course, edited. They do not perfectly map onto public
opinion. However, we can use them with caution to reconstruct the reception
of lines of reasoning and as a resource with which to get some sense of the

national mood. Opinion polls offer a tool of sorts for reconstructing world-views toward the periphery of civil society. These are usually hermeneutically weak but do provide robust information on the wider distribution of support for particular policy positions and sometimes, if the question wording is helpful to us, the endorsement of particular narrative frames. Finally, we can look to and interpret those forms of behavior that betray sentiment. For example, street demonstrations, sales of flags, and parliamentary uproar might offer evidence of collective effervescence, solidarity, or outrage.

Of course none of these information sources is perfect and all might contain some sample bias. Much the same could be said of any other form of information in social science—surveys have response rate problems, interview contexts influence what is said, participant observers are not neutral, and so forth. In combination, however, our diverse sources and forms of data allow a reliable picture to be drawn of what is being said and how such statements are organized. Because all these are directed toward diverse audiences (proximate or distant; partisan, bureaucratic or generic; as citizens, voters, or customers) and are produced by institutionally differentiated individuals and organizations they enable strong inferences to be drawn about the ubiquity of our culture structures and can counter the claim that we have uncovered simply media codes, not some more general coin of public discourse. They allow an accurate account of discourses both descriptive and performative that are oriented toward the public sphere and a somewhat less reliable one of the distribution of the belief systems that might underpin these. Private opinions and excluded discourses are, by definition, private and excluded. These are not our concern—they belong to another book and another research strategy. This book is about public language games and visible policy.

THREE

THE SUEZ CRISIS OF 1956

Largely forgotten today, the Suez Crisis of 1956 should be remembered not only as one of the most significant and perplexing events in the cold war but also as an object lesson in genre politics. The unexpected outcomes and paradoxes of the episode graphically demonstrate how interpretative frameworks influence policy choices and systems of accountability. We need to begin by outlining what happened. Performing this task is not so easy as it might seem. An implicit irony is unleashed when a text about the seemingly arbitrary representation of history proffers its own version of events. We cannot stand outside of genre choice here but we do have the benefit of hindsight and the advantage of a relatively disinterested, time-distant gaze. Some kind of story is required in order to set the ball rolling, to introduce the historical sequence, and to allow the narrative accounts more endemic to events to be subsequently played off one another. So here as in the other empirical chapters I offer a brief history. It attempts to sit squarely in the low mimetic genre, providing some relatively uncontroversial facts and event information to allow readers to make sense of the diverse native interpretations that follow.

In the early 1950s a military junta overthrew the administration of Egypt's King Farouk, whose regime was widely thought of at the time as corrupt and decadent. A prime mover in this coup d'état was a charismatic young officer named Gamal Abdel Nasser. The ensuing military government promoted a strange hybrid of socialist, pan-Arab, populist, and neutralist policy. Over the next few years Nasser's personal power grew and he soon became his nation's leader. In foreign policy Nasser assumed the role of *tertius gaudens,* courting both East and West and playing off their respective advances. The centerpiece of his ambitious national development policy was the building of the Aswan High Dam across the Nile River. This flagship project would provide not only national prestige but also power for Egypt's expanding industry and burgeoning population. After extensive negotiations, Nasser found that neither the United States nor the USSR was willing to fund the work. In July 1956, he decreed the nationalization of the Suez Canal claiming that his action would provide the necessary resources. Since its construction by colonial interests during the high-Victorian era, the Suez Canal had been a strategic and commercial waterway of considerable international importance. It remained, however, the property of private shareholders, most of them British and French, not Egyptian. As an expression of national sovereignty and autonomy this move was extremely popular among the Egyptian people. Wider diplomatic responses ranged from approval (Soviets and third world), to concern (Spain and the United States) to outrage (Britain and France). Throughout the summer of 1956 a series of conferences and diplomatic initiatives failed to resolve the issue of who was to control the canal. After an extensive military buildup, the British and French concluded a secret agreement with the relatively new state of Israel. Toward the end of October 1956, Israel invaded the Sinai Peninsula and advanced toward the Nile. On November 5, British and French forces invaded the Canal Zone, ostensibly to keep the canal open and to separate the combatants. Some 1,100 British and French paratroopers took control of Port Said at the head of the waterway. The military action had to be aborted just a few days later. In a situation unique in the history of the cold war, America allied with the Soviet Union and against its closest allies. There were threatening notes from the Soviets, diplomatic and economic pressures from the United States, and a run on the pound that chewed up some $420 million in scarce British reserves in just a few days. A cease-fire was declared (Eden 1960, 554ff.). In a subsequent humiliating United Nations session, Britain and France were censured by both the United States and the USSR. Their troops began to withdraw from Egypt soon afterward (For overview see Graebner 1979, 139; Schulzinger 1990, 250; Spanier 1977, 85ff.; Stoessinger 1979, 99ff.; Warburg 1966, 104; Yoder 1986, 57ff.). Within a few months the British prime minister Anthony Eden had resigned and in England the word "Suez" became forever tied to another: "Fiasco."

Why had this unlikely sequence transpired? The challenge of Suez for two or three generations of historians has been to understand why Britain and France embarked on a foolhardy and ill conceived military enterprise. They have misunderstood the issue. The real puzzle is to figure out why the United States did not go to war. Why did America split with its allies and stand shoulder to shoulder with the Soviet Union—a state that was not only a military rival but also culturally encoded as deeply antidemocratic, communist, and rapacious? Why did America, the defender of the capitalist system, fail to protect the vulnerable property rights of foreign corporations in exploitable third-world contexts? Why did Eisenhower split with Eden, his personal friend of the World War II struggle against tyranny?

THE UNITED STATES AND SUEZ

At least part of the answer to these questions lies in the genre politics of Suez. To put it briefly, within U.S. civil discourse we find a positive coding of Nasser and a low mimetic genre shaping perceptions of the nationalization of the canal. Why was this? The obvious answer is to suggest that typifications from events to big picture frames simply reflect interests and that in this case interests dictated a measured diplomatic and cultural response. In the work of political historians we can identify a raft of factors cited to explain such a relaxed U.S. policy toward Egypt. It has been argued that the proximity of an election made Eisenhower and Dulles unwilling to rock the boat through an aggressive anti-Nasser policy (Stoessinger 1979). An alternative form of explanation looks to national rather than party-political interests and suggests that there was a fear of Soviet reaction and the escalation of events to the status of a World War (Doyle 1999, 87). A third account focuses on the worries that a forceful response might engender antagonism to U.S. economic and political interests in the Middle East, the loss of support among non-aligned states and promote a movement toward the Soviet Union among the nations of the Middle East (Spanier 1977, 121; Yoder 1986, 59). A final, less complex, reason is that the United States simply had "no interests at Suez comparable to those of Britain and France" (Graebner 1979, 139). These all seem very sensible grounds for the emergence of a very sensible discourse. What I want to suggest, however, is that such argument explains less than meets the eye for it mates discourses, outcomes, and reasons after the cards have been placed face up on the table. Let me explain.

Hindsight, as they say, is 20/20 and the writing of history is a retrospective activity that all too often fails to reflect on the ways such a privilege might influence its patterns of accounting. As Roland Barthes (1975) has pointed out, knowing how a story unfolds provides an epistemological advantage to the reader that is simply not present the first time through. Once Time has closed the doors of possibility, we start to talk of what happened in terms of what happened, not what could have happened. Events are arranged post-facto into tidy patterns. What were only "clues" to onlookers and participants in a hazy and emergent sequence become fixed as self-evident "facts" and hard realities to those looking back. We reverse-engineer from action outcomes and identify and invoke reasons and interests that account for these. Yet when we open up what Time has closed off, such tidy explanations become problematic. Lived events are a messy business, replete with contradictory signals and possible future paths as they eternally unfold. Looking even briefly into these roads not taken and demonstrating their possibility is enough to show that "interests" are extremely problematic to define, that there is a vast universe of possible "interests" at play in any particular historical moment and that any given "interest" can call for several possible lines of action. The truth of the matter is that cultural systems determine the real-time perception of these interests, they determine which of these are more relevant and they determine what should be done to protect them. To explain outcomes post hoc in terms of interests and reasons is often to reify these as environments of action without exploring their situated interpretation by actors. We should instead unpack the world-ordering systems of meaning through which these take on relevance for real people in real historical sequences.

Thinking counterfactually enables us to destabilize the false certainty of the retrospectively imputed interest as an adequate explanation—so let us make this more concrete. It is quite easy, when we study the historical record, to locate a number of good reasons that could well have led to the United States joining the military intervention in Egypt. Had the United States gone to war these would no doubt have been cited by historians to account for a violent policy. Firstly, there were a number of ideological triggers for a hostile response to Egypt and its deeds. As British and French responses showed, there can be little doubt that Nasser's talk and actions provided more than enough fuel for vilification and intervention. Nasser's Egypt was continually skirmishing with Israel, a nation with a powerful lobby in the United States. Nasser himself had been in battle with Israeli forces. The military coup he had led was unashamedly and explicitly "revolutionary" in its rhetoric and had initiated various types of socialist style policy including land reform. The junta was actually called a Revolutionary Command Council. The Farouk government, in contrast, was exactly the kind of regime with which capitalists and major powers liked to deal. It was shortsighted, selfish, corrupt, compliant, and oppressive. More important still, Nasser's Egypt had extensive diplomatic, economic, and military dealings with the communist world. And if all this was not enough, his country came replete with Nazi style insignia, propaganda, and even hundreds of ex-Nazi advisors.

In terms of the American ideology circa the 1950s, then, a hostile understanding of Nasser was within the realm of possibility. What about those
allegedly objective realpolitik factors we have already cited? Do not these fully
explain American neutrality and its ability to overlook the categorical imperatives of its own ideology? When viewed counterfactually these become less
forceful by the minute. If Eisenhower was wary of conflict because of an impending election he might also have considered the well-known proposition
that the presence of a war or crisis is often significant in increasing presidential popularity. An attempt by Eisenhower, the military hero of World War
II, to inflate the importance of Suez could well have paid election dividends
as Americans went to the polls on November 6, 1956. Cynics have argued
that this is exactly what George Bush Jr. and George Bush Sr. were doing
some decades later. The issue of "interests" as defined by the Soviet threat and
the looming danger of escalation to World War III is similarly problematic.
Even profoundly anticultural sociobiologists agree that there are two ways to
deal with fear and risk in a given situation—retreat or aggression. Worries
about political and economic consequences were by no means sufficient to
prevent forceful U.S. actions both before and after Suez. The Berlin Airlift,
the Korean War, intervention in Vietnam, and the Cuban missile crisis were
all examples of crisis escalating policies undertaken in the face of the "communist threat" to support the "free world." There is no prima facie reason
why Suez could not have joined the basket. Certainly President Eisenhower
and his right-hand man John Foster Dulles were no strangers to strong-arm
tactics. Dulles even proposed the use of nuclear weapons in Indochina. As
John Stoessinger perceptively puts it, Dulles was a "crusader," " . . . cast in
the mold of the old Puritans" (Stoessinger 1979, 100). An ideologue in favor
of activism, Dulles was normally not content with a policy of containing the
communist menace. He wanted to actively roll back Soviet influence: "There
was, to him, no room for neutrality in the struggle between Good and Evil"
(Stoessinger 1979, 103). For these kinds of ideological reasons Dulles had already withdrawn America's offer of $56 million support for the Aswan High
Dam in a fit of pique following Nasser's recognition of communist China
(ibid., 113)—this is hardly the action of an appeaser. The argument that forceful anti-Nasser action would threaten U.S. interests can be confronted by one
that argues that *failing* to confront Nasser over Suez would damage these.
For example, two-thirds of the world's oil reserves lay in the Middle East,
and U.S. dominated oil companies controlled two-thirds of those resources
(*Time*, August 13, 1956). These too were vulnerable to nationalization. A show
of force against Nasser might head off such unpleasant possibilities. Indeed

it is arguably the case that British Prime Minister Eden's pitch to America was eventually proven right. Nasser was to become a de-stabilizing influence on America's Middle Eastern hegemony. As one historian points out, Suez resulted not only in the collapse of British power in the Middle East but also in "the strengthening of Arab nationalism, and the consolidation of Egyptian-Russian links" (Spanier 1977, 120). Would American have wanted this outcome?

There seems to be then a very strong case for the counterfactual possibility of American military intervention in Suez. An alternative history might have seen the United States move with its allies to consolidate and demonstrate Western power in Egypt, to secure oil supplies, and to forestall Arab nationalism and Soviet expansion. Such a hypothetical is made even more plausible by virtue not only of prevailing responses to Nasser in France and England, but also as we will see by the opinions of a minority in America. Realizing this undermines the faith we might have that reasons and facts can speak for themselves in accounting for actions. The temporal location of the historian is refracted in the sleek lines of the post-hoc explanation that invokes clearly identifiable interests and neat correspondences with outcomes. Yet it is not interests, but perceptions of what these are and what to do about them that determine national policy positions in the epistemological and ontological spaces of lived history. These perceptions are shaped by civil discourses and genre structures that work with the clues thrown out by events but are not determined by objective realities in any simple or unmediated way.

So why did an ideologically conservative 1950s America fail to engage in military action against a procommunist dictator who had nationalized a privately held asset, indirectly threatened oil supplies, and could have set up a Soviet beachhead in the Mediterranean? The answer lies in autonomous culture structures. These filter information and set out courses of action. They suggest which underlying interests need to be listened to and tell how relatively diffuse beliefs and ideologies might best be served in the here and now of ongoing crisis. Nasser's move in nationalizing the Suez Canal was a meaningless event—only when coded and narrated through familiar culture-structures could its clues be understood, complexity reduced, and context given.

Eisenhower and Dulles probably believed that they were acting rationally in accord with America's material interests and cultural values. Yet in the end their capacity for engaging in rational action was constrained by the horizons of their understanding, by their genre guesses, and by the genre politics at play in the wider public sphere.

NASSER THE HERO

Genre theory suggests that there is a certain path-dependence to interpretation. Once a particular typification of agents and events has fallen into place it can be remarkably difficult to turn this around. As with the scientific paradigms so famously discussed by Thomas Kuhn (1962), we see that new findings tend to be assimilated to old ways of thinking and contradictory clues are shrugged off or brushed aside. There are good reasons for stable beliefs of this kind. They allow for the efficient processing of bits and pieces of emergent information and provide the sense of ontological security that comes from knowing that the world is pretty much the same from one day to the next. As anyone who has lived in a quake zone knows, it is unsettling to have the ground move under your feet too often. We do not expect or desire the novel we are reading to switch from romance to tragedy and then back again with each new chapter. Likewise we do not anticipate political actors and nations behaving in ways that defy the ongoing expectations we have developed about them. In general, new events are woven into ongoing master narratives.

The stickiness of a genre attribution is a characteristic of genre politics that was to work to the advantage of Colonel Gamal Abdel Nasser. He was fortunate that on the eve of Suez his government, although avowedly revolutionary, was not considered in the United States to be "communist." Instead of being read as a profane figure and a potential threat to world peace, Nasser was viewed as a romantic if mysterious and slightly immature man motivated by high ideals. Egypt, the object of struggle in the early narratives of his rule, was seen as moving closer to a sacred state of freedom under modernity thanks to his efforts. In other words Nasser was represented as the charismatic figure responsible for leading Egypt away from the Discourse of Repression we identified in chapter one and toward the Discourse of Liberty. In the American media we see him narrated as a heroic protagonist in a folktale who had overcome a variety of antagonists in his journey—the corrupt *Ancien Régime* of playboy King Farouk, fanatical Egyptian communists and Muslims, and even starchy British colonialists. If it was true that he was a dictator, he was a "dictator by default" who "did not plan to rule." "Even his critics would absolve him of the charge of personal ambition," stated the *New York Times* (September 19, 1954). His policy seemed to be directed by good sense and the quest to fulfill universalistic ideals rather than by the ideological fanaticism expected of dictators and Arabs. Prior to Suez, discussions of Nasser's rise to power generally depicted a pragmatist and idealist, not a demagogue. Here was a moderate and sensible leader who could be explicitly contrasted with Marx, Hitler, and Islamic fanatics.

> The search continued for a program and a doctrine to express in concrete form the deeply rooted but ill-defined yearnings for social justice, political freedom, personal integrity and full national sovereignty. . . . It is the absence of any dogmatic blueprint—a *Mein Kampf* or *Das Kapital*—and the reliance on empiricism in the solution of problems that give the regime (its) . . . character. . . . While others ranging from the wild-eyed partisans of the Moslem Brotherhood up to President Naguib himself, ranted occasionally of a *jihad*, or holy war, to throw the British out of the Suez Canal Zone by force; Colonel Nasser recognized this as the course that could most surely bring the regime to ruin. (*New York Times*, September 19, 1954)

Time magazine (September 26, 1955) spoke of Nasser as an appealing and active figure. He was "the most powerful, most energetic and potentially most promising leader among the long divided, long misled Moslems in the Middle East," and an "All-American fullback." Likewise, the *New York Times* gave a nod to this powerful character, this autonomous subject who was the very antithesis of the Arab fanatic: "His face in repose is grave and thoughtful, accented frequently by a quick warm smile. Normally, he speaks quietly and courteously and only a handful of intimates have seen him in a rage. The overall impression he gives is of a man whose powers are carefully inventoried and controlled" (September 19, 1954). In Joseph Conrad's sense he was "one of us" rather than one of them. The details of Nasser's personal experiences with violence, demonstrations, secret plots, and the politics of the crowd could have threatened this characterization. They did not. Far from being a rabble-rouser, Nasser was injected into the archetype mold of the picaresque hero who moves from one unstable and temporary triumph to the next. He was a patriot, a heroic Gandhi-like figure fighting against the odds for the good of his country, struggling against oppression and injustice, blessed with *froda*, and willing to risk his own life to prove a point.

> Nasser led a group of students in a big demonstration on National Struggle Day in Cairo. Police and British troops fired on demonstrators swarming across the Nile in boats and on rafts. Nasser escaped the bullets, but again was clubbed. . . . The following year he was expelled from school for participating in another illegal demonstration, but was reinstated when fellow students threatened to burn down the school . . . in the Sudan he led a cabal against

the senior officers, the often corrupt products of royal favoritism whose rank increased with girth rather than professional ability. (*New York Times*, September 19, 1954)

As he rose to make his speech a man stood up in the audience and fired eight shots at him. Nasser remained standing and all the shots missed. (*Time*, 26/9/1955)

Astute readers will have noticed a series of evil others opposed to Nasser in such stories: fanatics, despots, and colonialists. This should not be surprising. As we discussed in the opening chapter of this book, an enemy is logically necessary for heroic storytelling. Given the way that events were to unfold the representation of the British in America deserves special attention here. They were associated with the Discourse of Repression. They used force to maintain an illegitimate domination and were arbitrary, disdainful, racist. They "ruled pretty much as they pleased and called the Egyptians 'wogs'" (*Time*, September 26, 1955). This identification of the British with the role of colonial bully was to re-emerge in a stronger form during the Suez crisis itself.

On the eve of Suez, Nasser's heroic status seems to have slipped a little as he engaged in a dalliance with evil communist powers. Yet the codes and narratives that had built up his reputation as an autonomous and independent spirit, qualities held to be inimical to collectivistic and robotic communism, prevented him from being tarred as a helpless Soviet satellite. For example, *Time* bewailed Nasser's major arms deal with the Soviet Union in 1955, likening the shipment of weapons to a "Trojan Horse" through which Soviet influence would be expanded. Yet at the same time it conceded that Nasser "behaved like a man convinced that his spoon is long enough to sup with the devil" (November 14, 1955). The mercurial Arab had become a kind of heroic trickster able to dice with evil and come out on top. And so it was that a few days before the Suez nationalization Nasser could be given a favorable report card: "In its four years in power, the military junta of 38-year-old Lieut. Colonel Nasser could boast of considerable progress. It had overthrown a corrupt monarch, broken a sordid feudal aristocracy's long-held power over Egypt's politics, disowned the murderous fanaticism of the Moslem Brotherhood and driven British troops from Egyptian soil after 74 years of occupation" (*Time*, July 2, 1956). How can we summarize this perspective on Nasser? Looking back to the structural model presented toward the start of this book we can see that we have all the elements of a romantic genre. Nasser is the protagonist. He is struggling to make headway against a series of antidemocratic dangers—Britain, Islamic fanatics, the Soviet Union. The object of struggle is Egypt and, more specifically its future destiny. The prognosis of the romantic narrative is optimistic—Nasser is pulling his nation into modernity and democracy, assisting it toward a closer correspondence with the Discourse of Liberty. He deserves America's trust and its moral and practical support in this task.

AMERICA THE SENSIBLE

Nasser carried the inertia of this narration with him into the period immediately following the nationalization. Throughout August 1956, we find pretty much the same cultural structures in place. If Nasser had become symbolically polluted by virtue of taking the canal, this was only in the weak sense of a cheeky boy who had stolen an apple from the lunchbox of the school bully. The big picture remained that of a patriot leading an Egyptian romance of modernization and emancipation. Commentary during the summer of 1956 reiterated that in place of a repressive and archaic regime he had installed "the most effective, certainly the most honest government in years" and that the Egyptian leader was "a man sincere in devotion to the improvement of his impoverished land and desperate people" (*Time*, August 8, 1956). Despite this high calling his personal life and character remained reassuringly familiar. As Americans strolled to their newsstands in the final week of August 1956, it was a smiling Nasser, top button undone, who greeted them from the cover of *Time*. This was a sympathetic and homely figure rather than a mysterious and alien Arab or an arrogant and imperious national leader hell bent on ruling the Middle East. When they turned the pages inside they could read about his appreciation of Jane Russell movies, his enjoyment of tennis and the beach, and how he loved to watch *Tom and Jerry* at home with his family (August 20, 1956). His residence was described as a modest five-room bungalow. Nasser, it seems, was a suburban American family man who just happened to be the Egyptian President. It comes as no surprise then to read that he practiced his marksmanship in time-honored American fashion by "lining up empty Coca-Cola bottles in the sand and shooting them up with his service revolver" (*Time*, August 27, 1956).[1] Discussions on the Suez Canal nationalization in U.S. debate invariably filtered information through the Nasser lens. The act was seen as a personal one and not as a state action. As Nasser was fundamentally good, essentially one of us, so it had to be that the action was well intentioned. Letters to the same *Time* (August 27, 1956) magazine made it clear that Nasser was trying to do the best he could for his people and that we should feel "some degree of sympathy with a man. . . . who seeks the deliverance of his country from a foreign yoke."

Although in Britain and France Nasser was seen as a tyrant on the march (we come to this understanding in a few pages), *Time* magazine made it clear that such a reading of the Egyptian leader was mistaken: "Nasser's *The Philosophy of Revolution* has now become must reading. . . . France's Premier Mollet calls it Nasser's *Mein Kampf.* In a time of tension, the comparison is pat, but overreaching" (August 27, 1956). This kind of "let's cool it folks" commentary is a tell that a deflationary, low mimetic genre is being advocated. Seen from Washington and New York Nasser was not Hitler, and Suez was not the Rhineland. Far from being an event of world-historical importance, Suez was simply a tiresome "squabble" (*U.S. News and World Report,* September 28, 1956).[2] A core feature of low mimesis is that moral differences between parties within a plot are only weakly drawn. So we find Nasser's modest pollution matched by that of Britain and France. America's great allies in the Second World War fight against dictatorship now found themselves characterized within the Discourse of Repression. They were emotive, aggressive, and uncompromising, reacting to Nasser's seizure with "white-lipped anger" and refusing the very reasonable path of taking the affair to the United Nations. Eden was seen as holding to unrealistic Victorian attitudes and making the wild "Palmerstonian boasts" about the capabilities of the Royal Navy (*Time,* August 13, 1956). Those in Europe calling for military action were denounced as irrational and emotional "hotheads" (*U.S. News and World Report,* August 17, 1956). As Eden put it in his memoir, Britain and France were perceived in America as "ganging-up" on Egypt (Eden 1960, 461). The impression of repressive colonial power was reinforced by continual news of violence in Cyprus, where British forces were struggling with separatist guerrillas. Only when we have this narration of Britain in mind can we understand why a middle-American clergyman should feel impelled to write: "Give the canal to Egypt as a moral debt long overdue. Long Live President Nasser" (letter, *Time,* September 24, 1956).

In chapter one it was argued that a hallmark of low mimesis is the belief that extreme, unorthodox, and violent solutions are not called for and that sensible, incremental, prudent actions can bring about modest positive results. In America, Suez was an international relations event of the "business as usual" kind—the administrator's and bank manager's mentality ruled. While the militant British and French rattled their sabers and held to rigid policies, Dulles and Eisenhower were busy preaching the virtues of flexibility and moderation. Dulles rhetorically condemned Nasser's action as a violation of law and property rights and argued for a pragmatic compromise. This move bore not only the stamp of patterns of thinking characterizing the low mimetic worldview, but also the imprimatur of that preexisting romantic understanding of Egypt whose themes of benevolent ascent suggested that an eventual rapprochement was possible. The matter should be solvable, Dulles argued, if it were investigated not in terms of "great slogans" but in "detailed ingredients" and the "concrete practical things" needed for "impartial, competent and efficient operation of the canal" (quoted in *Time*, September 10, 1956). "Patience and resourcefulness" (Dulles, press conference, September 26, 1956, quoted in *U.S. News and World Report*, October 5, 1956) would lead to a solution such as the Suez Canal Users' Association that he was proposing. The *New York Times* (editorial, September 30, 1956) for its part asserted that the United Nations would be useful not as a forum for moral denunciations, but rather because it could "suggest a solution or several alternative solutions; it can provide the technical and secretarial assistance without which the arguments might be nothing but a wild shouting in the desert."

The historian John Stoessinger accurately points out that Dulles's proposals for a Users' Association, "embodied the staggering assumption that somehow the problem could be resolved on a purely technical level" (1979, 17). The ideologue had become a fixer. Eisenhower himself reflected this mood arguing in an August 8 press conference that, "there is good reason to hope that good sense will prevail. Here is something that is so important to the whole world that I think a little sober second thinking is going to prevail in a good many quarters" (quoted in *U.S. News and World Report*, August 17, 1956). Such a climate of positive expectation generated by a low-mimetic can-do pragmatism may be traced throughout media reports and commentaries in August 1956. There was no real sense of impending conflict. The *U.S. News and World Report* captures this mood when it argued that war was unlikely because of interests and economics.

> Crisis at Suez looks like the real thing, the brink of war, but—Behind the harsh words and show of arms there are compelling reasons for both sides to go slow and work something out. Middle East oil, the real prize, is vital to Europe. But it isn't much good to anybody else, and Arabs know it. If they can't sell oil to the West, they'll have trouble finding other customers. Russia is a poor prospect. Same thing applies to Nasser and Suez. If the Canal is closed he is practically out of business. Result: Outlook is for a deal short of war. (August 17, 1956)

The *New York Times* agreed suggesting that, "It is a matter of dollars and cents and of common sense—and the general welfare" (editorial, August 3, 1956). Although "Nasser's bluff" would have to be called, it would be called "not by force, but by reason, economics and law" (editorial, *New York Times*, July 28, 1956). The State Department gave passports to Americans to enable them to take up jobs in Egypt that had fallen vacant following the withdrawal of British and French river pilots from the Canal Zone. Such policies paid dividends for the domestic reputation of Dulles, who was characterized as a practical man behaving in a professional and responsible manner and not as a flag bearer of the American Dream. *Time* spoke of a "Lawyer Dulles" who was "calm, bulky and phlegmatic" and who "took the position that Egypt as a sovereign nation had a legal right to nationalize the Canal Company" (August 13, 1956).

Although we consider British responses to Suez in a few pages time, we need here to introduce the efforts of Prime Minister Eden to change the American reading of events. Genre wars involve dialogical efforts to shift the reasoning of others. This is rarely done by providing new facts, but usually by providing an alternative narrative matrix within which those already in circulation can be inserted. The series of telegrams that Eden sent to Eisenhower is a perfect exemplar of this process. The telegrams are instructive for our implicit counterfactual reasoning because they capture exactly the way that events *could* have been seen in the United States. They also illustrate the tacit knowledge of genre that skilled political operators deploy in their routine activity. Think again of the desert island and the scraps of paper on the beach mentioned in chapter one. Imagine there are two people on our island, Eden and Eisenhower, who have collected the soggy lines of text from the tide line. Eden attempts to change Eisenhower's reading by arguing for the inclusion of items that Eisenhower has consigned to a separate story-pile, by redescribing the motivations of the characters they could both agree belonged and by expanding the scale of the object of struggle. Had Eden's interpretation been persuasive the interests and ideologies of Eisenhower and Dulles would have been channeled into a different policy flume. His first move was to suggest that Nasser was not so much a freedom fighter as a polluted figure of Hitlerian proportions whose actions were consistent with the Discourse of Repression rather than that of Liberty. The Suez Canal nationalization, in this reading, was only the first step in a more complex chain of negative events that might eventuate in the downfall of democratic civilization. The object of struggle was no longer just Egypt, but rather the fate of a free Europe: "In the Nineteen Thirties Hitler established his position with a series of carefully planned movements . . . similarly the seizure of the canal is, we are convinced, the opening gambit in a planned campaign. . . . When that time comes, Nasser can deny oil to Western Europe and we here shall be at his mercy. You may feel . . . it would be better to wait until Nasser has unmistakably unveiled his intentions. But this was the very argument that prevailed in 1936 . . ." (Telegram, Eden 1960, 485). Eden's second strategy was to prick America's ideological sensibilities. He painted Nasser in terms of the satire of dependence as an innocent and dependent pawn of an evil and calculating Soviet Union that was looking to dominate an entire continent. Now it was the Soviet Union rather than Nasser who was the evil enemy at the heart of the unfolding story, and Africa and the Middle East that were the prize. Here Eden is trying to expand the event set, to bring into the ongoing situation other players and characters that have been excluded by the American leaders. "I have no doubt that the Bear is using Nasser, with or without his knowledge, to further his immediate aims. These are, I think, first to dislodge the West from the Middle East, and second to get a foothold in Africa so as to dominate that continent in turn" (Telegram, Eden 1960, 452). Eden also took a bet each way, suggesting the active Hitlerian Nasser might be in collusion with the cunning Soviets in nebulous but indubitably sinister ways. Proactive military operations were needed to head off disaster before things got out of control with Nasser and/or the Kremlin controlling the world oil supply.

> In the nineteen-thirties Hitler established his position by a series of carefully planned movements. . . . In more recent years Russia has attempted similar tactics. . . . Similarly the seizure of the Suez Canal is, we are convinced, the opening gambit in a planned campaign designed by Nasser to expel all Western influence and interests from Arab countries. . . . [The] new governments will in effect be Egyptian satellites if not Russian ones. I can assure you that we are conscious of the burdens and perils attending military intervention. But if this assessment is correct, and if the only alternative is to allow Nasser's plans quietly to develop until this country and all Western Europe are held to ransom by Egypt acting at Russia's behest it seems to us that our duty is plain." (telegram, Eden 1960, 467)

Eden was no fool. His discourse could have worked because it tapped brilliantly into the conspiracy theme that is so thinly buried in American political culture (Bailyn 1967). Consider, for example, the remarkable similarity of the scenario painted in Eden's telegrams to that used by in 2003 by George Bush Jr. alluding to shadowy collusions between Iraq and al-Qaeda (we look at this in chapter five). Indeed it is an instructive exercise to reread the above telegrams and appropriately substitute the words "terrorists," "Iraq," "Saddam Hussein," and "Osama bin Laden" for "Egypt," "Nasser," and "Russia." Eden's discourse could have worked . . . it did not.

Why did Eden's arguments of impending doom fall on barren soil? In his autobiography the prime minister moans that "the old spoor of colonialism confused the trail" (Eden 1960, 459, see also 499ff.). This is correct insofar as it goes, but a more complete answer comes with the realization that America had already locked itself into a genre that made "colonialism" a relevant context for explanation. Having made its genre guess the United States fell into a rationalist and pragmatic interpretative orbit around a planetary complex of what it took as reasonably mundane gravity. And so it was that Eisenhower and Dulles pressed for negotiation and promised to use only "moral pressure" on Nasser. They considered Nasser's assurances that all nations would have free use of the canal to be valid. This is a noteworthy point. In our two other wars we will see that Saddam Hussein was considered to be immune to "moral pressure." Deeply coded with the Discourse of Repression he was taken to be an evil madman who was implicitly untrustworthy. Nasser, in contrast, was read as a man of honor. Should they be wrong Dulles proposed that oil could be just as easily routed around the Cape of Good Hope. Eden, however, was reading through a different genre—one where there could be no simple administrative or technical solution to a growing menace. It is no surprise that he felt aggrieved and frustrated at what he saw as American pedantry when Dulles spoke of the Cape route and petrol rationing (Eden 1960, 455), or drew attention to "technical difficulties" or procrastinated on whether the "problem in the language of the [UN] Charter was a 'dispute' or a 'situation' " (ibid., 459).

OUR POLLUTED ALLIES

David Lloyd George once remarked that wars make enemies of allies. He was right. Already depicted as colonial bullies the British and French found themselves headed for the sin bin after their November 1956 invasion of the Canal Zone. Although a process of narrative inflation finally took place in the United States, it was not one that worked to their advantage because tragic genres came to supplement the low mimetic one. America's great allies had fallen from grace. They had made the wrong choices, moved closer to the Discourse of Repression, failed to live up to the high ideals expected of them, set in motion a course of avoidable and regrettable events describable in terms of themes of descent. On hearing the news Dulles exploded: "How could they do this to me? . . . They are shoving us, they are showing contempt for us, they have betrayed us!" (cited in Stoessinger 1979, 120). For *Time* magazine Britain had shown its true colors. An "aggression bound" Eden had issued a "ruthless ultimatum and armed attack on Egypt." In doing so he had replaced cooperation for force as the basis of human relationships, returning to "the nineteenth century pattern of a big power's imposing peace and demanding of the rest of the world that it accept the result" (*Time*, November 12, 1956). Assisting this genre shift was the mobilization of a discourse of conspiracy. As

Bernard Bailyn (1967) has pointed out this has been at the core of America's political culture for centuries and juxtaposes open and progressive rational relationships with images of plots, covens, and counterdemocratic forces. In this case the military compact of Britain, France, and Israel was seen as an under-the-table move driven by utterly selfish motivations that would harm innocents. Correspondents for the *New York Times* captured this reading of events as polluted.

> Britain and France have finally unveiled their premeditated conspiracy with Israel to execute a well timed and sinful scheme to destroy Egypt and its present regime, particularly President Abdel Nasser. . . . the spilled blood of the Egyptian men, women and children—innocent victims of that butchery—will fall on the heads of the invaders and those who have helped them and condoned their barbarous aggression. (letter, November 5, 1956)

> They arbitrarily took the law into their own hands. . . . They violated every legal and moral code. . . . They tried to justify their heinous deigns by the hollow pretext of "stopping all warlike action near the canal and securing freedom of navigation therein." (letter, November 5, 1956)

Consistent with the logic of the Discourse of Repression these coolly manipulative actions were tied to attributions of dependency rather than control. The colonialists had acted according to "a blind and slavish adherence to the discredited power politics of another age" (*The Nation*, November 10, 1956). Timing in politics is everything. In bombing Cairo, Britain and France had the misfortune to find that easy parallels could be drawn with the Russians, whose tanks had clanked into Hungary in the very same week. As another letter writer to the *New York Times* (November 3, 1956) concluded, "there is really no difference between Russian and Western policies toward their respective 'spheres of influence.'" Britain and France had betrayed the democratic world. They had pulled the rug of morality from under the feet of the Western powers. They had undertaken a "betrayal of mankind's best hopes" such that as the Soviets crushed the heroic Hungarians "the embarrassed West could not even cry shame with one voice" (*Time*, November 12, 1956). It is no surprise to find that the Eisenhower administration made haste to disassociate itself from the evil acts of America's cold war allies. In his television broadcast of November 1, 1956, Eisenhower metaphorically threw up his hands in astonishment claiming that, "The United States was not consulted in any way about any phase of these actions. Nor were we informed of them in advance" (reported in *New York Times*, November 1, 1956).

A different reading from this dominant position was possible. Some Americans found the British action to be legitimate. Scattered letters published in the *New York Times* demonstrate the presence of a minority position that mimicked that of England in claiming Nasser was sinister and that murky Soviet plans were afoot that threatened the free world. In this version of events the British were heroic protagonists confronting evil. Their action would "help Egypt for it will rid her of a tyrant and the agony which a tyrant always brings to his country. It will help us, for it will smash the sinister plans of the Russians to use Africa as a base of operations against us" (letter, *New York Times*, November 6, 1956). For those inhabiting this narrative position it was the American government that was coded in terms of the Discourse of Repression, Eisenhower who had failed to interpret America's interests correctly. America was guilty of weakness, indecision, and passivity rather than decisive and principled actions. "Russia's intentions in the Middle East are well known. It is only regrettable that our Government has not realized this fact. Instead of helping an ally defend our avowed policies it is frustrating its cause" (letter, *New York Times*, November 6, 1956). The American Left was quick off the mark in attempting to make political capital from a situation that had left the United States allied with a polluted Russia in the United Nations. "Do we have to side with the Kremlin and the Dictator of Egypt?" asked Eleanor Roosevelt in a full-page newspaper spread (*New York Times*, November 3, 1956), pointing to passive leadership that had "let our relationships so deteriorate with our closest allies." She argued that America needed the strong leadership of Adlai Stevenson in the forthcoming presidential elections. The fact that most of America did not share this point of view was demonstrated in the landslide victory that Ike scored three days later (see Yoder 1986, 59).

MAKING UP

Juvenile delinquents today are often subject to a judicial process known as "reintegrative shaming" (Braithwaite 1989). Not considered real criminals, they are allowed to rejoin the community after appropriate expressions of societal disapproval had been made and sufficient apologies given. Something rather similar took place in the weeks following Suez. In the United States the low mimetic genre had resulted in the attribution of relatively little importance to the events in Egypt, and this facilitated a surprisingly rapid symbolic reintegration of the guilty parties. The comparatively weak narrative inflation, which had never made it past the stage of tragedy, allowed the moral/discursive redemption of Britain and France easy to achieve. The transcript of a phone conversation held between Eden and Eisenhower on November 6, illustrates this theme. Eden repeatedly states that he is committed to a cease-fire, Eisenhower congratulates him on this and, back in the low mimetic mode, talks about how the cease-fire and a hand over to UN troops could be accomplished. Consistent with this genre position he tells Eden that the "technical things of it would be settled very quickly" once hostilities stopped (in Doyle 1999, 89).

The political obituaries in America subsequent upon Eden's resignation in January of 1957 confirm that the stain of pollution was water soluble and that repair could be effected. Suez was read as an unpleasant and unusual aberration on a great career. His stepping down from office was regrettable, his actions in Egypt a mistaken "blunder" driven not by bad intent but rather by the democratic principles that he had held throughout his life.[3] It was the *longue durée* that provided the true frame for biographical evaluation. Hence the *Los Angeles Times* (editorial, January 11, 1957) drew attention to Eden's heroic stand against fascism as evidence of an underlying virtue. He had "resigned from the cabinet in protest at the appeasement of the European dictators, Hitler and Mussolini. Sir Anthony sought to cultivate the closest relations with the United States and his launching of the Suez adventure without consulting the United States also took a good deal of moral courage." Likewise the *New York Times* (editorial, January 10, 1957) saw high ideals as the root of mistaken practice, writing that, "(Eden is) one of the best known statesmen of our age—a statesman who has fought for liberty and human decency against totalitarian tyranny and who in that cause played a vital and constructive role in the world-shaking events of the last two decades. . . . in deciding on this intervention Sir Anthony was only true to himself and to the principles he had long represented. These principles called for opposition to the appeasement of dictators." Eisenhower and Dulles publicly realigned themselves with the departing statesman who had fought so long for freedom.

Sherlock Holmes was puzzled by the dog that did not bark in the night. In the last few pages we have been looking at a similar puzzle—the question of a military involvement that did not happen but that according to several predictors and parallels and counterfactuals might very well have. We have also proposed an answer. This lies in cultural codes and narratives that framed events and proposed responses. In the course of this exposition we have seen how genres that largely downplayed the significance of events and refused narrative inflation underpinned an American stance opposing military solutions to crisis and favoring legal, technical, and administrative ones. We turn next to a national context in which very different culture structures became dominant within civil and political discourse and where domestic politics was marked by a far more violent genre war.

BRITAIN AND SUEZ

At the start of this chapter I pointed to the dangers of retrofitting interests to actions, indicating the ways that this tends to close out thinking on contingency and choice, and to reify and essentialize interests. There are other reasons why hindsight can be misleading. For example, when things go right for actors we tend to point to the rational foundations for their actions and congratulate them on their wisdom. When things go wrong we start speaking of the "irrational" cultural motivations that led them down the wrong path. To take this common sense view is a mistake. Actions that turn out well have cultural inputs just as there can be good reasons for those which lead to failure. It can be less insightful to speak of miscalculation and bias in accounting for policy disaster than to explore the more positive effort that goes into making sense of the world, to uncover the storytelling activities through which strivings for rationality and accurate interpretation work together to define interest-orientations and shape action paths. To understand Britain's Suez fiasco we need to come to terms with this cultural process.

Conventional explanations of Britain's belligerent response and fatal miscalculation speak of both reason and unreason. These are invoked in ad hoc ways and replicate the fault line that we saw in the first few pages of this book marking discourses on the causes of war more generally. On the side of "reason" we see that the Suez Canal was of greater strategic importance to Britain than to the United States, providing, as it did, an important conduit between the United Kingdom and much of the rapidly dwindling remainder of its Commonwealth. Although this greater level of "objective interest" might explain the national response, historians have tended to steer clear of accounts that focus on the immediate logistical importance of the canal. Their geopolitical arguments regarding the origins of the war rest on a different and in some ways rather cultural explanation. This revolves around the need of Britain to appear a strong nation for reasons of deterrence. In other words a robust military response was performatively rational as a demonstration of hegemonic power. Another set of explanations refer to the personal political ambitions and needs of the British prime minister, Sir Anthony Eden, particularly his desire to appear a strong leader in the vein of his wartime boss Winston Churchill. Then there is the mire of the irrational. The consenting attitudes of the British people to Eden's militarism are often attributed to psychological drives, frustrations, and contradictions arising from the end of empire (see Skidelsky 1970 for review of theories). In his autobiography Eden manifests a remarkable personal hatred of Nasser. This internalized orientation does not correspond to arguments that his evaluation of the crisis was cool, calculating, and self-interested in a strategic way. And if Suez were the action of a rationally acting state it is hard to see how it could have blundered on such a massive scale and proceeded with plans for war despite a plethora of negative signals from the United States.

What are we to do with this trifle of layered, poorly integrated explanations? One way to proceed is to step back and understand that both perceived interests and experienced emotions are the product of narrative. Nasser nationalizes the canal. OK, so what are Britain's interests here? They might have been to regain the canal, or to regain the trust of the Arab world, or to regain military hegemony, or to exact compensation for shareholders, or to stand up to Russia. Events do not determine the interests at stake but rather call for them to be identified, prioritized, and acted upon. How should we respond emotionally to the event? Do we shrug it off, feel outraged and humiliated, or experience solidarity with Nasser? Taking a cue from Robert Musil's (1953) *Man without Qualities,* we may argue that political life, like everyday life, is lived in the subjunctive mode. Many possible scenarios and complexes of interests and emotions are readable from any given geo-political text. But this is not wholly so. For at certain points we settle upon particular understandings as definitive—at least for the present and for practical purposes. Decision rather than uncertainty and ambivalence becomes possible only once there has been this Schutzian operation that reduces the complexity and uniqueness of each new context. The geo-political facts and interests subsequently invoked in responding to a crisis are, in some sense, artifacts of this prior cultural ordering through which raw information becomes typified into cooked knowledge. Then we feel a corresponding collective emotion and we do something. Let us explore this process a little further.

THE ROMANCE OF THE NILE

In contrast with the United States the years immediately following the Second World War were physically hard in Britain—rationing, shortages, and a sluggish economy seemingly belied the promise of the utopian post-Nazi world order. With the coming of the 1950s the country had seemingly turned a corner. New technologies such as the jet airliner and the television not only contracted space but also indicated that a better future was finally rushing toward the present. The coronation of Queen Elizabeth, ushering in what was quaintly termed a "New Elizabethan Age," provided for many a symbolic moment in this rejuvenation of a weary nation. The promise of the epoch was further displayed in a reformulation of the relationship between Britain, her colonies, and ex-colonies. The British Empire was conceptually—and to some extent organizationally—transformed into a Commonwealth. The term itself derives from the Tudor conception of the "common weal" (Elton 1953), which denoted a diffuse community of gentlemen and equals with a collective interest in sociable, contractual, and cooperative social relations. In this spirit the Commonwealth was to be an association in which a shared good was to emerge from friendly, indeed familial, relationships among nations. As might be expected Britain saw itself as having a special role within this organization. By freely granting independence the vertical ties of Imperial domination were voluntarily broken and replaced by horizontal affections. Britain's moral and cultural leadership was to remain. Under this paternalistic conception it was to be Britain's role to guide and advise her former children. In return for these services and in gratitude for the gift of their freedom, the fledgling nations within the Commonwealth were expected to reciprocate by behaving in the British way and exhibiting a certain deference to the mother country. Putting this in terms of the binary codes of civil society this meant that they were expected to work toward the conception of the good society embodied in the Discourse of Liberty—even if they were not quite there yet! The highest extant exemplar of this discourse as concretely manifest was, of course, Britain itself. Although no longer the economic or military leader of the world Britain still considered itself to be the moral leader and exemplar. After all, had she not stood alone against Hitler?

It is fair to say that neither Egypt nor Nasser held much interest for the British until the Suez crisis. Still, those who paid attention to that Nile-watered nation and its youthful leader, gave a thumbs up (Fullick and Powell 1979, 3). As in the United States, Nasser himself was contrasted favorably with typical Orientals. "He is a driving force for realism," wrote a *Times* (February 26, 1954) correspondent who went on to assert that the "common idea that he is an icy fanatic derives mainly from misquotations of what he has said from time to time. The British have found him an intelligent but hard bargainer." It was this "balanced approach" that had enabled Nasser to reject the violent terrorism of the Muslim Brotherhood, and also to acknowledge the value of the 1946 Sidqi-Bevan agreement, "unlike many nationalists" (ibid). Nasser was narrated as a bulwark against the profane tides of fanaticism that threatened to turn Egypt away from its path toward modernity and civilization and out of the Commonwealth. Commenting on his rise to power the *Times* (February 26, 1954) noted that "the main danger of the change is that the new regime may run into domestic difficulties with the older political leaders and with the Muslim Brotherhood. If this happens it may be tempted into still worse chauvinistic extremes against Britain in order to preserve its authority." The implication of this statement is that such anti-British sentiments as Nasser might express would be purely rhetorical and in no way a reflection of his true, underlying beliefs.

The available evidence suggests such a positive evaluation of Nasser continued through 1954 and 1955 right across the political spectrum. He was held to be sufficiently trustworthy for an agreement to be signed for the withdrawal of those British troops who had remained to protect the canal after Egyptian independence. Many of these Tommies departed from Egyptian shores ahead of schedule. Only a small minority of Tory backbenchers, known as the Suez Group, were sufficiently wary as to oppose the demilitarization. In February 1955, Eden visited Nasser in Egypt and, in a joint communiqué, they declared their satisfaction at the progress of Anglo-Egyptian relations. Complementing the success of this cooperative demilitarization was a wave of social and cultural reform sweeping Egypt toward modernity: "Egypt has undeniably acquired a vivid new dynamism . . . the boulevards are broad, white and expensive; the new government buildings are big and boastfully bureaucratic, the new hotels are white and shining. Slums are slowly being destroyed. There are big new steel mills and fertilizer plants; the Aswan dam is being electrified; land reform is being implemented" (*Times*, June 22, 1956). This narrative is a romantic one that matches that of the United States at this time. The modernization of Egypt was going ahead. Nasser's administration seemed to have a moderate and realistic tenor when contrasted with the "fanatical" Muslim Brotherhood and hard line nationalists. Egypt was moving from dependence and irrationality toward rationality and autonomy. Nasser was helping his country in this transition. He had also demonstrated his ability to behave in a civilized way by negotiating with Britain over the demilitarization of the Suez Canal and in sticking to the agreement. If not a model Commonwealth citizen or all-American hero, Nasser was at least making a pretty good show of it.

Through 1956, however, the increasing intensity of Nasser's anti-Western vituperation and his dalliance with communist powers slowly undermined this dominant impression. Genre revision began to set in. Doubts bubbled up that did not break the surface in the United States. By the eve of the nationalization of the Suez Canal, Nasser and his regime were in a somewhat ambiguous position. His increasing levels of contact with Russia seemed to betray the patron/client expectations of the Commonwealth. Whereas before Nasser's anti-Western expressions had been instantly repairable now they were a mystery. If it was unclear to observers to what extent Nasser was responsible for Egyptian foreign policy, it was nevertheless true that he was in part responsible for the country turning its back on Britain. Nasser started to slip from statesman to enigma as signs of a self that was consistent with the Discourse of Repression began to be noticed: "If the style is the man, which is Colonel Nasser's style—the frank fireside reforming statements he makes to his western visitors, or the vicious mischief-making of his radio programs? . . . Will the next few months prove him to be the wise and restrained statesman the world hopes him to be, or shall we find that the malicious diatribes of Cairo radio truly represent his level of thought?" (*Times*, June 22, 1956). In view of his accumulated capital of trust, it is perhaps the case that most British people would have opted for the homely fireside figure as the true Nasser. Few would have anticipated that a dramatic new clue would soon be available to assist their thinking.

A HINGE OF HISTORY

The nationalization of the canal moved Nasser from Sideshow Alley to the Big Top and ended this brief period of ambiguity. A broad spectrum of majority opinion in Britain rapidly and definitively encoded him in terms of the Discourse of Repression (Stephens 1971, 138). Nasser's act destroyed the romance of the Commonwealth. He had failed to play cricket. The control over the Canal Zone (the strip of land along the side of the canal) had been transferred to Egypt in "all good faith. . . . The only restraint on her was honest dealing and that has been brushed aside" complained the *Times* (editorial, July 28, 1956). The spokes of fraternal decorum and progress that supported the Commonwealth umbrella had been decisively broken. An already faltering romance of the Nile was emphatically replaced by another and far more inflated genre. Parallels were made to the situation that had brought about World War II (which it should be recalled had ended only eleven years before). The essential message of the new narrative was apocalyptic. The world and not just Egypt was the object of struggle. Events had implications for the direction of history. Nasser was no longer the leader of a tin pot third-world nation. To the contrary he represented a powerful threat to the sacred qualities of freedom, law, and democracy throughout the entire world. In collusion with the Soviet Union he threatened to bring the developed nations to their knees by cutting off the oil supply and destroying their economies. No longer could he be expected or trusted to participate in a felicitous process that aligned modernization with democracy and reason. Future events could take either of two paths, with the world drawn toward slavery or freedom. As in 1940 the key factor in determining this outcome would be the courage of the hero—Britain.

As so often happens in times of perceived national crisis the process of narrative inflation was accompanied by remarkable political unity (Foot and Jones 1957). As Eden put it afterward, "The Leader of the Opposition and the large majority of speakers in the debate on both sides of the House were at that time in general agreement. The House did not seem to be divided on party lines" (Eden 1960, 440; R. R. James 1986). On the political Right, Harold Macmillan branded Nasser an "Asiatic Mussolini." From the Labour Party benches Hugh Gaitskell condemned the nationalization as an arbitrary event that had happened "suddenly, without negotiation, without discussion." Drawing attention to Nasser's desires to create an Arab Empire he urged that "this episode must be recognized as part of the struggle for the mastery of the Middle East" (Hansard). Gaitskell insisted that Nasser's attitude was "exactly the same that we encountered from Mussolini and Hitler in those years before the war" (quoted in Eden 1960, 440). Consistent with this Hitler parallel the *Daily Telegraph* puffed: "If there is anywhere a lurking desire to appease Colonel Nasser, it should be brought into the open" (editorial, July 28, 1956). In those initial days there was a strong sense of the gravity and purport of events and that Britain was engaged in some epochal struggle. For example, it was not only the case that Prime Minister Eden's speech on July 30, 1956, was repeatedly cheered, but he himself was when he entered the House and also when he rose to speak. Overnight he had turned from the perpetual boy wonder of British politics into a genuinely charismatic leader, a symbol of the nation who had to be acclaimed as such in an interlude of Durkheimian collective effervescence. The Labour leader's speech was similarly received. The presence of Sir Winston Churchill in the House could only magnify the portentous mood of the proceedings and enable the mobilization of collective memory motifs derived from the struggle against Hitler. The understanding that events were pivotal was nicely captured by the *Times* and its metaphors: "If Nasser is allowed to get away with his coup all the British and other western interests in the Middle East will crumble. The modern world has suffered many acts like Hitler's march into the Rhineland or the Stalinist overthrow of freedom in Czechoslovakia . . . they were in fact, hinges of history" (editorial, August 1, 1956). A structure of feeling that encompassed anxieties over potential future catastrophe, the tense anticipation of mortal struggles to come, the honor of calling, shameful memories of appeasement, and heroic ones of standing up to Hitler in World War II formed an emotional vortex that swirled around this apocalyptic core. This was so well captured in letters to the *Times* that it is worth quoting these at length. Notice how in each of these a vision of national interest is at play, how in each this is shaped and defined by a broader genre context, and how a particular emotional/moral response is both exemplified and demanded. The rational and nonrational are fused by the narrative matrix through which understandings are generated.

We are faced today with a challenge in the Middle East potentially no less mortal than that in the Europe of 1938—though far more easily countered if we have the courage. We shall never have another last chance as we did in 1939–40. Unless we and our American allies now act together in defense of interests which in the long run are vital to us both . . . then indeed for us both the bell will toll. (letter, *Times*, August 1, 1956)

What is at stake is the power and position of this country, the life or death of its people . . . our duty is to see that we survive. We must not flinch from any means that will ensure survival. (letter, *Times*, August 8, 1956)

If a country will not stand up for its rights it will surely loose them. The spirit of giving in is the most fatal disease to which nations are subject, and it is apt to attack them, like a cancer, when they have arrived at the meridian (editorial, *Times*, August 1, 1956).

Is it surprising that a British committee banned Egyptian swimmers from the annual Channel race? Although the strong initial reaction faltered somewhat in the succeeding weeks, Eden still caught the mood of the nation when he invoked the world-historical implications of Nasser's nationalization in an August 8 radio broadcast. The free use of the canal was, he asserted, "a matter of life and death to us all." Invoking the national "we" that attempts to mobilize the imagined community Eden went on to conjure memories of World War II: "The pattern is familiar to many of us, my friends. We all know this is how fascist governments behave, and we all remember only too well what the cost can be of giving in to fascism. . . . With dictators, you always have to pay a higher price later on, for their appetite grows with each feeding" (reprinted in *The Listener*, August 16, 1956). To avoid this future trajectory, this escalation of danger "we must make sure that the life of the great trading nations of the world cannot in future be strangled at any moment by some interruption to the free passage of the Canal" (ibid.). No doubt Eden's personal biography as an opponent of Hitler's appeasement was a conditioning factor that made it more likely for him to adopt this interpretation of events.[4] Perhaps many in his audience had World War II in mind as they listened to his speech. Apocalyptic concerns about the future of democracy and freedom had allowed militarism to become a legitimate response. The mass mobilization of army reserves and a buildup in the eastern Mediterranean went virtually unopposed.

ALTERNATIVE NARRATIONS IN BRITAIN

Powerful as this majority opinion was in the United Kingdom it was not fully hegemonic. Opposition to a policy of military escalation in preparation for war was vocal and considerable even during the early stages of the crisis. The Left in particular made use of an unsettling array of strategies—this scattering and instability perhaps diluting their message. Inverting the dominant codings and narratives, some used the discourse of civil society to encode the United Kingdom as evil and Nasser as a hero. This historian A. J. P. Taylor, for example, claimed that the real Hitler was not Nasser but Eden. Others tended toward U.S. style low mimesis and attempted to ratchet back Eden's apocalypticism and promote what they thought of as a cool-headed and rational debate. Hence the *Manchester Guardian* (editorial, August 10, 1956) argued that Eden in linking Nasser with Hitler was manipulating public sentiment and "creating an emotional readiness for war." The Trades Union Congress spoke out angrily against the fact that Britain was being dragged into an "unnecessary war." Coming in from left field was the former ambassador to Egypt Sir Frederick Leith Ross, who pointed out that "Egypt has always had the physical control of the canal," and that "faced with nationalist Egyptian opposition, we would almost certainly be compelled to occupy not only the Canal Zone but the whole of Egypt." Observing that Egyptian funds amounting to 130 million pounds sterling were frozen in London he saw "no reason why Egypt should not pay adequate compensation" from them (in *Times*, August 7, 1956). This last point is a tell that a low mimetic stance is at play. Within the world of business as usual the media of money can be used to balance out disputes because the motivations for action are routine rather than extraordinary, ambitions modest and defined rather than unlimited. For Leith Ross, then, the Suez crisis was not about ultimate values and the need to safeguard future generations but about fair remuneration.

Somewhere between this low mimetic stance and the inverted apocalypticism of A. J. P. Taylor was the position that was to become increasingly influential in Britain during the late summer. This was first espoused in a prescient letter to the *Times* sent in by two politicians who would later become key players in the British Labour Party: Denis Healey and Douglas Jay. Their stance aligns the sides in terms of the contrasting Discourses of Civil Society but the polarization is weak, the labeling somewhat tentative, and a door is left open for reconciliation. Nasser is condemned as unrealistic and arbitrary, as having acted in an "ill-judged, high-handed and untrustworthy fashion." He has been naughty, but he is hardly an incipient Antichrist. Britain is described by the Discourse of Liberty, but only on a provisional basis. So long as she abided by the law and genuinely sought a negotiated settlement or undertook at most a blockade the government would remain legitimate. However, if Britain went to war it would lose this status. Such a war against Nasser's Egypt would be a tragedy because it would be a demonstration that the United Kingdom and the Eden administration was characterized by irrationality, a lack of realism, and a disdain for the law. In contrast with this negative future a peaceful policy would allow agreement and reconciliation permitting the romance of the Nile to be resuscitated. What was essential for this future to be realized was that Britain act out its part in accord with the Discourse of Liberty and be calm, just, realistic.

The critical decisions now facing us must really be taken with a calm understanding of the realities and not in a mood of impatience or anger . . . a unilateral act of force would be a stupendous folly—unless and until Colonel Nasser resorts to force himself . . . should . . . Colonel Nasser accept [plans for international control of the canal] the way will be open for new talks on economic development. If we thus keep right scrupulously on our side and act resolutely, we shall have by far the best chance of vindicating the essential principles at stake. (Healey/Jay letter, *Times*, August 7, 1956)

As August and September 1956 wore on, this deflationary perspective gained favor. In large part this was due to Nasser's own performative competence. Although he railed against imperialism in his speeches to the Egyptian people, he was scrupulous in allowing ships of all nations to pass unhindered through the canal. The fears of the alarmists appeared unfounded, the more so when calculations showed that oil could be brought around the Cape for a very small extra cost. Nasser's move had not been followed by any significant further aggression against Western interests in either Egypt or other Arab nations as was feared. If this position gained ground it did not mean that Nasser became cleansed of his symbolic pollution. Rather it meant that he was reclassified. The emerging frame saw him as a criminal who should pay for his crime, not as the next *führer*. Genre deflation was accomplished, then, according to the standard formula of downgrading the object of struggle and reducing the narrative polarization between the protagonists.

I have argued elsewhere that charismatic leaders require powerful enemies (P. Smith 2000). Hence, when apocalyptic concerns waned and Nasser became framed as a small-scale evil, Eden's brief moment of charismatic authority came to an end. His continuing military buildup suddenly seemed to many to be out of step with the more moderate narratives and polarizations that were emerging. His unwillingness to take the issue of the possible use of force to the United Nations led to the Discourse of Repression being used against him with greater plausibility. By the middle of August the Labour front benches had joined in this new typification, leaving the Eden and his Tories isolated—a condition that continued until the outbreak of the conflict.

THE FIASCO AND A NATION SPLIT

The declining credibility of the apocalyptic scenario is nowhere better demonstrated that in the justifications put forward immediately after the Suez invasion. The official explanation for the military confrontation made use of a genre of low mimesis not that of apocalypse. Anglo-French forces were ostensibly upholding stability, law, and order by "policing" the Canal Zone and separating Israel and Egypt. Eden insisted that this was a temporary measure designed to meet the dangers of the ongoing situation. In order to sustain this role as the peacemakers the allied air raids were supposedly carefully designed to minimize civilian casualties. Notwithstanding such a genre deflated story line, in the eyes of the invasion's more robust and visible supporters the apocalyptic narrative remained valid. For supporters of the war, who seem to be mostly Tory old guard and possibly the working classes (Blake 1978) the mobilization and invasion was an act of moral courage redressing the wrongs of the appeasement policy of the 1930s. It was a heroic moment giving spine and backbone to a United Nations that could be characterized in terms of the Discourse of the Repression as feckless. Lord Bridwood, appearing before the House of Lords in the full dress uniform of Lieutenant-Colonel, Probyn's Horse, Indian Army, spoke out against the "wicked folly of a man who had become the victim of anti-western obsessions of his own fertile imagination and creation" before going on to hope that we "might belatedly witness the ever-shifting current of world opinion record its gratitude for the courage of this country in giving life and decision at last to a body [the United Nations] which for years had faced the charge of ineptitude" (reported in the *Times*, November 7, 1956). A correspondent to the *Times* (letter, November 7, 1956) asked whether those who supported this organization were "prepared to support . . . its masterly and verbose inactivity until those nations who can still resist evil and real aggression have been so sapped of their moral and material strength that they are powerless any longer to take a stand?" Thus for the conflict's strongest supporters, the invasion was still heroic, not merely proper like a police action: "I think recent events have shown that Colonel Nasser is the conscious, or unconscious, tool of the Kremlin, whose world campaign to spread Communism would have been well suited by an Arab revolt. . . . As it is that danger has been minimized by the strong, prompt action of Great Britain and France" (letter, November 7, 1956).

Despite this applause from those holding onto the apocalyptic scenario, there were considerable cultural liabilities to the military action. We have seen that with moderates Eden had the benefit of a positive cultural coding only on condition that he performed in ways consistent with their genre guess of low mimesis: negotiation, compromise, common sense, and so forth. The move to war without UN backing decisively eliminated this possibility. Eden's action came to be seen as unreasonable, aggressive, and irrational by larger and larger sections of the political community and civil society—students, newspapers, the church, the Liberals, and the Commonwealth all protested. Two Tory ministers resigned in disillusion. With this reclassification came the move to the genre of tragedy. In this new frame Britain had become tainted and tarnished by her actions, its great claim to the moral leadership of the free world, and the spiritual leadership of the Commonwealth was gone.

In the parliamentary arena it was the Labour Party that led the assault. Hugh Gaitskell now decided to split the House and argue that it was Britain and Eden who were violating the Code of Liberty: "this is war. . . . It is not a police action. There is no law behind it" (Hansard, November 1, 1956). There could be no greater contrast than that between the House sessions immediately following the nationalization and those immediately following the invasion. The former, it will be remembered, were characterized by a solidaristic collective effervescence in which Eden, as a symbolic extension of the nation, was cheered even before he spoke. The session of November 1 was suspended after an uproar in which the two parties hurled insults back and forth across the floor. The Labour members made it clear that in their opinion the government was behaving in an unconstitutional, illegal, and aggressive way. As for the church, the Archbishop of Canterbury declared that "Christian opinion is terribly uneasy and unhappy" (quoted in Time, November 12, 1956). This is Anglican-speak for strongly disapproving. The General Secretary of the Church Assembly was less veiled in asserting that "the government . . . have decided to take the law violently into their own hands" (quoted in Times, November 3, 1956). After a mass meeting in Trafalgar Square thousands of demonstrators tried to smash their way through police cordons near 10 Downing Street. Among the intellectuals 240 Cambridge and 350 Oxford dons wrote to the Times protesting the intervention, while a rival prowar group could muster only thirty. Student riots and demonstrations broke out spontaneously all over the country and the Manchester Guardian, the Economist, and the Observer called for Eden's resignation.

It is often said in accounts of British twentieth-century history that Suez "split the nation." For the past few pages we have opened up the cultural foundations and dynamics of this process. It was a divide that was not just about whether invasion was the most efficient or rational policy for protecting the national interest, but rather one that involved concepts of right and wrong, efforts to preserve a sacred national identity, and understandings of the direction of history. It was a split made possible by contending readings that defined what was rational or reasonable, it was at heart a genre war.

In wars there are legitimate and illegitimate failures. The Suez invasion was an illegitimate failure for many pivotal elites. For the mass of the electorate, however, the case can be made that it was a legitimate one. An opinion poll in the Daily Express showed approval increasing over time. From October 30 to November 5, support for the military action grew from 48 percent to 51 percent, while opposition fell from 39 percent to 30 percent (see Eden 1960, 546). During the following fortnight satisfaction with the government rose from 51 percent to 60 percent and that of the opposition fell to 30 percent. Even after withdrawal from Egypt the government's popularity remained sufficient for them to win the next election. The case can be made that the Labour Party's narrative switch from the apocalypticism of August to the low mimesis of September and finally the outraged tragic frame of November had lost it core blue collar support—and with this political power.

BRITAIN AFTER SUEZ

As in the United States the period after Suez saw polarization abate. On Tuesday, December 17, 1956, Eden returned to Parliament after his recuperative vacation in Jamaica. The atmosphere on this occasion was very different from that which he had experienced when he went away and serves as an indicator that a ritual process of the kind discussed by Victor Turner (1969) was in hand with its sequence of breach, separation, and reintegration. This last phase was underpinned by a shift in the language of the Commons toward a comedic genre. Questioning was integrative rather than hostile. This reintegration proved so successful that Eden's subsequent resignation—on the grounds of ill health—came as something of a surprise. It was by no means the historical necessity that is so often assumed. While the diplomatic problems of Suez rather than ill health were generally considered to be the true cause of his resignation there was no domestic symbolic reason why Eden could not have toughed it out. As in the United States, British political obituaries reflected this reintegration by suggesting that actions that had previously been understood in terms of the Discourse of Repression could be more truthfully described in terms of the Discourse of Liberty. This is not to say that the actions were now taken to be correct, but rather that Eden had been mistaken or misinformed. The integrative discourse also took other paths. Unimpeachable aspects of Eden's past were located, such as his exemplary life as a "model Parliamentarian—not only skilful but punctilious in his respect and duty to the House of Commons" (editorial, *Times*, January 12, 1957). Likewise the actual decision to resign was seen not as cowardice or as pragmatic but rather as an act that "needed courage, strength, and a disinterestedness which has not always been found—not even in Prime Ministers" (editorial, *Times*, January 10, 1957).

So the widespread acceptance of Eden's resignation cannot be conceptualized in any simple way as the result of enduring symbolic pollution. More accurately it reflects a loss of faith that he could get the job done. It was Eden's failure to attain mundane political goals—such as maintaining credibility in British strength and a good relationship with America—rather than symbolic ones that were the proximate causes of his fall. Yet perhaps we should not conclude with such an anticultural resolution. The fact that these prosaic ends were seen as important reflects the cultural filtering of priorities. The Suez crisis had marked a brief period of collective effervescence in which the business as normal rules of political life had been suspended. By January 1957, Britain was out of the apocalyptic mode and back in profane time. The usual standards of evaluation could apply once more.

FRANCE AND SUEZ

General de Gaulle once quipped that it was impossible to unite a country that produced over 246 types of cheese. Even those who attempt to rewrite the history of the Fourth Republic in a positive light would agree that for the most part the experiences of that unhappy period were consistent with this observation (see Courtier 1983; Fonvieille-Alquier 1976). The cultural currents and political forces that had split the nation during the Dreyfus Affair—clericalism, republicanism, militarism, communism, socialism, nationalism, regionalism—were still around. These divergent interests and values left a series of weak governments struggling to find common ground and to execute consistent, coherent policies (Hanley, Kerr, and Waites 1984, 8). On the eve of Suez, Prime Minister Mollet's government faced an economic crisis along with political dissent over fiscal policy. Nasser's nationalization solved these immediate problems, leading to the spontaneous mobilization of discourses of crisis and movement toward national unity. Mollet's controversial economic legislation could now pass. Only the communists were in opposition

(Bourdache and Miquel 1980). Mollet, for once enjoying widespread support, argued the case for a firm response to Nasser, stating that, "The French government has decided upon an energetic and severe riposte, which must take the form of an action together with the Western allies, guarantors of right and justice" (quoted in Bourdache and Miquel 1980, 167).

We can easily identify the requisite rational grounds for this proposed course of vigorous action. Some 48 percent of French crude oil came through the canal (Bourdache and Miquel 1980, 166). Rebels in Algeria, then struggling for independence from France, were receiving arms and other aid from Nasser's Egypt. Mollet and his government had looked weak and ineffectual in the light of their failure to deal with the Algerian problem (Bourdache and Miquel 1980, 188). Striking at Nasser could thus kill several birds with one stone. It would remove a material ally of Algerian nationalists, secure France's oil supply, and show Mollet to be a decisive leader. On first inspection securing the oil supply stands as a strong, extracultural motivation for conflict. Looked at more closely it starts to fall apart. Counterfactually the calculation could have been made that compromise rather than conflict would best guarantee supplies in the long term. That this idea did not find sponsorship reflects narratively embedded assumptions about Nasser's long term plans and trustworthiness that operated as a context of bounded rationality. Likewise, the national interests at play in the Algerian question could not be fully identified or made relevant without reference to cultural presuppositions. Attitudes to Algeria were shot through with value choices and passionate commitments. As was the case with the British Commonwealth, support for a French Algeria was based on a cultural belief in universalism and modernity. Maintaining the tie was widely held to be in the best interests of both France and Algeria. Consequently, the Algerian war received widespread support on a gamut that ran from the Maurrassian Right, through independents, Gaullists, radicals, and socialists. On the one hand, the Right believed in protecting the French empire and its territorial sovereignty in the interests of a strong, independent nation. This proud, but nationalistic ideology was well summed up by General de Gaulle's belief that France "isn't really herself unless she is in the first rank [of nations]" (De Gaulle in Hanley et al. 1984, 214). The Left, on the other hand, considered that better economic and social conditions would emerge under French rule than under native administration (Courtier 1983, 99). This explains the irony that although repression was strongest under the government of socialists and radicals from 1956–57, Mollet held that far from oppressing Algerians, France was bringing to them the benefits of civilization (la Gorce 1979, 366; Hanley et al. 1984, 13).

This Algerian context decisively filtered French readings of Nasser. Because he openly supported the Algerian rebels it is no surprise that, as one historian has argued, Nasser "incarnated . . . for Guy Mollet, the dangers from which Algeria must be protected as well as the rest of that region of the world" (la Gorce 1979, 366). France like other Western democracies of the time wanted a moderate, secular Egypt. From their perspective the Arab League and Nasser threatened to bring only nationalism and Islamic fanaticism. By contrast with the United States, in the French *conscience collective* Nasser was narrated as a regressive rather than as a progressive force—one of several demons dragging Algeria away from the civilizing influence of the French *patrimonie*. These readings were reinforced in their consequences by the lack of a tradition of de-colonization, or a positive narrative for this, such as could be found in Britain. For the French the loss of empire was less the inevitable result of societal evolution and a confirmation of the success of the civilizing mission of colonialism than a "national catastrophe" that promised relegation from the Premier League of world powers (Duroselle 1982, 341). It was this fear of falling that allowed the Algerian war to absorb an incredible 28 percent of the national budget (Hanley et al. 1984).

With this broader context in mind it is hardly surprising to find that cultural dynamics in France followed the pattern in Britain. Apocalyptic narratives and polarizing codings fell into place insisting that the Suez nationalization simply could not be taken with a pinch of salt. It was not just the case that "for France and Great Britain, Nasser was the devil in person" (Bourdache and Miquel 1980, 166), but also that his nationalization seemingly confirmed that there was, as Paul Isoart puts it, an "anti-French conspiracy, of which Egypt was the center" (Isoart 1978, 448). In other words the Suez move was part of a larger event-set and this gave it special relevance. Paralleling the British scenario, collective memory references to Munich and Hitler dominated civil discourse and reinforced this hatred of the Egyptian leader. Mollet reminded those listening to his speech of July 30 that the "apprentice-dictator" wished to establish an empire from the Atlantic to the Persian Gulf (in *Times*, October 3, 1956). The Hitler motif was echoed by the influential Catholic/Right paper *La Croix* (editorial, July, 31, 1956) when it declared: "Gamal Abdel Nasser's action over Suez was brusque and unforeseen, however, it does not give the impression of anything new. The West has been, for a long time, accustomed to a similar style. The Egyptian decision singularly recalls, in its tone and modalities, the arbitrary thunderbolt with which, twenty years ago, Hitler re-occupied the Rhineland, annexed the Sudetenland, and violated Prague. . . . The most disturbing thing is that Colonel Nasser probably takes such a re-mark for a compliment." Laughable as this scenario might appear today it was repeated on the Left. Commentary in *Le Monde* suggested that serious problems required drastic measures. The untrustworthy Nasser could understand only force, not law, and immediate action was required: "The example of the years 1933–1939 is clear . . . in the face of the megalomania of a dictator one must reply, not through inefficient legal procedures which hold up to ridicule that which is right, but through force" (Maurice Duverger in *Le Monde*, quoted in Bourdache and Miquel 1980, 166). As we know, this call to move beyond legalism and pedantry to action is a hallmark of the apocalyptic scenario.

For the French, what was true of Nasser's policies also held true for his personality. To an extent not found even in Britain public attacks on Nasser became personal and vitriolic. Where *Time* magazine in the United States had drawn a picture of a clean-cut freedom fighter and family man, in France Nasser was depicted as an irrational half-animal. Telltale signs of this breeding according to a contributor to *Le Figaro* included "the military step, the strong jaw, the long teeth, the fierce laugh and the snarlings in the depths of the throat" (Thierry Maulnier, *Le Figaro*, cited in Rioux 1983, 12). The American failure to understand the true nature of the crisis in Egypt was experienced as deeply frustrating. A full-page picture in *Paris Match* (September 15, 1956) shows a maniacal Egyptian soldier thrusting a bayonet toward the reader. The caption underneath reads: "What America Refuses to See." Not only Nasser and his military were enraged, ambitious, and dangerous. Above all it was the crowd, the Islamic masses, who were emblematic of Egypt's Oriental status, the barometer of its moral climate. They were read as an irrational, dependent mass rather than as an autonomous and critical civil society. *Paris Match* (August 4, 1956) reported in Orientalist tones that, "The burst of laughter which announced the confiscation of the Suez Canal was more primitive than any tone of hatred. The crowd listened to it as if it was listening to a tune of revenge, just as the Nazis listened to the *Horst Vessel Lied* in their collective delirium. . . . The stupid masses, the flock of human sheep . . . bleated their support and mirth." Its photographic reportage reflected this vision. Roland Barthes (1977), Stuart Hall (1973), and others have spoken of the subtle ways in which visual imagery works in conjunction with text to anchor hegemonic discourses. We find this process at work in *Paris Match* with one departure from theory—there was no subtlety. In the edition of September 1, 1956, there is a photograph of a giant illuminated eagle dominating an Egyptian street. The caption reads: "Illuminated every night for the last two months, Nasser's eagle strangely resembles Hitler's emblem." On the facing page is a reproduction of a street poster of Nasser, sporting moustache and military uniform, and looking remarkably like the *führer* himself.

Fighting fire with fire the communists tried to confront the predominant apocalyptic narrative by means of the discourse technique of I have elsewhere termed inversion (P. Smith 1991). This involves retaining institutionalized discourses but switching their empirical referents. Echoing A. J. P. Taylor's efforts in Britain *L'Humanite* spoke of Nasser's action as a "new stroke to the colonial system" (quoted in Bourdache and Miquel 1980, 166) and argued that the real Hitler was the West. "People cry *coup de force* and evoke the remilitarization of the Rhineland. In fact, if one must make a historic parallel it is the Western threats which recall the comportment of Hitler . . . the same call to arms, the same brutal effort to interfere in the interior affairs of a sovereign state, the same imperialist views" (Yves Moreau, *L'Humanite,* cited in *La Croix,* July 31, 1956). The results of public opinion polls broadly suggest that this communist interpretation did not have a wide currency. Some 58 percent in a September Gallup Poll stated that Nasser did not have the right to act as he did, as opposed to 18 percent in favor of his nationalization (24 percent no opinion). This negative coding of Egyptian policy is further confirmed by the fact that the most frequent response to a question relating to Nasser's motivations for the nationalization was profane: "personal prestige" (Gallup 1976, 202, 207), and also by behavioral data: French cinema audiences whistled when Nasser appeared on newsreels (*Paris Match,* August 11, 1956).

If our indicators of public opinion are weak, we can have more confidence that Mollet's vision was shared in the political community—communists excepted. We find the prominent Socialist Max Lejeune claiming that Nasser had the ambition to be the *führer* of the Arab world, and the Christian Democrat Pierre-Henri Teitgen railing that "the xenophobia, the racism and the violence of Nasser are of the same type as the racism and violence of Hitler" (Winoch 1978, 57). Within this apocalyptic context events became of world-historical importance. The struggle was no longer just about Egypt and Algeria, for "We are living in times comparable to the great moments in the past when the decisive struggle is played out between expansionist totalitarians and the forces of liberty" (*Le Populaire,* quoted in Winock 1978, 61). This position mimics the Hinge of History motif we have already seen used by the London *Times.*

When we have chosen our genre, the readings that others make need to be accounted for and explained away if we are to have faith in the validity of our interpretation. We need not only to articulate our own position but also to discount and discredit rivals—even if we do not directly challenge them to debate. So we find the failure of the United States to engage in strong political condemnation or to support France explained. Consistent with the Discourse of Repression it was unwilling to face the facts. America lacked a realistic perspective and "closes its eyes so as not to see at all the evidence" argued one critic (Robert Bony, *L'Aurore*, quoted in *La Croix*, August 8, 1956). Its ideas about compensation and negotiation were quite simply unrealistic given the true nature of the enemy: "Washington believes yet again that the dollar can hold back the sorcerer's apprentice" (Jean Fabiani, *Combat*, quoted in *La Croix*, August 2, 1956).

We have already seen how political unity and apocalyptic codings faltered in the United Kingdom as the summer of 1956 wore on. This was not the case in France (Bourdache and Miquel 1980, 169–71). Pivotal in this respect was the interception by the French of the ship *Athos* filled with arms for the FLN in Algeria. This clue was taken as proof of Nasser's deep complicity with Algerian rebels. When the French parliament reassembled in October after its summer recess only seven "interpellations" were tabled instead of the usual sixty (*Times*, October 3, 1956)—a clear signal that the government had a political mandate to get on with the job. The communists, of course, continued to resist the government's policy. In his speech on the reopening of the National Assembly, Marcel Cachin mobilized the Discourse of Repression. He spoke of the dated and unrealistic nature of the French government's Algerian and Suez policies arguing that it was impossible to put back the clock on colonialism. Cross party unity, however, was such that the chamber "sat in silence whilst the Communists enthusiastically applauded the speech" (*Times*, October 3, 1956).

In a context where a hegemonic interpretation of an apocalyptic tenor was widely shared, the invasion of Egypt was far more enthusiastically received in France than in Britain. As in Britain the conflict's apologists argued that Britain and France had played a heroic and self-sacrificing role and that time would show that "the voice of the two old democracies, faithful to their obligations, steadfast in their decision, will have the deepest reverberations" (*Le Figaro*, quoted in *La Croix*, November 3, 1956). By contrast the United States was a fair-weather friend, for "It is only too easy to accept [an alliance] when it serves your interests and to reject it when it does not agree with your views" (Francois Roussel, *La Croix*, November 27, 1956). The historian Alfred Grosser remarks that although called the "shortest war in history" the Suez conflict remained despite the setbacks a popular one. He contends that, "Rarely have the public opinion polls given such clear results" (Grosser 1961, 372–73). Perhaps this is overstating the case. A poll of December 1956 showed 42 percent supported the use of force in Egypt, 33 percent opposed and 25 percent had no opinion (Grosser 1961, 373). In a poll of March 1957, 43 percent claimed they had been for the invasion of Egypt as opposed to 28 percent against (8 percent indifferent, 21 percent no answer) (Gallup 1976, 209).

These are hardly spectacular figures, although they do suggest a pattern of moderate popular support like those revealed in the British surveys discussed earlier. What is remarkable, and more accurate as an interpretation, is that the war was extremely popular among the elites who engaged in civil discourse construction and political decision making. What the British quickly decided had been a fiasco, the French saw as a half-success foiled only by the Americans (Rioux 1983, 114). Whereas Eden was considered not up to the job and resigned, Mollet easily survived a vote of no confidence held in the *Assemblée National* on December 20, 1956. The French were even keen to continue the war after the British had given up. Practical reasons unrelated to domestic politics meant that they could not continue alone in fighting the good fight.

That said, the war was subject to subsequent critique. Leftist objections came in both narratively inflated and low mimetic modes. The communists continued their prior discourse pitched at the former level, maintaining in effect that colonialism was wrong and that France was an oppressor. It was Pierre Mendès-France who best articulated the emergent opposition to the Suez war founded on low mimesis of the kind the Jay and Healey had made in England. Subscribing to the fiasco interpretation he argued that the Suez invasion was badly thought out and organized. He contended that he had pointed out to Mollet the danger of the military option unless it was "crowned by an immediate and decisive success" and that the prime minister "failed to foresee the reactions on the part of the Soviets, the Americans, the Arab countries and the United Nations" because "he did not want to envisage these hypotheses" (Mendès-France 1987, 247. [1956, "Pourquoi je me suis abstenu"]).

In both Britain and France a culturally legitimate military intervention in response to Suez required an apocalyptic scenario to be institutionalized in civil discourse. In each of these countries such a footing was achieved, albeit incompletely. This result, as we have seen, contrasted with that in the United States where polarizing codings of Nasser and collective memories of Hitler never gained more than a toehold. Even efforts to expand the event set to include plot roles for the Soviet Union were unsuccessful. Our theory predicts that Spain, which did not participate in the Suez military action and also tried to broker an agreement, would exhibit discourses similar to those in the United States. We turn very briefly to this case in concluding this chapter.

SPAIN AND SUEZ

Spain provides a useful test case with which to examine some important questions about civil discourse and war. Do countries on the sidelines of world politics use the same discursive and narrative structures as those who are players? Are the culture structures we have identified unique to democratic contexts or do they have some wider relevance that allows them to assume a role even in dictatorial environments? These questions are investigable because Spain was a politically impotent quasi-Fascist backwater in the 1950s. Of course the presence of heavy censorship in the media and elsewhere makes the press of Franco's era less a reflection of a public sphere than the expression of a dominant ideology, or legitimate political language. Nevertheless, such efforts at media control suggest that even manipulative elites in nondemocratic contexts take ideology seriously enough to try to justify their policies to some kind of a broader public. For example, although the Civil War in the 1930s had demonstrated that Spain was rent with ideological cleavages, these divisions were masked and repressed by Franco's regime, which continued to appeal to universalism in promoting its particular value set (Edles 1998). Looking to public discourse in Spain can help us understand the nature of such claims-making activity.

Spain had emerged from its Civil War and the Second World War under the leadership of General Franco. Franco's dictatorship was underpinned by a variety of conservative factions and ideologies—the military, the church, fascists, nationalists, landowners, and capitalists. Political opponents, especially regionalists, socialists, and communists were ruthlessly suppressed (Gallo 1973). Once a great power, Spain's centuries of decline had culminated in a self-inflicted and crippling civil war. It was now a weak and marginal state, albeit one with an attractive climate. After attaining power Franco's problem was to define a new role for this failed nation. In his Columbus Day speech of 1946 he expressed his hopes for a "cultural empire." An important part of this empire would be the Arab world with which Spain (like England and France and America!) thought it had a special relationship (Grugel and Rees 1997, 174). Yet colonial expansion was an impossibility given Spain's limited economic and military capabilities and its lack of international allies (Trythall 1970). Politically, then, Spain's guiding concern in responding to the Suez crisis was to continue to "pose as a protector of Arab interests" (Payne 1967, 39) and to stand against the dominant powers of Western Europe in an effort to build political influence in North Africa. Obsequiousness toward the United States was likely also part of Franco's game plan. By playing upon anti-colonialist feelings there he had long hoped to enlist U.S. diplomatic support for his claims to British controlled Gibraltar (Preston 1993, 601) as well as secure a supply of economic aid. If considerations of realpolitik would tend to lead Franco's elites to approve of Nasser and to decry the Suez invasion, some ideological considerations pulled in the other direction. Nasser was liable to negative typification in Spain because he could be connected to the profound pollution that the atheistic and communist Soviet Union embodied for the dominant factions in Spanish society. It is this strange mixture of a steely ideological conservatism and a rusting geo-political impotence that explains Spain's moralizing, yet detached, low mimetic approach to the Suez affair. As in the United States both Nasser and the British were cast in mildly negative roles. Only when Nasser moved toward the Left did he become a potential target for markedly more profane coding. Let's look at this process in more detail.

Although not defined in terms of a Discourse of Repression, Nasser had the latent potential for such a designation one the eve of Suez. His attacks on "imperialism" and "feudalism" were dangerously revolutionary, his government—presumably in contrast to that of Franco himself which, of course, represented the true will of the Spanish people—an imposition on the Egyptian nation. Using sneer-quotation marks the dominant newspaper La Vanguardia Española (editorial, June 26, 1956) encouraged an ironic and skeptical view of events. "A movement such as that of Nasser" it wrote, "is characteristic, in part, of those latitudes. A group of young radical officials who undertake a revolution against pre-existing 'medieval' and 'feudal' regimes and then enter upon a path of reconstruction based on an iron dictatorship." In this quizzical gaze Nasser was taken as a potential puppet of the Soviet block: "It is beyond doubt that Shepitlov, head of Kremlin diplomacy and 'inventor' of the 'new line' for Moscow's Middle Eastern policy will do everything possible to push Nasser in his far-reaching ambitions. Ambitions from which, of course, the Kremlin hopes to be co-beneficiary" (ibid.).

There was some leeway here for the Egyptian leader. Nasser and his ambitions were not seen as inherently sinful. Rather they were utopian, somewhat naïve, and potentially capable of being perverted by the true evil of a cynical and manipulative Soviet foreign policy. Likewise, the British and French could be viewed with some ambiguity. In a revealing interview about Suez, General Franco pontificated: "It cannot be forgotten that although imperialism and colonialism are now dead . . . they live on in the minds of certain governments, who are not resigned to recognize the loss of certain situations, whilst in their turn formerly subjugated peoples embody their own nationalisms. It is a phenomenon which always shows up in the progress of peoples towards independence" (interview in ABC, October 28, 1956).

If Franco condemned the conflicting parties in terms of the Discourse of Repression, then this was a weak condemnation. To be sure, the players were driven by powerful sentiments and lacked realism and, by implication, a mature perspective on events such as that of Caudillo himself. Yet they were sincere in their beliefs and desires. This empathy is understandable in light of the fact that the Falangist strand of Franco's own ideology stressed the importance of sentimental attachment to the nation and the pursuit of national interests. This was an important local condition that permitted the Spanish right to view unfolding events in Egypt without malice. Franco's maverick cabinet member José Luis de Arrese y Magra, however, found Nasser's nationalism preferable to that of the European powers. He lobbied for a stronger demonstration of support for a man whose agenda he saw as consistent in spirit with the virile energies of Falangism and as a blow to Gibraltar-owning Britain (Preston 1993, 660). A consideration of the need to remain in lockstep with the United States prevented the *Caudillo* from adopting this policy. Nevertheless, the belief that there was common ground with Falangist ideology on all sides prevented strong profanation of the interested parties and made predictions of a negotiated settlement appear plausible. Nasser, Eden, and Mollet were perhaps misguided, but they were all doing what they thought was best for their nations.

This common ground provided modest cause for optimism. Hence, Spain felt impelled to try to broker a solution. It was admitted that Nasser had been rather high handed, but his sin was simply a legalistic peccadillo, not a transgression betokening world-historical ambitions. *La Vanguardia Española* (editorial, June 28, 1956) was able to write that, "One does not violate a single vital principle in proclaiming a sympathy or antipathy. Another thing altogether, however, is the violation of a formal international treaty." This understanding that events had the mundane qualities of a legal breach allowed a certain optimism to prevail with respect to the prospects of Spanish sponsored negotiations. "It does not appear likely," wrote *La Vanguardia Española* a few weeks later (editorial, August 4, 1956) that "anything gravely disturbing will occur, and Nasser, diluting the extreme violence that gave rise to the crisis, will assume a much more prudent attitude. . . . Past the initial xenophobic frenzy of the initial hour, the Colonel is sufficiently wise to understand that a retreat, which will be toasted with honor, is, in his case, a great victory." Similarly the "rival" newspaper *ABC* (editorial, August 18, 1956) confidently predicted that "the Suez crisis will be resolved, fortunately, according to the dictates of reason and in no case by the force of arms." The next day it asserted that "the declarations of the Egyptian president a week ago surprised the world by their comparative moderation" before going on to argue that, "Extreme solutions, such as . . . an armed invasion with incalculable consequences must be forgotten. And this is exactly what the Spanish proposition tries to achieve with its reasonable, moderate and balanced tone and content" (editorial, August 19, 1956). Again on August 22, an *ABC* editorial on the Muslim Brotherhood—probably with an eye to the Magreb—argued for an even-handed and careful approach and expressed the low mimetic belief that money could solve the problem. "Spain understands the longings of the Arab peoples with whom it maintains a spiritual solidarity. Our country does not practice racism, nor imperialism nor the incomprehension of East and West. It recognizes the right of Egypt to nationalize an Egyptian Limited Company, even if it has foreign capital. On the other hand, it has demonstrated on numerous occasions its respect for the legitimate interests of the shareholders and hopes that the members of the Universal Company will be compensated in accord with the solemn promise of the Egyptian President." A few weeks later Franco argued within the same genre. In a reply to an Associated Press interview, which is worth quoting in full, he nicely captures the tone of this understanding. Just like "lawyer Dulles" his discourse is dominated by references to technical, fiscal, and legal matters rather than by references to ultimate values, salvation, or this-worldly evil.

> In this as in everything it is necessary to leave the passions to one side if we wish to see clearly and find the solution. The fight, in this case, between one or two peoples is more artificial and apparent than real. The general interest of one and all is the same at the bottom; that the natural flow of petrol to Europe . . . isn't interrupted. If the interruption of supplies could be disturbing for Europe, in turn it would represent a greater loss for the suppliers and the canal itself. For this reason it is in the general interest that everyone agrees on the need for a peaceful solution to the discussions. The problem . . . is clear; freedom of navigation as affirmed in the Treaty of 1888, security of the passage, . . . technical guarantees of preservation and improvements, a technical problem which does not affect sovereignty and which all agree on guaranteeing, and the moderation and normality of the tariffs . . . compensation and indemnization for the nationalization. (General Franco, interview, *ABC*, October 28, 1956)

For the Spanish neither Britain nor France nor Nasser was a source of profound evil. They were all players with common sense and goodwill who should be able to resolve their differences amicably and contractually. Any real sense of drama was provided by an off-stage presence—the Russians were lurking in the wings. The Soviet Union was attributed with profoundly negative motivations and relationships. It showed no interest in peace, but rather a self-seeking interest in chaos and war that was betrayed by "inscrutable reserve, only broken by periodic incitements to Nasser to be intransigent . . . this is a typical case of blowing on the fire so as to keep it alive every time it could go out" (editorial, *La Vanguardia Española*, September 14, 1956). From the Spanish perspective responses to the whole event should be subsumed into a broader agenda: obstructing Soviet ambitions in North Africa. Discord between the major players—Britain, France, and the United States—had to be condemned as a dangerous state of affairs. "Through their disunity," wrote *ABC*, "they have destabilized in a disturbing way the solidarity of the Atlantic Treaty and have given a direct triumph to the Afro-Asian Bandung bloc and another, indirectly, to the Soviet imperialism" (editorial, *ABC*, September 8, 1956). The power of the Soviets, it was argued, could only be broken by unity. The Western powers should "seek his [Nasser's] friendship, his inclination towards the western world and prevent perilous flirtations with the Soviet bloc" (editorial, *ABC*, September 13, 1956). This kind of wishful thinking was made possible by the low mimetic frame, which held that negotiations and interests could bring people together and a compromise could be reached. In contrast a bellicose approach might lead to disaster, for "A false tactic in the problem of Nasser could push the whole of that world [the emerging nations], young and full of spiritual energy, into the hands of the Kremlin" (editorial, *ABC*, October 2, 1956). With the Middle East a "powder keg," then "any carelessness whatsoever could cause a catastrophic explosion" (editorial, *ABC*, October 14, 1956). Consistent with this narrative that prioritized prudence and restraint in the effort to prevent Soviet expansion we find that at the London conference designed to locate a peaceful solution, Spain was a major proponent of negotiated settlements and put forward an initiative— a "just mean" situated "above the passions" (editorial, *ABC*, September 23, 1956)—which effectively gave the canal and control of it to Egypt (editorial, *ABC*, August 18, 1956).

If Spanish low mimesis during the summer and fall of 1956 by and large matched that of the United States, post-invasion discourses did not. In the United States attention was drawn to the moral equivalence of Britain, France, and Russia as lawbreakers and force-users. In Spain the stronger reading of Soviet pollution, reinforced by the invasion of Hungary and the suppression of a heroic uprising that was seen to have nationalistic and Catholic foundations, assisted a divergent account to emerge. According to *ABC* (editorial, November 14, 1956), one could not compare "a purely military attack on strategic objectives without more cruelty than that which any military operation brings, with the inhuman slaughter by the thousand Russian tanks in Budapest." While the Suez invasion was "full of risks and difficulties; imprudent or at least bold" (editorial, *ABC*, November 16, 1956), the invasion of Hungary was an act of "barbarous assassination" (editorial, *ABC*, November 14, 1956) by forces "under the hoof of the anti-Christ" (editorial, *ABC*, October 31, 1956). Here was the real apocalyptic struggle.

In brief: Spain's response to the Suez crisis closely paralleled that of the United States. Despite ideological and structural differences between the two regimes, the low mimetic genre underpinned a common expectation that a nonviolent compromise could and would be attained. In our next war we will see these two nations diverging in their genre choices, a situation leading to a very half-hearted war effort from Spain and a strong push for violent confrontation from the United States administration. But first let us recap some lessons from this chapter that has opened up our empirical analysis of the genre politics of war. We have seen how (1) talk in crisis situations takes on a narrative form with defined features such as protagonists, antagonists, motivations, and objects of struggle, and that (2) these fall out in ways predicted by genre theory; (3) that perceptions of risks and interests are shaped by these genres, and that (4) political actors and military actions are held accountable to them; that (5) a sharply divided civil sphere can form around genre stances, and that (6) the success or failure of a reading in political life can depend not only on its ability to conform to the objective crisis events but also on the distribution of genre positions among other players both at home and abroad. In the discussion of the 1991 Gulf War you might experience déjà vu for we will see these lessons repeated in both their generality and details.

FOUR

THE GULF WAR OF 1991

Our next conflict takes place some three and a half decades after Suez. In August 1990, Iraq invaded and took control of the small but rich emirate of Kuwait with which it shared a common border. The reasons behind this attack remain the subject of debate. There are several commonly cited factors. Iraq needed cash. It had a debt of some $90 billion after its long war with Iran during the 1980s. Yet Kuwait and the United Arab Emirates had failed to agree with OPEC policy on restricting output. Oil prices had fallen and so, consequently, had Iraq's own oil revenues. There was a long history of border and territorial dispute between the two Middle Eastern nations. These revolved around extractions from the Rumaila oil field that straddled the border, and access for landlocked Iraq to the Persian Gulf. Most important of all, many argued, was the fact that Iraq had a large army in need of gainful employment and an ambitious leader—Saddam Hussein. In his diverse self-aggrandizing statements Hussein claimed to be inspired by the pan-Arab philosophy of Nasser and the empire building achievements of Saladin and Nebuchadnezzar. In combination these provided the structural possibility, leadership, and material and ideological motivations for the takeover of Iraq's neighbor.

Observers and politicians throughout the world were quick to denounce the invasion. Only Arab nationalists and the "rogue" states of Cuba and Yemen openly approved of Iraq's action. The U.S. president, George Bush, and his secretary of state, James Baker, played a crucial role in the assembly of an international coalition of forces in the Middle East. The United States was equally instrumental in assuring that there were United Nations resolutions providing a legitimating charter for forceful intervention. Under Operation Desert Shield the United States led a military buildup in Saudi Arabia in the second part of 1990. This was putatively a defensive and containing action aimed at deterring further Iraqi aggression. A United Nations—approved sanctions policy was also set up, isolating the Iraqi economy. Following Iraq's refusal to respond to a deadline for withdrawal from Kuwait specified in UN Resolution 678, Operation Desert Storm was initiated. From mid-January 1991 onward Iraq's cities and armed forces were subjected to an intense bombardment from air strikes and cruise missiles. There was little resistance in the skies. After five and a half weeks during which over 100,000 sorties were flown, U.S. led ground forces invaded Kuwait and then southern Iraq, achieving an easy victory. Iraq had managed to lob a few missiles and set fire to some Kuwaiti oil wells, but its army had proven otherwise unable or unwilling to confront the United States and its allies. The military engagement was essentially a rout. In the so-called Battle of Medina Ridge, for example, three hundred Iraqi tanks were lost in forty minutes at the price of one American casualty. In all the Gulf War lasted forty-two days with a ground war phase of just four. America sustained only 137 confirmed deaths (Woodward 1991, 376). Yet Saddam Hussein and his weakened forces remained in power. There followed a lengthy civil war in Iraq. Kurdish and Shiite populations rose against Saddam Hussein, his Baath Party and centralized state. Viewed as a purely internal matter, their efforts did not receive international military support even though their resistance was violently suppressed. Eventually the UN stepped in and established a security zone for the Kurds in northern Iraq (for a brief overview see Atkinson 1993; Greene 2000; Powell 1995).

THE UNITED STATES AND THE GULF WAR

In the previous chapter our comparison was largely between nations. The primary finding was that the same events were narrated in systematically different ways in Britain and France on the one hand, and in the United States and Spain on the other. Each narration had corresponding implications for policy and legitimacy. Because this chapter introduces a second historical sequence to this book it also opens up possibilities for an alternate mode of comparative sociology. We can now think about how each nation responded over the two event sequences, looking for similarities and differences in cultural patterns and gaining analytic and ironic purchase in this way. This approach is most evidently relevant in the case of the United States. Detached and censorious during Suez, in the case of the 1990–91 Persian Gulf crisis the United States was the prime mover and shaker in political and military arenas. It provides what we might think of as a crucial experiment. That is to say it is a site of difference that needs to be explained. Because of this methodological centrality and also the objective importance of the United States in providing military and diplomatic leadership the focus in this chapter is disproportionately on the American case. We shall go into greater detail on historical contingencies, alternative discourses, and the strategies used to challenge or effect repairs upon the dominant genre. The argument that will unfold is that by contrast with the low mimetic reading of Suez in the United States, apocalyptic narratives gained ascendancy in representations of the Gulf crisis and the ensuing war.

THE MYSTERIOUS MR. HUSSEIN

"In retrospect, it's difficult to reconstruct why the Western powers should have looked so favorably upon the President of Iraq and upon his dictatorship," moaned Martin Peretz in *The New Republic* (September 3, 1990) shortly after Iraq's 1990 invasion of Kuwait. The answer to this puzzle lies not just in the objective interests of these nations but also in the narrative frames through which these were filtered and clarified in the decade before the Gulf War broke out. We can begin an illustration of this theme with the American case. Here we find collective representations of Saddam Hussein that were ambiguous and weak, but also mildly positive. That is to say exactly what Iraq represented was unclear and few cared very much anyway, but when all was said and done it did not look too bad for a country in that part of the world.

Why did Iraq enjoy a broadly positive representation in the United States? The answer in one word: Iran. Saddam Hussein's nation spent a fair proportion of the 1980s in military conflict with its fundamentalist Islamic neighbor, a country that was coded in the strongest possible terms within the Discourse of Repression. Iran was America's number one third-world nemesis. It was perceived as the home of fanatical Islamic terrorists, it was the powerbase of the cunning and inscrutable Ayatollah Khomeini and it was the site of the humiliating hostage crisis and bungled rescue attempt that had shamed and destroyed Jimmy Carter's presidency. For 1980s America, Iran and not Iraq was the monster that had to be caged. There was a primitive logic at work here wherein my enemy's enemy must be my friend. Iraq appealed mostly because it was involved in containing and confronting the evil of Iran. There were other reasons too. Iraq had additional attraction because it appeared to be more socially progressive, more secular, and more civilized than many of its immediate neighbors. It was rewarded by the Reagan administration with $1 billion in agricultural commodity credits and the approval of export licenses for military technology purchases. In 1989 the Bush administration increased the agricultural credits while making faint diplomatic noises about Saddam Hussein's attacks on Iraq's Kurds—attacks that had involved the use of chemical weapons (Greene 2000, 109–10).

Nobody it seems cared too much about Saddam Hussein or saw much possibility for evil because, like Nasser's Egypt in the early 1950s, the Iraq of the 1980s was scripted in terms of the romance of modernization. After a certain frisson in the 1970s, the renewal of Iraqi-American diplomatic relations in the mid-1980s seemed to herald a new era. To be sure Iraq had flirted with communist Russia and was a trifle authoritarian, but it was headed in the right direction. What Northrop Frye has called themes of ascent could be mobilized by invoking local standards against which Iraq could be evaluated, rather than global or universal ones.[1] As the *New York Times* (editorial, December 4, 1984) put it, the renewal of diplomatic relations in 1984 would allow America and Iraq to locate "shared interests" and "in the fractured Middle East that is progress." This "delayed rapprochement between Baghdad and Washington" was not the fault of Saddam Hussein's regime. It had been made possible by the "American policy maker's erroneous stereotyped image of Iraq as radical and pro-Soviet" when in truth "Iraq's Communist Party's leadership is in exile and almost all Soviet advisors have been expelled." Even if there were human rights problems Iraq had agreed, "unlike Syria, to invite Amnesty International representatives" to discuss these. Moreover President Hussein had accepted "Israel's right to secure borders" (*New York Times*, November 28, 1983).

Iraq resembled 1950s Egypt not only in that it was perceived as an oasis of comparative reason and tolerance in the shifting whispering sands of the Middle East but also because it was a place where everyday life was getting better and better for ordinary people. These themes of ascent are for all practical purposes identical to those we saw applied in the previous chapter. President Hussein's Iraq was represented as a country characterized by dynamism and social progress. A reporter writing in 1982 commented favorably on children going to school early in the morning. This was "Not an unusual sight in the West. But here in Iraq it was a testament to the introduction of universal education by Saddam Hussein." Iraq's citizens were also to benefit from infrastructural changes and the growing prosperity of a nation that was starting to approximate the American Dream of wealth, activity, and enterprise: "The highway into the capital from the dazzling new airport is dark, but everywhere else lights blaze outside all-night snack bars and gas stations. . . . Thousands of cars, lights blazing, stream through the city at night. The Government's construction and the big new hotels have drawn workers from all over Asia" (*New York Times*, November 26, 1982).

Of course there were some who pointed out Iraq's negative qualities. Human rights activists in particular tried to indicate that there were fundamental problems with the heartwarming vision of secular progress. Nobody was listening—Iraq was a good guy. This cultural framing is demonstrated by American responses to three events. (1) A survey conducted in September 1987 asked whose airplane had fired a missile at the USS *Stark* the previous May, killing some thirty personnel. Only 29 percent correctly named Iraq, 25 percent named Iran, and 43 percent said they did not know. In the same poll 43 percent said they hoped Iraq would win its long-running conflict with Iran, while only 8 percent said they hoped that Iran would win (*New York Times*, September 24, 1987). Iraq, unlike Iran, simply did not register as an embodiment of evil. (2) The gassing of Kurdish civilians by Saddam Hussein's forces in August and September 1988 confirms this pattern. The claims of Kurdish refugees were disputed, and newspapers devoted much of their space to running articles on the difficulty of diagnosing such attacks (e.g., *New York Times*, September 18, 1988; September 13, 1988). Fifteen years later the U.S. administration would be obsessed with Saddam Hussein's weapons of mass destruction, invoking their prior use as a reason for war with Iraq and leaving no stone unturned in the search for stockpiles. Yet in 1988 the Reagan administration sat on its hands. This inactive posture did not raise too many eyebrows in the domestic media. Rather than condemning Iraq on the basis of pretty strong evidence the jury handed in the Scottish verdict: "Not Proven."

The pattern of wishful thinking and apathy built on a weak but romantic underpinning genre also explains (3) U.S. responses to the Israeli bombing of Iraq's nuclear reactor in 1981. Israel was apparently alone at the time in thinking it was a bad idea for Iraq to have a nuclear program of this kind. A State Department figure noted that "the US does not share Israel's sense of immediate threat" (Dean Fischer quoted in *The New Republic*, June 20, 1981). President Ronald Reagan was no great lover of Arabs or Arab nations. His efforts to bomb the Libyan leader Colonel Qaddifi in his tent—a man he had called the "mad dog of the Middle East"—demonstrated as much. In this case, however, The Gipper called the air strike a "tragedy" and decided to suspend the sale of military aircraft to Israel (*Cambio 16*, June 22, 1981). The *New York Times* (June 22, 1981) accused Israel of hypocrisy in claiming a nuclear monopoly for itself.

An optimistic belief that Iraq's infractions were petty and that events would sort themselves out for the best continued right up to the invasion of Kuwait.

On April 12, 1990, five U.S. senators placated Saddam and assured him that a *Voice of America* commentator who had spoken of Iraq's threat to Israel had been removed from his post (*U.S. News and World Report*, September 10, 1990). Just weeks before the invasion Congress authorized renewed aid and trade with Iraq. Just days before the invasion on July 25, the U.S. ambassador to Iraq, April Glaspie, had told Saddam Hussein that the United States was seeking better relations with Iraq. She reassured him that a negative television profile on ABC news had been "cheap and unjust" and that the United States had "no opinion" on inter-Arab border disputes (Woodward 1991, 211). Hours *after* the invasion President George Bush told reporters "We're not discussing intervention. . . . We're not contemplating such action, and I . . . would not discuss it if we were" (*The New Republic*, September 3, 1990, 12; Powell 1995, 466). Strong words from Margaret Thatcher and an emergent apocalyptic narrative in civil society led to a rapid reassessment of the situation by the president. He returned from a short weekend stay at Camp David and declared to the press waiting at the White House: "This will not stand, this will not stand this aggression against Kuwait" (quoted in Powell 1995, 466).

The story we have been telling so far indicates profound structural similarities in American collective representations of Nasser and Egypt in the 1950s and Saddam Hussein and Iraq in the 1980s. In both cases the regimes and their leaders were understood as secular and progressive influences in a chaotic and irrational part of the world. Although the level of priority in the attention space was low, it is possible to identify a romantic genre at work, with optimism and themes of ascent allowing the benefit of the doubt to be given. There was however a subtle difference that needs to be noted here. At the time of Suez, Nasser had the advantage of a strongly positive *personal* characterization. This provided him with the momentum of good faith once things got sticky. As we have seen, he was the all-American freedom fighter who just happened to be Egyptian. Saddam Hussein did not enjoy such a profile—he was rarely the object of comment. Iraq's military, domestic, and diplomatic actions tended to be represented as those of the nation, not those of a single leader. During the 1980s, Iraq was Iraq, not a metonymic extension of Saddam Hussein. The Iraqi leader lacked a reservoir of heroic mythological capital, and this was to prove an important factor in the possibility for a genre switch toward apocalypticism after the invasion of Iraq. Saddam Hussein did not have to be comprehensively and systematically rewritten because he had been only thinly sketched. Now he could be fulsomely colored in as an incarnation of evil without fear of contradiction.

FROM CRISIS TO APOCALYPSE

When President George Bush declared on August 8, 1990, that "a line has been drawn in the sand" (in McGrath 2001, 92) and announced that he was sending military forces to Saudi Arabia he was making a firm statement. Yet just a few days earlier he had been dithering. The U.S. ambassador to Iraq, April Glaspie, had requested that Washington "ease off criticism" and Bush had responded with a message to Saddam Hussein stating that he continued to desire "better relations with Iraq" (Powell 1995, 462). Although Bush had now upgraded to a more resolute posture, he was outpaced by civil discourses that had already inflated the crisis to one of apocalyptic proportions. Just as Nasser's Suez nationalization had world-historical implications in the eyes of the British and French, so did Saddam Hussein's invasion of Kuwait seem to threaten the rather utopian dream of the postcommunist, post—cold war "new world order" with its "thousand points of light" that President Bush himself had recently been proclaiming. Exactly what these catchphrases meant was unclear. However, they conjured up an optimistic vision of the rule of law, mutual cooperation, and trust. Such a romantic understanding of an exciting new era in world history was now looking terribly vulnerable. U.S. citizens became conscious of the fact that Iraq had the "fourth largest army in the world," and that Saddam Hussein "made the entire world quake, weak-kneed, at his raw power" (*Time*, August 13, 1990).[2] Saddam Hussein's true ambitions had become apparent. Far from being a minor figure in a forgotten country, he now dominated front pages and threatened world peace and democracy. The need to do something about Kuwait was about more than just protecting abstract notions of sovereignty and supplies of sticky black fluids—it was a matter of stopping a new Hitler hell bent on world domination. Narrative inflation set in with powers of action becoming more awe-inspiring, objects of struggle more global and less local, and motivations for action less routine, less rationally accountable and more maniacal, more diabolical.

When *Time* (August 13, 1990) asked, "Does America really want to let the Saddams of the world shape the new global power structure?" the question was rhetorical but not facetious. For many the world would not be safe "so as long as Iraq, with or without Hussein, has the kind of military arsenal that he has built up. Whoever rules Iraq commands a million-man army with the biggest tank force in the region; the fastest-growing chemical weapons industry in the world; a $1 billion ballistic missile program; and a nuclear program believed to be only five years away from producing the bomb" (editorial, *New*

Republic, September 3, 1990). As for Israel's previously censured bombing of Iraq's nuclear reactor—this could be converted into what Martin Peretz applauded as "a providential unilateral act of nuclear nonproliferation" (*New Republic*, September 3, 1990).

The apocalyptic scenarios that took root with such virulence in August and September of 1990 projected the scenario of Saddam Hussein mobilizing his vast army along with pan-Arabic sentiment, taking control of the world's oil supplies, and eventually bringing global and nuclear war through his programs of weapons development. With the benefit of hindsight these stories might appear to some as amusingly out of touch with realities. At the time they made sense. Hussein really was understood by the majority of Americans as a figure analogous to Hitler. Some 61 percent of respondents to one opinion poll responded positively to the statement that "Saddam Hussein is like Adolf Hitler of Germany in the 1930s and it is important to stop him." Only 33 percent thought that "Saddam Hussein and Adolf Hitler are not a good comparison" (Hastings and Hastings 1992, 225). Among those who identified themselves as "following news of the Iraqi invasion closely," support for the Hitler parallel was even higher at 73 percent. By confronting the dictator, Bush found himself enjoying a 75 percent approval rating in August 1990 (Greene 2000, 124). As it is so central to the apocalyptic mood, let us illustrate this narrative theme a little more. Just like Hitler, Saddam Hussein's activities were understood as threatening to envelop the entire world in a web of evil. He was a kind of secular Antichrist, the person responsible for the direction of forces of destruction that threatened civilization itself. In this sense Saddam Hussein was not merely the figure at the center of political events, but also constituted a symbolic and discursive epicenter. He was "the most dangerous man in the world" (*U.S. News and World Report*, August 13, 1990). *Time*'s feature on Saddam Hussein on August 13, 1990, fixes this new understanding in its crystalline form. There is a vignette of Saddam-as-Octopus in the top corner of each page. The article consists of a series of typifications to the Discourse of Repression made through portentous reference to historical and biblical events. Saddam, we are told, believed himself to be "heir . . . to the blood thirsty Mesopotamian kings" such as Nebuchadnezzar. "Despite a bout of insanity," we are reminded, "Nebuchadnezzar made his name in history by destroying Jerusalem in 587 BC and driving its inhabitants into 70 years of captivity. It is fair warning." Such biblical parallels were welded to the Hitler themes to which we have already alluded: "Even in the fine points of his strategy," continues the article, "Saddam evoked echoes of the past. He excited his people with impassioned speeches full of grievances toward their neighbor. He exploited a border dispute, scheduled negotiating sessions that were intended all along to be fruitless, and cooked up a request for intervention by supposedly downtrodden locals. The invasion sequence itself was classic '30s; bluff, feint and grab."

Whether right or wrong these alignments of Middle Eastern leader to mad German were ubiquitous in America much as they had been for the British and French in Suez. They were a resource of infinite flexibility that could be used to make sense of Iraq's military policy and its domestic politics, to interpret Saddam Hussein's strategies and the risks they posed, and to suggest lines of action for the Western powers. They explained, for example, the puzzling fact that Iraq had not engaged in further aggression after seizing Kuwait: "As Germany did after blitzing Poland, Saddam is consolidating his position and gazing across the frontier as his foes assemble their armies" (*Time*, September 3, 1990). They could be used as shorthand for Saddam's style of rule: "Hussein is daily creating new parallels between himself and Hitler, compounding a record that already includes rule by torture and terror, the launching of aggressive war, and the use of poison gas against civilians as well as soldiers (editorial, *The New Republic*, September 10, 1990). They were invoked in arguments against appeasement: "Hussein's neighbors can rely only on the same assurance Hitler offered the European powers half a century ago when he pushed into Czechoslovakia and Poland: 'It is them I want, step aside and you shall be spared.' No one wanted to die for Danzig then. Hussein's gamble is that few will be willing to die for Kuwait and that the *fait accompli* he has created will become the new order of things" (Fouad Ajami, op-ed, *U.S. News and World Report*, August 13, 1990). In some respects Saddam Hussein was even worse than the Nazi leader: "there were signs that should have put him beyond the pale: Murdering ethnic minorities, brazenly flouting the 1925 Geneva Protocol against chemical warfare, which even Hitler respected." (*U.S. News and World Report*, September 10, 1990). This being the case a war against Iraq was necessary to prevent some future *Götterdämmerung*: "We are not in Saudi Arabia to protect our supply of oil. The real justification for being in Saudi Arabia is to stop World War III before it starts" (letter, *Time*, January 14, 1991).

If the apocalyptic vision was sustained by a Hitler narrative, this was made possible in turn by the use of the binary codes of civil society in describing Iraqi society. When arguments are made that someone is a tyrant of global ambition and distilled evil, evidence of popular support for that person becomes deeply problematic. As we will see more clearly in the next chapter, from the liberal stance it is only "natural" that citizens should crave freedom and despise the demagogue. If Saddam Hussein was a new Hitler, then why did his people put up with him? Two forms of explanation were used to account for Saddam's appeal to the Iraqi people as well as to his sympathizers in the Arab world. The first of these, perhaps not surprisingly, was an Orientalist discourse that drew upon the Discourse of Repression. From this perspective Saddam Hussein's supporters were not fully rational or sovereign subjects. They were emotive, dependent, and driven by unrealistic and nostalgic visions that were several centuries out of date. "Logic in the Arab world is often eclipsed by emotion," wrote a *Time* journalist (August 27, 1990) before going on to suggest that, "Saddam's populist message against corrupt regimes kept in control by American and Zionist powers, and the swagger of a leader who can and will fight them, has had an intoxicating effect on the dispossessed across national boundaries. . . . Few foreigners understand how Arabs yearn for a return of the puissant and united Arab world that dominated the globe in the 7th and 8th centuries."

The second account for Saddam's appeal was more widespread and pointed not to motivations but rather to the deeply problematic structural relationships and institutions within Iraq. These had eliminated a differentiated and autonomous civil society and created a kind of syncretism in which a coercive political party invaded all aspects of life. Like *Time*, *The New Republic* mobilized the octopus motif to capture this sinister pattern of control.

As opposition was rooted out, Iraq's Ba'ath Party built itself into a gigantic octopus-like body. From fewer than 20,000 members and followers when it seized power in 1968, the Ba'ath Party expanded to a million and a half in a decade, with tentacles reaching all strata of Iraqi society. Members were recruited by intimidation as well as by inducement. Educators were required to become informants, to submit regular reports on colleagues, friends and even family members. Their own comportment was subject to close scrutiny, and punishment for deviation was more severe for them than for others. Once you were in the Ba'ath party, there was, literally, no way to leave except feet first. (October 29, 1990)

The movement of hundreds of thousands of American troops into the Middle East during the second half of 1990 can be understood, at least in part, as a response to this dominant narrative of impending doom, unmitigated evil, and societal dependency. Minimally these civil discourses made the military buildup legitimate and so helped pave the way for an eventual war. A CNN survey as early as one week after the invasion of Kuwait found an 81 percent approval rating for military involvement (*U.S. News and World Report*, August 13, 1990). A war in which it was calculated between three and fifteen thousand American troops would die (Powell 1995, 498–90) was now an acceptable option. The low mimetic themes of cost and efficiency that usually prevail were no longer central to governmental decision making and decision justification. Traditional problems attending to what sociologists call "collective action" could be pushed to the side, such as who should pay for the war. As *Soldier of Fortune* so eloquently put it, "we can bring in the bean-counters later—when tyrants march, the free world can't afford to get into a pissing contest over how to split the tab" (editorial, November 1990).

By the end of 1990 President Bush seems to have finally given up on diplomacy toward Saddam Hussein and joined in enthusiastically with the popular apocalypticism. He frequently used the terms "Hitler," "madman," "rapist," and "evil." In remarks to the Reserve Officer's Association he conjured up the image of appeasement and suggested that "turning a blind eye to Saddam's aggression" would only lead to "a far more dangerous, a far more costly conflict" (in McGrath 2001, 146). Perhaps this was his genuine view. In a letter to his children dated December 31, 1990, he declared, "I look at today's crisis as 'good vs. evil'—yes, it is that clear" (in Greene 2000, 122, 129).

As Congress debated authorizing military action Bush said in private, "I'll prevail or I'll be impeached." This statement, according to Colin Powell (1995, 499), suggests that he was prepared if necessary to ignore his constitutional duty to obtain the support of Congress for war. The president seemed to have moved beyond the point where what Max Weber had called legal-rational authority was central. Even Colin Powell himself—famously dubbed a "reluctant warrior" by Bob Woodward—seems to have shared this vision. Recollecting his testimony before the Senate Armed Services Committee on December 3 in his autobiography, he claims to have given a "cold, hard appraisal of what we faced." Yet for all this talk of clinical rationality, the descriptors he uses carry the telltale signs of the apocalyptic vision, for in addition to the "fourth largest army in the world . . . hanging like a specter over the desert was the Iraqi biological arsenal and Saddam's feverish drive for nuclear capability" (1995, 493). A few pages later he says that Saddam Hussein's "way was madness" (1995, 497). Enough said.

EFFORTS AT GENRE CHANGE

So we have a narrative structure in place in the United States that is remarkably similar to that which was encountered in France and Britain in the summer of 1956. Yet if dominant through the second half of 1990, apocalypticism did not remain so without effort and without challenge. In order to account for war in a voluntarist way we need to understand not only which genre was calling the tune but also how it managed to stay on top. We also need to demonstrate the presence of plausible alternatives. By showing that there were stories that related events differently, reality can be decoupled from its representation, and the constitutive, humanly constructed qualities of civil narrative made clearer. Once events can be shown to no longer speak for themselves, acts of ongoing interpretation become apparent as pivotal elements of cultural process. Between August 1990 and January 1991, the tidal force of the apocalyptic master narrative was to ebb as a series of themes and disputes threatened the integrity of the dominant picture. Although widely disparate in subject matter, these assaults share common structural properties as predicted by our model. For example, they appealed to the binary codes of civil society, but in ways that narrowed the moral divide between characters in the unfolding drama of the Middle East. The negative typification of Iraq's leader was a taken-for-granted feature of the discursive landscape. Nobody was arguing that he was a freedom fighter or saint as some had seen Nasser. However, a process that I have elsewhere termed "reclassification" (P. Smith 1991) saw Kuwait, the United States, and President Bush also located within the Discourse of Repression. As we saw in the case of Suez, such a process of depolarization can allow violence-averse low mimetic and tragic genres to replace those of a more heroic and apocalyptic tenor.

It should come as no surprise to find that liberal intellectuals and peace groups considered both sides to be symbolically polluted. *The Nation*, which is essentially a liberal/Left journal for and by intellectuals, provides an excellent and convenient source for understanding the structure of this discourse. In its articles we discover a deep cynicism as to motivations. President Bush was described as seeking violence rather than as trying to avoid it through serious and sincere diplomacy. The war was no longer just Saddam's war; it was Bush's too. As *The Nation* put it, Bush was like a gung-ho action hero rather than a true statesman: "Each day President Bush ratchets up the Rambo rhetoric and closes more alleys of diplomatic escape" (editorial, September 10, 1990). George Bush and James Baker were seen as manipulative and devious in their machinations, with the military alliance and the war really just about oil. According to *The Nation* they were rapists like Saddam, engaged in deception and without true respect for legitimate institutions: "The party of death . . . has since August 2 seen sanctions as a kind of ritualistic foreplay to the violent penetration of the entire region of the globe. President Bush manipulated the various United Nations sanctions votes as he sent Secretary of State Baker to bribe and buy a favorable 'use of force' resolution, putting a specious international gloss on his deadly designs for war" (editorial, December 24, 1990). James Baker's own confused justifications for the war only assisted this view that interests and not morals were behind America's action.

With the fall of Kuwait, Saddam Hussein had control over 21 percent of the world's oil supply. If he went on to capture Saudi Arabia this would double (Greene 2000, 115). At the very time when the president shifted toward apocalypticism and increasingly spoke of confronting evil, Baker spoke about the need for oil, seemingly fearing that the American voter remained in low mimetic mode. On November 13, he suggested, like Eden before him that, "We cannot permit a dictator such as this to sit astride that economic lifeline," before going on to blunder, "And to bring it down to the level of the average American citizen, let me say that means jobs" (cited in Greene 2000, 123). Remarks such as this could only encourage protestors armed with slogans such as "No blood for oil." The president implemented some damage control when he declared a few days later, "We're not talking simply about the price of gas; we are talking about the price of liberty" (in McGrath 2001, 110).

Domestic as well as foreign policy goals were read by many on the Left as objectives of this insincerity. It was believed that Bush had "plotted" a "roller coaster ride" designed to "rip public opinion from its moorings and allow the Administration to have its way" (editorial, *The Nation*, December 3, 1990). An antidemocratic strategy was afoot to convert civil society into a quivering jelly of incoherent thought: "The idea is to create so much confusion that rational public response is impossible" (ibid.). Needless to say, the aims of all this plotting were particularistic. In contrast to the dominant narrative in which America was enacting the good for the benefit of all in the New World Order, this alternate narrative was grounded in a cynical realism according to which, "All Bush is doing is asserting America's post-Cold War role as the un-opposable, nuclear-tipped world cop, enforcing rules of its own making for its own narrow, short-term interests" (editorial, *The Nation*, September 10, 1990). Some, like Christopher Hitchens (1991) writing forcefully, argued this pattern of principle-less politics could be traced back through years of morally problematic Middle Eastern foreign policy that had included the cosseting of Saddam Hussein himself. With both the United States and Iraq having doubts cast on their motivations in such a manner, critics suggested that only the universal "sacredness of human life" (Douglas Hostetter, Member of Fellowship of Reconciliation, cited in *U.S. News and World Report*, November 12, 1990) should be used to guide action. The result of this form of analysis, we are told, was to blockade not fight. Much of *The Nation*'s leader for December 24, 1990, for example, consisted of a two-page litany of the costs that would result from the use of force. Following on what Albert O. Hirschman (1991) has called the perversity thesis, it was argued that the policy of war would lead to consequences in direct contradiction to those that were intended. A scenario was envisaged that included thousands of dead Americans and Iraqis, greater political chaos in the Middle Eastern region, and disaster for the world economy. This, of course, is a tragic genre at work. There is a sense of pathos and an awareness of missed opportunities for more prosocial outcomes.

More surprising than the familiar and to some extent predictable views of the antiwar Left were those of the antiwar Right. The Left's story, we have seen, was one suggesting Americans should be wringing their hands because of the moral failings of their leaders and the pointless loss of sacred human lives. This was a mildly inflated genre where points of principle and transcendent values such as democracy and equality were at stake. Critics on the Right, in contrast, selected a low mimetic genre that pivoted around a worldly cost-benefit analysis. Here there was no strong effort to morally condemn Iraq and no real attempt to make predictions about distant possible futures. Because the threat of Russia's evil empire was no longer around, events in the Middle East were not really that portentous. What was important was to keep things in proportion and to do exactly what *Soldier of Fortune* had counseled against—count the beans. These included "American lives" (by contrast the Left almost invariably spoke of "human lives") and dollars. "Before we send thousands of American soldiers to their deaths," said the right-wing Republican Pat Buchanan, "let's make damn sure America's vital interests are threatened" (quoted in *Time*, September 10, 1990). Buchanan claimed, "Saddam is not a madman, he is no Adolf Hitler." Sure he was a "ruthless menace to his neighbors," but he did not threaten America (quoted in Greene 2000, 124). Calculations would show that Saddam's threat did not justify the expense. We were really just looking at a sordid third-world struggle that should be ignored. As Pat Buchanan again put it, "There are lots of things worth fighting for, but an extra 10c for a gallon of gas isn't one of them" (quoted in *Time*, September 10, 1990). Ted Carpenter, the director of the libertarian Cato Institute asserted that "making the US the guardian of global stability" was simply "a blueprint for the indefinite prolongation of expensive and risky US military commitments around the world" (quoted in *Time*, September 10, 1990). In short, America's interests, defined in dollars and sense, dictated isolationism.

The assaults from both Left and Right reached a peak in December 1990, when Bush's policy shift from sanctions to war became increasingly explicit. The release of foreign hostages by Saddam Hussein came at a critical moment, reinforcing these coherent challenges to a weakening apocalyptic master narrative. On December 17, 1990, *Time* reflected this mood when it ran a lead article entitled "Options for Peace." In its pages in August it had somewhat gleefully noted that a sample of Saddam Hussein's handwriting had exhibited signs of "megalomania and paranoia" and spoke of his "snake eyes . . . the eyes of a killer" (August 13, 1990). Now the dictator appeared to be a man with some measure of rationality. Taking the hostages had been wrong, of course, but in releasing them Saddam Hussein had shown that he "responds to pressure. That somewhat undercuts the belief that nothing short of war is likely to nudge Saddam out of Kuwait."

SUSTAINING A NARRATIVE: REPAIR WORK
AND SECONDARY ELABORATIONS

Writing on the witchcraft practices of the Azande tribe of southern Sudan, the anthropologist E. E. Evans-Pritchard (1937) pointed long ago to the ingenious ways in which a cosmology that believed in supernatural forces and the divination powers of an oracle could be sustained. When presented with contradictory messages from the oracle or empirical evidence that suggested it had made a false prediction, the Azande were always able to come up with an explanation to account for seemingly problematic information: Witches had interfered with the oracle, the techniques of divination had been faulty, the oracle was signaling in an oblique way that the right questions had not been asked, and so forth. Something rather similar goes on with the genre guess. Once a reading is in place it is remarkably robust, but it still needs to be sustained against logical and empirical challenge by work that discounts alternative readings or that shores up a faltering genre choice through ad hoc accretions and layers of additional complexity. Minor concessions are made, the veracity of evidence questioned, aspersions are cast on the motives of competitors and the validity of the big-picture reading is affirmed for all practical purposes.

To understand the precarious survival of the apocalyptic narrative in the United States we need to acknowledge such a process as central. This activity of genre repair and justification involved more than just responding to the contending, systematic claims made by the Left and Right we have just reviewed, for spontaneous or organic challenges also eventuated that did not seem to have any clear political sponsors. Whereas the Left attacked the Bush administration as manipulative and self-interested and as a ruthlessly efficient political machine, and the Right called for more cost counting and prudence, a more diffuse discourse in civil society spoke of feckless, weak, indecisive, and self-contradictory American policies.

It is often the case that major crises begin with affirmations of unity but that soon a kind of postmortem activity transpires in which the following kinds of questions are asked: Why did we let things get to this state? How come we were caught by surprise? What went wrong? Then fingers start to be pointed. We saw this sequence play out, for example after the terrorist attacks of September 11 and the space shuttle disasters in the United States, and in Britain after the unexpected invasion of the Falkland Islands by Argentina in 1982. Such activity can undermine binary imagery because negative social outcomes are no longer attributed exclusively to an external enemy. Narrative complexity eventuates that can only generate deflation toward low mimesis as heroic visions of the world are replaced with those replete with ironies and unintended consequences, with pictures of failed agency and weak leadership. Such storytelling in turn undermines the certainties of belief that make the loss of life and risks of war readily acceptable.

In the fall of 1990 an emergent critique of U.S. involvement and complicity with Saddam Hussein during the 1980s and immediately preceding the invasion of Kuwait replicated this pattern.[3] The United States had to take some responsibility for a debacle: "George Bush may be full of resolution now, but before the invasion the signals sent to Saddam by his administration were, at best, mixed. At worst, it can be argued, Saddam was given a green light to gobble up his oil-rich neighbor. If it comes to war, Saddam will be fairly cast as the villain, but the ultimate responsibility cannot be said to rest with Iraq alone" (*Newsweek*, October 1, 1990). George Bush's failings as president were a persistent deflationary threat. Even if his previously vacillating policy toward Iraq could be consigned to history, his perceived weakness in domestic affairs was an ongoing burden to him throughout the period of military buildup. Structuralist poetics makes it clear that heroic narratives require some kind of protagonist with remarkable autonomy, prophetic vision, and powers of action. President Bush, however, appeared unable to resolve even a mundane budget crisis; he "flopped back and forth," "made incomprehensible jokes," and "looked goofy" (*Newsweek*, October 22, 1990). This passive, weak, and indecisive figure was "a political wimp" (*New York Times*, cited in *Newsweek*, October 22, 1990), rather than a decisive world savior. Opinion polls indicated that such a negative discourse had polluted Bush to the extent that his October popularity plummeted to only 54 percent (*Newsweek*, October 29, 1990).

Also propelling Bush's ratings decline was the fact that the symbolic representation of Saddam Hussein's danger had also deflated. I have argued elsewhere that the charismatic power of leaders and their ability to be strongly coded in the terms of a positive discourse often depends upon the presence of an evil enemy over whose actions they have limited control. Hitler railed against Jews and Bolsheviks, Churchill against Hitler, and Martin Luther King Jr. had the cultural advantage of a sequence of brutal and performatively inept southern sheriffs as opponents (P. Smith 2000). Bush's problem was that since August the Iraqi leader had done little visible evil except for his "human shield" policy that had involved retaining some western hostages in Iraq. Yet if the textures of Bush's character were scumbled during the fall of 1990, they were not beyond redemption. Pivotal here was a secondary elaboration that saw the mobilization of contrasts internal to Bush himself. When mirrored against his own weaker moments in domestic policy and diplomacy, the U.S. president's forceful postinvasion politics could gain that disproportionate merit accorded to the good works of the apostate. The contagion of the potentially heroic Bush by his polluted doppelgänger was prevented by conceptually partitioning the domestic and foreign president and the preinvasion and postinvasion leader. *Time,* for example, was able to argue that the two "George Bushes" were its "Men of the Year": "If Bush ignored the Iraqi threat for weeks, if his Administration miscalculated Saddam's messianic intentions and engaged in a quiet appeasement of Baghdad for the better part of two years, if America is at greater risk because Bush, his predecessors and Congress failed to develop a credible energy policy that reduced the country's dependence on foreign oil, at least since the Iraqi invasion of Kuwait the President has proved adroit, even brilliant" (*Time,* August 20, 1990). Kuwait's image suffered alongside that of Bush. In August 1990, it had been seen largely as a minnow swallowed by a shark, as a small and innocent nation that had been brutally invaded by Saddam Hussein's armies, as a maiden in a tower who needed to be rescued from an ogre. As the crisis dragged on with little action on the ground, Kuwait came under the analytic spotlight. Such activity saw the oil-rich nation coded in terms of the Discourse of Repression. Had such a story stuck, then the narrative motivation for war could have been weakened. After all, why should lives be lost in the effort to return a stolen country to its rightful dictators? As we have seen before in this book, local standards came to the rescue as a secondary elaboration. *Time's* lengthy article of December 24, provides an eloquent and representative defense of Kuwait in these terms. Accusations that it was an "arrogant, undemocratic" nation are dismissed as "pernicious." Kuwait's leaders are exhibited as kindly, western educated, and charitable. The oligarchic ruling system was seen as a "quasi-democratic tradition" founded on "popular consent." Although by no means perfect, Kuwait could be considered as accountable in terms of the Discourse of Liberty for all practical purposes. It was "an essentially decent nation despite some glaring blind spots, Kuwait before Saddam was a good country in a bad neighborhood" (*Time,* December 24, 1990).

Notwithstanding such creativity, the apocalyptically framed master narrative did weaken, and with it support for vigorous action. A *Newsweek* poll of October 1990 showed that a surprisingly low 21 percent favored immediate military action, while 73 percent wanted to see sanctions given more time, and 69 percent diplomatic solutions given more effort. A *Los Angeles Times* poll discovered that support for Bush's more aggressive policies fell from 75 percent in August to 50 percent in December. Only 42 percent supported increased troop deployments (for polls see *Economist*, December 1, 1990). The nation was split: 49 percent of respondents to one December poll advocated waiting a further six months for sanctions to work, while 48 percent opposed (Hastings and Hastings 1992, 228). George Bush's hawkish policy was in crisis when in mid-January 1991, Congress debated whether or not to authorize the use of force by the president, thereby unleashing some of the military power that had been building up for months in Saudi Arabia and the Gulf in Operation Desert Shield. Reading through these debates we can see a titanic battle of genres—apocalypticism confronted low mimesis and tragedy—and a reiteration of the themes we have already tracked. All parties agreed that Saddam Hussein was evil and that the occupation of Kuwait must end. All agreed on the sacredness of U.S. servicemen's lives and the fact that a war should be a last resort. Speakers from both sides alluded to the immense import of the debate, and made reference to the cultural authority of the Constitution and to the wisdom of the founding fathers. Where they differed was in their understanding of the plot trajectories that would result from diverse actions and inactions—in other words in their genre-inflected thinking about events with consequent predictions and injunctions.

Those in favor of authorizing immediate war argued that only violent intervention could prevent Saddam from eventually accomplishing his diabolical ends. To recap, under this scenario Saddam, like Hitler or the Devil, was a man with a desire to dominate the entire globe. His plans to control the world's vital oil supplies were only a stage in a far grander strategy. Delay could not be countenanced because it would only increase the danger. Pivotal here were beliefs that Iraq was developing a nuclear capability. According to Senator Pete Domenici, Saddam Hussein was "an international outlaw with unlimited ambitions" who was "getting dangerously close to possessing nuclear weapons" (*Congressional Record* 137 [January 12, 1991]: S 323, 324). Likewise, Senator Warren Rudman pointed out that we stood at "one of history's critical junctions" (remember that "Hinge of History" from Suez?) and that "if he is not stopped now . . . how credible will our response be when his aspirations are further buttressed by a deliverable nuclear weapons capacity." The senator goes on to remind us that "the lack of a concerted response by the League of Nations to Axis aggression in the 1930s contributed to the global carnage which followed" (*Congressional Record* 137 [January 12,

1991]: S 325).[4] For Mr. Alfonse D'Amato, Saddam Hussein was a "geopolitical glutton" who would just keep "grabbing and gobbling" (*Congressional Record* 137 [January 12, 1991]: S 384). Mr. John Seymour argued that Saddam Hussein's goal was to manipulate "the entire oil supply of the Arabian Peninsula," and that consequently nations from The Netherlands to Japan would face the risk of economic collapse." History had taught us that sanctions were of no use in "averting conflicts and stopping injustice," just as "American and European sanctions did not stop the Axis power of World War II from trying to absorb the lands that they invaded" (*Congressional Record* 137 [January 12, 1991]: S 384).

Those who advocated the maintenance of sanctions in the congressional debate mobilized the Discourse of Repression and attacked the move toward war as irrational and imprudent. The narrative they proposed was one of tragedy. The choice of war, albeit well intentioned, would be counterproductive, leading to increased levels of violence and chaos and death. War should only be used as a last resort. We had not reached that point yet because America was not faced with an immediate, clear and present danger of apocalyptic proportions. Senator Robert Byrd suggested a need to assess the "national interests by a totally calm and rational standard," whereas he believed America was being "hurried into war" (*Congressional Record* 137 [January 12, 1991]: S 371). Senator Dan Moynihan was even more explicit in attacking the cultural processes that had made war seem like good sense. He did so by drawing in implicit ways upon a theory of narrative. America, Moynihan argued, was trapped into a genre inflated mode of thinking that was no longer appropriate: "The problem is that the Cold War mode of decision making does not admit of such proportionality . . . the tiniest issues roar to the fore with armegeddonic fury. . . . What I have pleaded for, however, is a sense of proportionality" (*Congressional Record* 137 [January 12, 1991]: S 394).

The argument for a narrative deflation was further enhanced by pulling the rug of sanctimoniousness from under the feet of the United States and thereby narrowing the gap between the players in the unfolding drama. Senator Fritz Hollings, for example, indicated that America had itself been on the wrong side of many UN resolutions. If American resembled Iraq in diverse ways, then rhetorical condemnations grounded in Manichean visions were deeply problematic. "The President likes to rile us all up about this wild man Saddam Hussein saying that Saddam has attacked two of his neighbors in the last 10 years. But that is exactly what the US has been condemned for in the United Nations in 1983, not by 12 votes as in the case of resolution 678, but by 109 members of the United Nations condemning the United States for an act of aggression in Grenada, and by 75 votes just December a year ago for an act of aggression in Panama. . . . So let us cool down around this place and talk sense" (Senate. *Congressional Record* 137 [January 12, 1991]: S 328).

Bush's war plans survived votes in the House and Senate. But only just. An antiwar resolution was defeated in the House by 250 to 183. In the Senate the margin was only 52 to 47, a victory that required nine Democrat defections to support the Republican president. This cleared the way for House Joint Resolution 77 authorizing military force against Iraq (Greene 2000, 127; Powell 1995, 505).

AMERICA AT WAR

The move to war in the middle of January 1991, saw many of the doubts evaporate that had allowed only a narrow margin of victory in the Senate debate. The failure of Saddam Hussein to respond to aerial bombardment was undoubtedly an important factor. American and allied airpower was so superior that it seemed the war could be undertaken without substantial human costs—or at least human costs as measured in American lives. The actuarial critics at least could be placated if not those holding to the tragic genre. The scenario of bloodless "technowar" (Gibson 1986) could have led to a more deflated narrative falling into place that framed conflict as a primarily managerial and logistical problem. Equally, a more tragic narrative could have resulted, feeding off the one-sided nature of the fight. This did not happen. Apocalypticism remained in vogue. Why? Because it seems that only a dangerous madman could continue to resist such an onslaught. Saddam Hussein's failure to withdraw from Kuwait or make diplomatic initiatives after the air war began simply confirmed the long-held belief that he would have to be destroyed. Genres overcode information. Hence more than 90 percent of respondents to one January poll, regardless of gender, race, or party, believed that Saddam would fight to the "very end," and 83 percent in another considered themselves to feel proud of what the United States was doing in the Persian Gulf (*The American Enterprise,* March/April 1991).

Other events assisted in reinforcing the credibility of the binary codes and narratives on which the war was justified. American military technology did more than promise an apparently effortless victory. It also had a cultural valence, symbolizing the peaceful and universalistic mission on which Bush had sent his nation. The "smart bombs" and Patriot missiles pushed into the limelight by U.S. military briefings appeared to be clean technologies that could kill and protect in a discriminating, civilized manner (see *Policy Review,* Spring 1991). Iraq's Scud missiles, in contrast, were described by *Time* as "unwieldy and inaccurate, practically antique, a dinosaur compared with the sleek precise Tomahawk cruise missile" (*Time*, January 28, 1991). Consistent with the World War II frame, treatments of the Scud usually described it as Nazi derived and pointed to a legacy extending back to Hitler's V2 rockets. In point of fact the Scud could be more accurately seen as a B-grade Soviet missile (Powell 1995, 511). With Gorbachev's regime in support of the coalition and Saddam already coded as a sequel to Hitler such details passed unnoticed. The display of brutalized military hostages on television further confirmed the image of a barbaric Saddam Hussein, of an untrustworthy man addicted to violence who was incapable of conforming to civilizing codes such as the Geneva Convention (see *Time*, February 4, 1991). As the war unfolded a collective effervescence became manifest in the behavior of many American people. Ordinary routines were interrupted as citizens sought information by television, radio, and telephone. Church attendances increased dramatically (see *Time*, January 28, 1991). Desert Storm paraphernalia ranging from books to T-shirts, to yellow ribbons and American flags to display on cars and trees, even a board game—it all sold in vast quantities.

The triumph of the apocalyptic master narrative during the fighting was as contingent and contested as it had been in the buildup to war. Although objectors on the Right shifted ground rapidly and supported the war once it appeared that events were moving smoothly and that material costs of confrontation would be low, the Left and its intellectuals continued to attribute polluted, Discourse of Repression qualities to the United States. The neo-Marxist academic Robert Brenner (1991), for example, attempted to deflate Bush's motivations by indicating that "US action is in no way motivated by Saddam's awful regime or his violation of democratic rights," before going on to characterize the war as an "obsessive" attempt to maintain the illusion of hegemonic power. Radical sociologist Todd Gitlin attempted to question the exercise by suggesting that it was driven by, "The rationality of the think tank and the thrill of the video game," which could only "generate fantasies of neat war and neater settlement" (*Dissent*, Spring 1991, 153). Whether obsessively and cynically calculating, or self-deluding and excitable (or indeed all of these at the same time, for the Discourse of Repression admits such seemingly contradictory combinations), America's leaders, it was argued, were not acting in responsible ways. Once again this discourse had limited impact outside of Leftist circles. Once again more important for confronting the cultural foundations for war were the unanticipated and seemingly unsponsored narrative opportunities that arose.

Because military technology was taken as a material embodiment of American universalism, a point of semiotic vulnerability was opened up. The positive coding of the use of force was provisional upon the minimal victimization of Iraqi civilians who, as we have seen, were framed by civil discourse as innocents who had been deluded and coerced by Saddam Hussein. The bombing of the Amiriya shelter in Baghdad with the loss of numerous civilian lives in the middle of February 1991 kicked this Achilles heel. Military and administration officials moved quickly to defend the action. The first secondary elaboration was that the site was "an active command-and-control center that was working, that was communicating with the leadership" (General Neal, quoted in *New York Times*, February 14, 1991). If this was the case, then the presence of civilians had to be explained as a devious trick of Saddam Hussein who had "set us up" ("A Senior Officer," ibid.). Such an account allowed Pentagon officials to insinuate that "the Iraqi Government was ultimately responsible for the deaths by having allowed civilians to take refuge at a military command post" (*New York Times*, February 14, 1991). Forced in the end to concede that the bunker was not even a command center, American spokespersons fell back on a discourse of confession. It was admitted that the deed was wrong and that a "mistake" had been made.

"Mistakes" have the language game property of simultaneously recognizing causally efficient culpability while denying moral responsibility at the level of intent. They are a powerful cultural resource for those seeking honorable ways to account for bad actions, a useful if sometimes last ditch secondary elaboration for a code typification under attack. Related mistakes were conceded—reluctantly but also as required. When a "biological weapons factory" was bombed on January 22, it was discovered by CNN that it was manufacturing infant formula. Analysis: faulty intelligence. Patriot missiles had a mythology constructed around them that they could not live up to. Only after the war did these failures enter into public knowledge. Analysis: faulty technology. Around a quarter of the coalition deaths were due to "friendly fire," a condition suggesting chaos rather rationality and efficiency. Likewise, this information was slow to emerge. The final analysis: these things happen in war. The overall picture is of an administration keen to align its war with the concepts of rationality specified in the Discourse of Liberty. The war had to be witnessably directed at targets of evil, be proportional, to be driven by cool heads with high ideals. Military technology and professionalism had apparently enabled these objectives to be reached with minimal collateral damage to the prevailing genre regime. The concept of the "mistake" allowed damaged binaries to be repaired. By and large the media did little to challenge this perception of precision and purity. Corralled in Saudi Arabia and fed information in choreographed briefings, it had only limited capability to discover new clues that could have shifted the narration (Greene

2000, 134–35) and had to content itself with grumbles about this sad state of affairs.

THE TRAGIC DENOUEMENT

During the conflict, then, apocalypticism was sustained despite the objective weakness of Iraqi forces. Saddam Hussein became an increasingly gothic figure, a composite Hitler/Devil in a Hell of his own making. *Newsweek* (March 4, 1991) captured this imagery precisely and eloquently:

> Saddam's last stand was Wagnerian in its madness. He backlit himself with the flames of Kuwait's oil wells, which he turned into torches. As the air filled with the stench of rotten eggs, his troops shot civilians in the streets of Kuwait City. One moment he swore defiance, the next he tried to get Mikhail Gorbachev to save him. When that failed he withdrew into his bunker, playing Hitler, who wanted to take everyone with him when he fell, rather than Hirohito, who surrendered to save his people from annihilation. Cornered, bloodied, he still had one infernal device in his arsenal: his stocks of nerve gas and chemical weapons.

If this is the way that Saddam Hussein was represented at the end of the war it should come as no surprise that Bush gained kudos from his defeat. He was judged to be a hero, a leader who had taken the difficult steps and summoned up the moral courage necessary to stand up to such a madman. As the *New York Times* (editorial, March 1, 1991) put it, the American president stood as "unchallenged winner in an enterprise of high risks and high ideals." On March 6, Bush announced before a Joint Session of Congress that Kuwait was free. This cultural victory for Bush was to be short lived. In the postwar period, initial euphoria following an easy military victory over the dictator was replaced by dismay. The plight of the rebels who had risen up against Saddam Hussein started to dominate headlines. In his autobiography Colin Powell remarks that he had felt unease at Bush's anti-Saddam rhetoric during the buildup to the war (Powell 1995, 491). He suggested to Dick Cheney and Brent Scowcroft that they should find a way for the president to turn down the demonization. As U.S. military objectives did not include regime change in Iraq, he "thought it unwise to elevate public expectations by making the man out to be the devil incarnate and then leaving him in place." Powell places too much emphasis on the role of the White House in setting the narrative mood. As we have seen, at the start of the crisis it lagged behind the wider civil discourse in shifting to apocalypticism. Yet he is otherwise right on the money. The public wanted Saddam eliminated and Bush had helped create this wish by pushing the narrative best suited to legitimate the war. He ended up being held accountable to his own words. In addition, the very success of Bush's military policies had created a climate of inflated expectations. As victory had been easy why not keep going all the way to Baghdad? Bush's moral capital, carefully accumulated through coalition building, leadership, and rhetorical denunciation was squandered when he failed to support the Shiite Muslims in the South and Kurds in the North fighting against Saddam Hussein, or indeed to take any steps whatsoever to try to remove the evil dictator. The policy switch toward laissez faire was justified in terms of realpolitik—specifically the need for a strong Iraq in the Middle East. America did not want to see Iran or Syria dominant in the Gulf region. The decision not to intervene was further justified with reference to the technicalities of United Nations resolutions. These had allowed force to be used to remove Iraq from Kuwait, not to enforce a regime change in Baghdad. These are "good reasons" only in routine politics. In a cultural environment where normative horizons had been shaped by apocalyptic logics, they were bean-counting, pen-pushing nonsense. Whatever its merits as a rational policy that may or may not have accorded with America's objective interests, in cultural terms the decision to revert to the politics of low mimesis was a massive blunder.

There was a further cultural contradiction that might have driven the administration's decision to halt the war against Iraq. As U.S. military superiority over Iraq became manifest in the final days of the conflict, the apocalyptic narrative finally started looking implausible. Images of charred bodies and blown-up tanks made it appear as if norms of restraint and proportionality were being breached. Without a fair fight Iraqi deaths could become encoded as carnage and the United States as barbaric and in breach of the Discourse of Liberty. Awareness of such as issue was present in the White House. Colin Powell (1995, 520–21) relates concerns that "the television coverage . . . was starting to make it look as if we were engaged in slaughter for slaughter's sake," and a worry that the United States would "lose the moral high ground" by fighting past the "rational calculation." The decision to end the war, then, was not simply a military or political decision shaped by environments of power and law but also one influenced by cultural codes and expectations about the appropriate and inappropriate use of overwhelming force.

All this created a horrible dilemma for President Bush. Satisfying legal obligations, keeping the international coalition and the UN happy, and demonstrating that war was subject to rational constraint meant calling off the dogs and keeping out of Iraq. Yet this meant leaving Saddam Hussein in power and ignoring the categorical imperative of the apocalyptic narrative: destroy evil. As Saddam crushed rebels within his own country, the American president became more and more vulnerable to narration as a kind of Pontius Pilate washing his hands of the affair. America's new policy of nonintervention was seen as an act of "cynical" desertion of the rebels (op-ed, *New York Times*, April 3, 1991). The United States had become an unwitting ally of Saddam, for "by betraying the rebels the US is truly intervening—on the side of the killer Hussein" (op-ed, *New York Times*, April 2, 1991). According to Senator Al Gore, Bush's treatment of the Kurds "revives the most bitter memories of humankind's worst moments" (quoted in *New York Times*, April 13, 1991). Members of Bush's own party shared these sentiments. Senator Orrin Hatch spoke of the shame that would result from such a betrayal when he argued that, "Not since the Cambodian holocaust under Pol Pot's Khmer Rouge has the West so callously stood by while a brutal dictator's forces wiped out an innocent people. . . . Rightly or wrongly, the Kurds joined with the US and its coalition in trying to bring down Saddam Hussein. If we refuse to take steps to protect them from his vindictiveness, we will taint our troop's victory in Operation Desert Storm" (op-ed, *New York Times*, April 13, 1991).

So the political culture in part nurtured by Bush during the build-up to war had put him between a rock and a hard place. It is a scenario that illustrates a theme elaborated in chapter two. Whether or not Bush and his supporters actually believed what he had said earlier about Saddam is beside the point. We need only understand that words are performative and that actors are held accountable to their rhetoric. Bush's poll ratings plummeted. Some 54 percent of respondents to one poll claimed that they would "support . . . US forces resuming military action to force Saddam from power [37 percent oppose, 9 percent D.K.]" (Hastings and Hastings 1992, 231). This public pressure eventually forced Bush to replace a polluted and profane policy of passivity and inactivity with one that took some faltering but effective steps. A security zone was established in Kurdish Iraq and half a million refugees began returning. The full costs of Bush's policy were not to become apparent, however, until the presidential election campaign of 1992. Because Bush had "betrayed" the Kurds and failed to oust Saddam Hussein, he was unable to mobilize the Gulf War as electoral capital. Fear of reviving the pollution obliged Bush to maintain an astonishing envelope of silence about the crowning glories of his four years in office: the assembly of a multinational coalition, the execution of a brilliant battle plan, and the liberation of Kuwait. William Jefferson Clinton became the forty-second President of the United States of America. It is a supreme irony that Bush, the victor of the Gulf War, was out of office and Saddam Hussein remained in power. It is a supreme irony that indicates the power of genre politics to shape outcomes in ways every bit as real as more material military and political process.

BRITAIN AND THE GULF WAR

Broadly speaking, the narratives and justifications in the United Kingdom replicated those in the United States. This cultural pattern explains in part why Britain entered into the material preparations for war with greater enthusiasm than was perhaps strictly necessary, for its troop and hardware commitment was much more substantial than that of continental neighbors of similar size and wealth. Opinion poll measures confirm a higher level of hawkishness in Britain than in mainland Europe. As early as August 1990, 42 percent of those polled supported "the bombing of civilian and military targets in Iraq." Amazingly, some 12 percent agreed with the use of nuclear weapons should oil supplies become seriously threatened by Iraq, and 18 percent with the "limited use of nuclear weapons on military targets" in order to "restore independence to Kuwait." Some 31 percent supported the World War II—style internment of Iraqi civilians in the United Kingdom (Hastings and Hastings 1992, 209ff.). Once an apocalyptic narrative had gained wide currency there was little choice for political parties but to jump on the bandwagon. It is probably the case that the Tories were genuinely in favor of war. With the Labour Party this is less certain. However, mindful of the damage caused by its vacillating policy during the Falklands War, it kept a low profile, silenced its Left wing, and eventually accorded the war the formal legitimacy of bipartisan support. An important consequence of this decision was that antiwar sentiment was deprived of a high-profile institutional forum. This contrasts with the situation in the United States where congressional debate and vociferous lobbies on both the Left and Right had generated a more diverse expression of opinion.

During the 1980s, prevalent attitudes in Britain had much in common with those in the United States. Interest in and information about Iraq was sketchy and events were judged piecemeal, yet there was a generally positive assessment of the Middle Eastern nation. We can see this by looking back again to June 1981, when Israeli jets bombed the Iraqi nuclear power station near Baghdad. The Israeli claim that Saddam Hussein was a potential aggressor trying to develop nuclear capability was considered risible. The Israeli leader Menachem Begin offered an apocalyptic scenario in a postraid press conference: "Saddam Hussein, the ruler of Iraq, who with his own hands killed his own friends to become the sole ruler of that country had an ambition. He wanted to develop nuclear weapons so that he could either bring Israel to its knees on behalf of the Arab world, destroy her menfolk, her infrastructure, and the greater part of her Army" (reported in *Times*, June 10, 1981). This vision was not shared in the United Kingdom. Israel's action was "an act of barely credible international piracy" (letter, *Times*, June 12, 1981), viewed as motivated less by genuine fear and more by impending elections. The British prime minister Margaret Thatcher joined the United States in speaking of the raid as unjustifiable and as a "grave breach of international law" (Hansard, June 9, 1981). Iraq here was the innocent victim. After all, unlike Israel it had signed the nuclear nonproliferation treaty.

It is instructive to compare the comments of Menachem Begin with those produced in Britain and America nine years later. The same ruthless character for Saddam Hussein is established by reference to biography, and the very same ambitious plans for mass destruction and domination are touted as futures to be avoided. It is equally instructive to contrast Begin's understanding of Saddam with those prevalent in Britain in the early 1980s. Begin speaks not of Iraq but of "Saddam Hussein." In the United Kingdom, like in the United States, Saddam Hussein was not yet synonymous with the evil of his nation. His cult of personality was viewed with bemusement. It was entertaining rather than sinister, and Saddam was considered to be a puppet rather than a puppet master. According to the London *Times* he was simply the appealing face of the more sinister Baath Party.

He is everywhere, staring out from every shop window, dominating every street corner and square. Big Brother could not compete for sheer omnipresence. What saves him is the enormous variety of his costumes and poses. Almost every shop seems to have its own version, which makes his popularity seem a little more spontaneous and genuine that it would if he were an unchanging image. It's a fair bet that President Saddam himself is more popular than the austere, ruthless Ba'ath Party that keeps him in power." (*Times*, May 8, 1984)

President Saddam Hussein has adopted a brash new image in the past few months. . . . Gone are the slogans urging workers to labor yet harder for socialist fulfillment, or encouraging the Arab nation to withstand the latest twist in the Zionist conspiracy. . . . Instead there are cozy pictures of Saddam Hussein." (*Times*, August 1, 1980)

Likewise, Saddam Hussein's grandiose schemes were viewed in the 1980s as harmless amusements rather than as evidence of a dangerous megalomania that would one day boil over into ambitions for global dominance.

A *Guardian* (May 8, 1984) reporter had a good chuckle at Iraq's kitsch civic architecture: "Two of the most monumental buildings are actually war memorials. . . . One is the tomb of the unknown soldier. It covers about an acre and is shaped like some science fiction jellyfish. . . . The other monument, more successful to my philistine eye, is the Martyrs' Memorial. . . . The effect is of an onion sliced in half." Notwithstanding this poor taste, Saddam's Iraq was on the right track. It was making healthy political and economic progress and converging with the virtues of modernity. As in the United States this positive characterization was achieved through invoking "local standards" as the appropriate reference frame. "A moderately fair election anywhere in the Arab world is an achievement . . . most Iraqis seem to accept the Ba'athist rule, admitting even in private that stability under President Hussein is preferable to the social chaos that might occur if the freedoms of liberal western thought were suddenly introduced. . . . Iraq's oil has given the country a gloss of wealth that is transforming the dusty towns into modern cities. Four-lane highways have replaced the bumpy tracks that the British built" (*Times*, August 1, 1980). The romance of modernization allowed Saddam Hussein the benefit of the doubt. Hence a book by Iraqi exiles and critics of the Baathist regime was given a far from enthusiastic review in the *Times:* "their sweeping denunciation of the regime's political, economic and social policies is not uniformly convincing. . . . The regime's drive against illiteracy, for example, is derided for its Ba'athist purposes, but we are not told that it has been, on the whole, a success" (July 4, 1986). Only toward the end of 1989 did Iraq's coding gradually shift. For the majority of the 1980s it had enjoyed a provisional location on the fringes of the Discourse of Liberty. The gassing of Kurdish refugees initiated a classificatory slide toward the Discourse of Repression even if it did not merit sustained analysis or denunciation. During the first half of 1990 a series of further events hinted that a more evil image Iraq might be required. Evidence was obtained that Saddam was planning the construction of a so-called supergun and had tried to export components from the United Kingdom, a British journalist was executed for spying, and various nuclear naughties were intercepted. The previous genre guess was starting to look problematic. The stage was set for the Gulf War.

The invasion of Kuwait enabled an aggressive and insane Iraqi leader to be discovered as the solution toward which these puzzling clues had been pointing. With this new understanding of Hussein himself came a respecification of his prior achievements. The progressive, socialist benefactor of a few years before was replaced by a cruel tyrant. "In reality," wrote one commentator, "he has been a disaster for his own country, which he has bankrupted and ruled by murder and terror, and for the Arabs, whose cause he has associated across the world with ruthlessness and cruelty" (*Independent*, January 15, 1990). Mobilized in binary contrast to Iraq was Kuwait. It was now Kuwait which, although far from perfect, approximated more closely the model of an ideal Islamic nation according to a criterion that should by now be familiar to readers of this book—local standards. Thus on the eve of war the *Economist* admitted that "Kuwait was no democracy" before going on to qualify the remark: "but by the standards of the Arab world it was a decent place, tolerantly run, with a freeish press and freer politics than any Mr. Hussein could ever countenance. An artificial state? Yes, but no more artificial than the other nations of the modern Middle East—Jordan, Lebanon, Syria, Iraq itself—which were given their borders by former colonists" (*Economist*, January 12, 1991).

In keeping with the inflated, heroic genre the activities of Britain and America were situated within a quest narrative that had a structural resemblance to those sung by medieval troubadours. This depicted the allies as heroic liberators, Kuwait as a helpless victim held to ransom somewhat like a maiden in a tower, and Iraq as the evil violator. As the *Sunday Times* (editorial, January 13, 1991) put it on the eve of the aerial bombardment: "There is a war to be fought to rid the world of a tyrant who has ambitions to extend his tyranny far and wide and who has already ravaged a small, innocent nation in pursuit of that aim." Yet as in the United States these cultural breezes, so propitious for war, had weakened in the passage from August 1990 to January 1991. Public perceptions of the inevitability of violence had dropped—a sure sign of the deflation of an apocalyptic prognosis. Whereas in August, 39 percent of the British surveyed thought it very likely that a "shooting war" would break out in the Middle East, by December the proportion had declined to 25 percent (Hastings and Hastings 1992, 213). Again, the numbers of people in favor of military action should the blockade "look like failing" declined from 67 percent in August to 61 percent in December (ibid.). Between August and December support for British military action, given certain objectives, fell across the board: the defense of Saudi Arabia and the Gulf from 86 percent to 66 percent, restoring independence to Kuwait from 84 percent to 69 percent, the defense of Israel if attacked from 66 percent to 47 percent, and protecting oil supplies from 87 percent to 69 percent. The smallest decline in support— 69 percent to 62 percent—came for "toppling Saddam Hussein's regime in Iraq" (Hastings and Hastings 1992, 214).

Notwithstanding this slide, on the eve of the war the damage to the master narrative in the United Kingdom was considerably less than in the United States. As the U.S. Congress wavered and divided almost 50/50, the British political community at least could put up a show of near unity behind the apocalyptic narrative, with Leftist intellectuals and the Labour Party maintaining a curious silence (see *Sunday Times*, January 27, 1991).

As the war unfolded from January 1991 onward, established sets of themes and contrasts were reiterated time and again. This repetition is to be expected for the legitimacy of war is the product of continuous work that asserts difference again and again and again. Readings of Saddam Hussein's character constituted perhaps the key focus for repetitious moralizing discourses during the war. Although his character was repellent to all "civilized" people, it also exercised a perverse fascination. Saddam embodied in its most refined form the negative charisma of evil. This made him a prime mover of history, the person to whom all Iraq's actions could be attributed, the cultural shortcut that reduced complexities into an icon. The war was "Saddam's war," the failure to make peace his failure. Hussein's methods were seen as manipulative and coercive rather than as contractual, his drives as selfish and insane, and his goal as pure power. His failure to capitulate or agree to foreign peace terms was yet another sign of his evil and irrational nature. With the invasion Hussein had succeeded in taking over the mantle of public enemy number one from Colonel Qaddafi. Unlike Libya's Qaddafi or Iran's Ayatollah Khomeini, Hussein appeared in Western-style suits and military uniforms. He rarely gave vent to impassioned tirades, but rather spoke calmly and informally. Such comportment did not suffice to exempt Hussein from a negative typecasting. The contradiction between behavior and imputed motivations was resolved by the attribution of what in other times was called a "natural depravity," a cold and fiendish cunning, outwardly rational, that works in the service of malicious and arbitrary inner drives. Writing in another context Herman Melville captures this personality type: " . . . though the man's even temper and discreet bearing would seem to intimate a mind peculiarly subject to the law of reason, not the less in his heart he would seem to riot in complete exemption from that law, having apparently little to do with reason further than to employ it as an ambidexter implement for effecting the irrational. That is to say: toward the accomplishment of an aim which in wantonness of malignity would seem to partake of the insane, he will direct a cool judgment sagacious and sound" (Melville 1924, chapter 12). This pattern had, of course, commonly been attributed to the Soviet Union and was grounded in the Civil Discourse of Motives. Cunning, cold calculation and manipulation are the means through which the lust for power, greed, and an unrealistic world vision are translated into lines of action. Yet in the case of Saddam Hussein, his "ambidexter" rationality was more flawed than it had been with the Soviets. In the British vision, Saddam Hussein calculated and machinated ad infinitum—but to no avail. Far from being "sagacious and sound," Hussein's efforts toward Machiavellian state-craft were irremediably corrupted by his faulty understanding of the world. Although the British press might have spoken of Saddam Hussein's ability to stay in power as a sign of political talent, it preferred to point to his errors. "Strategically his grasp of international affairs has been limited. The Iraqi invasion of Iran was a blunder . . . the attack on Kuwait counts as another," wrote the *Times* (editorial, January 16, 1991). Likewise, the *Independent* (editorial, January 15, 1990) asserted that although "President Saddam is still often regarded to be a skilful tactician. In reality he has been a disaster . . . the only causes close to his heart are his own self-aggrandizement and personal survival."

"Is Saddam Hussein a maniac?" asked the *Times* (January 17, 1991). The answer was yes. The emphasis placed on Hussein's "insanity," and its dominance over a rationality that was now describable as purely vestigial, had significant consequences. It threw gasoline onto the fires of militarism by making eventual victory in a military conflict seem likely—after all a mad leader will make poor strategic decisions. It also made war seem necessary and inevitable. The option of peace would appeal only to a man capable of rationally evaluating the political and military environment—and realizing he was out-gunned. Carrots and sticks only work when they can be understood. While some held out hope that Saddam "may well be rational enough to reach a moment at which he recognizes that he is doomed to loose Kuwait" (*Daily Telegraph*, January 22, 1991) others believed that his mind was in a spiral of decay that had eroded the last remnants of his calculative ability. This assumption was based on a logic that had as its Archimedean fulcrum the knowledge that any rational person would have withdrawn from Kuwait. Although "many observers had been counting on Saddam's past record of Machiavellianism, the streetwise cunning and hard head for power-broking to pull the world back from the brink," they were to be disappointed. The Iraqi leader, we were told, had suffered a "severe nervous breakdown and is now obsessed with dreams of his own immortality" (*Observer*, January 20, 1991). In January 1991, there could be no guarantee that even the most carefully thought out diplomacy would work for "his cost-benefit calculation is entirely different from that which we would be making were we in his shoes" (*Times*, January 17, 1991). Saddam Hussein had "lost any sense of what constitutes his own, or Iraq's, self-interest" and was suffering from an "intransigent megalomania" (editorial, *Times*, February 22, 1991). As the renowned military historian John Keegan put it, only Saddam "can avert a war" but "perhaps the fantasy which grips him is so strong that he does not known how to do so" (*Spectator*, January 1991).

The same qualities that made Saddam Hussein a sure-fire bet for war also made him a bad bet for peace. Faith in the contracts of international law is predicated on the existence of a sense of responsibility and obligation in the actors bound by them, or more minimally by their understanding of the negative sanctions that can flow from noncompliance. But how, when dealing with a mind like Saddam Hussein's, could one have any confidence in a negotiated settlement? After all he had been "consistent only in the ruthlessness with which he has broken treaties and promises" (editorial, *Independent*, February 23, 1991). Speculation as to Saddam's mental state did not abate once the ground war started. To the contrary, Hussein's continuing and frustrating failure to capitulate in the face of superior military power provided evidence for a more precise diagnosis of his insanity. By the end of February 1991, it became common to argue that the main force in his psyche was no longer a dream of immortality but rather a suicidal streak. Having been identified, this ailment of the mind could then be projected back to earlier events as well as be used to explain present episodes. An editorial in the *Independent* epitomizes this discursive complex. The signifiers of madness and rationality are folded into a narrative that typifies Saddam Hussein to a particular class of evildoer and then uses this to explain his past successes and to predict his future downfall.

Dictators have a tendency to spurn the calculation of likely profit and loss that less despotic leaders make. Men such as President Saddam discount the loss of life that their military adventures are bound to inflict on their own people as well as on their opponents, and hope that by acting with irrational audacity they can win amazing victories. They are able, after all, to achieve total surprise, which is of huge value in war. For some years Adolf Hitler prospered by ignoring conventional military opinion. By launching a surprise attack on Kuwait, President Saddam won an easy victory, but one whose suicidal nature is now being confirmed." (editorial, *Independent*, February 25, 1991)

If Saddam Hussein's discursively constructed irrationality heightened the apparent need for war in one direction, it could potentially weaken it in another. It opened up possibilities for him to appear a pathetic, comic figure—an opera buffa idiot capable only of failure like the Hitler caricatured by Charlie Chaplin in *The Great Dictator* or the Idi Amin so relentlessly lampooned by British satirical magazines of the 1970s. There was little world-historical threat in a clown or a tin pot dictator with delusions of grandeur. It might not be worth losing lives over a man whose "pudgy, jowly face so often seen on television is scarcely the stuff of which nightmares are made"; whose "guttural monotone mangles the rhythm of a language that lends itself to great oratory"; and whose "supporters in the Arab world concede that he lacks the charisma of a Muammar Gaddafi and the conviction of Ayatollah Khomeini" (Times, January 16, 1991). Fortunately for hawks, the comic Hussein remained for the most part confined to the daily political cartoon and rarely surfaced in other speech genres to bring about a narrative deflation away from apocalypticism. What did surface, time and time again, were binary contrasts between the evil and irrational Saddam Hussein and the usually uninspiring British and American leaders. These drew upon the Discourse of Liberty. Character evaluations of the leading Western political figures pivoted around the civil discourse code elements "open" and "honest," "sane," and "realistic" whose presence is indicated by a perceived authentic naturalism in interaction, and reluctance to use hyperbole. The American president and the British prime minister, John Major, in particular were praised for their exhibition of these qualities. In a seeming paradox, their lack of charisma was transformed into a virtue. The Times (editorial, January 18, 1991) for example, used this pattern to make telling contrasts with the Iraqi leader: "Eloquence is not his greatest virtue, but yesterday the President found a directness that surpassed eloquence. Mr Major's impromptu speech in Downing Street yesterday morning, after an exhausting night, displayed a quiet command of events, with no attempt to hide the seriousness of war behind a shield of rhetoric. The comparison with the extravagant bluster of President Saddam Hussein could hardly be sharper or more telling." Britain's famously "grey" prime minister, the bank manageresque John Major could be explicitly and favorably contrasted with his predecessor at the time of Suez: "The Prime Minister looks calm and unabsorbed. The possibility of him 'doing an Eden' and cracking under the strain . . . seems a remote one" (Economist, January 19, 1991). So Bush and Major "conveyed a calm sincerity" and "were cautious in eschewing bellicosity, and in denying false optimism" (editorial, Times, January 18, 1991). They had even "gone out of their way to puncture the absurd euphoria that characterized some of the first media reports" after fighting started (editorial, Times, January 20, 1991). The prime minister had "eschewed the fancy tricks and rhetorical flourishes of the seasoned television professional . . . he spoke briefly and to the point with . . . no diplomatic niceties, no military jargon; no ersatz Churchilliana; just the plain sentiments of the common man. Like his counterpart in the White House, Mr. Major was not big on 'this vision thing'" (Observer, January 17, 1991) but exhibited "cool determination and lack of posturing" (editorial, Independent, January 22, 1991). A performative fusion had been achieved (Alexander 2004b) with outward actions understood as inwardly sincere.

Calm and rational leaders require calm and rational followers if binary contrasts of nations are to be sustainable. Hence there was a moral expectation that civil institutions and the general public would behave in the same spirit as Bush and Major. There was a need to "keep our collective nerve and maintain a sense of balance" wrote the *Daily Telegraph* (editorial, January 19, 1991), invoking such a civilized imagined community. Commentators were pleasantly surprised to find that contrary to their expectations neither the perceived jingoism of the Falklands conflict, nor the so-called Rambo streak in American culture became manifest. This allowed contrasts to be drawn with the Iraqi people. In Britain, as in America, the firm support of the Iraqi people and others in the Middle East for a "cruel" and "insane" leader who was busily engaged in loosing a "hopeless" war was a potential problem not only for military reasons but also because this seeming contradiction could destabilize the master narrative. After all, who wants to be a slave? As in the United States this dilemma was solved by invoking an Orientalist (Said 1979) discourse. Like the Egyptians at the time of Suez the Iraqi people were interpreted as dependent, unrealistic, emotive, and childlike. They also lived in fear and therefore lacked true autonomy. Their support for Hussein was based on both bread (necessity) and circuses (irrational excitement). This inherent propensity was, needless to say, understood to have been cynically exploited by Saddam's manipulation of traditional elements of Arabic culture. He had appealed to "the very ancient codes of honor and shame which are current throughout the Mediterranean basin, to be found in the Bible as in the Mafia. Honor makes life worthwhile whilst shame is a living death. Much that seems destructive and even suicidal in Arab life stems from these codes" (*Independent*, February 27, 1991), but "fortunately, an ever growing proportion of the Arab world appears to have decided to break with this losing-side psychology and to face up to reality" (editorial, *Independent*, February 2, 1991).

If mass support for Saddam Hussein was understood using a psychologistic discourse of emotion that drew upon the themes of dependency and irrationality in the Discourse of Repression, the institutions and institutional figures that supported him were accounted for in terms of another set of code elements. These related to calculation, secrecy, and lies. There were shady personages and organizations dedicated to propagating homogeneity within Iraqi society and expanding Saddam Hussein's power. Iraq's media, for example, was taken to be little more than a puppet of the government helping to propagate an unrealistic world vision—"that victory against America in battle is possible" (*Times*, January 16, 1991). The specter of terrorist organizations was raised. By using a discourse of conspiracy (Bailyn 1967) the lack of any firm data was made dismissible. The very fact that not much was known about the terrorist groups only added to their mystique. For example, in one *Times* article entitled "Baghdad's Shadowy Allies Wait to Attack," the only named group is the PLO. Nevertheless, the reader is assured that, "In the darkest corners of the Middle East, Saddam has other allies. Their real capacity to inflict damage is a mystery, but their intentions are clear" (*Times*, January 16, 1991). Even children were subject to Saddam's profaned relationships and institutions and thereby indoctrinated into his philosophy through institutions such as a "secret school" in the middle of London. Set up for the embassy staff it had "blatantly flouted" the law requiring all schools to register, and children were "taught to idolize President Saddam Hussein" while surrounded by their own artwork depicting "men toting machine guns" (*Daily Telegraph*, January 22, 1991).

Like leaders and followers, the question of respect for peace, order, and international law was a major resource for asserting difference in British civil discourse. In contemporary Western thought war cannot be justified except as reluctant undertaking of last resort. Consequently even in the dominant prowar narrative a violent showdown was held to be a reluctant choice for the allies, but a preferred option for the Iraqi leader. While the British considered themselves and their allies to have done all that was possible to avoid the conflict, Hussein was understood to have set out in search of violence from the start. Saddam Hussein it was argued "did not grasp any of the olive branches that were extended to him months, weeks, days and even hours before the launch of operation Desert Storm. He'd turned away one negotiator after another. He rejected all the proposals put forward by experts in the art of compromise. He did not attempt to make use of the few hours granted to him after the expiry of the January 15 deadline. . . . And he did this all for one reason and one reason only. Out of all the possible scenarios, he had chosen to take up the challenge of war, thereby rendering war inevitable" (*Guardian*, January 18, 1991). Closely allied to the theme of wanton aggression was that of legality. References to the United Nations and its resolutions were used to identify allied violence with universalism and with policing functions. In contrast, Saddam Hussein was understood as having violated the sacredness of the law in two important ways. He had invaded Kuwait, and he had taken and used civilian and military hostages. Like the abuse of captured airmen, Saddam's use of civilian hostages was a key factor in maintaining his typification as "outside the law."

War, I have suggested at various points, should be understood not only as the rational pursuit of military objectives. It is also a performative action directed to various audiences—one's own troops, the enemy's troops, the enemy leaders, citizens of the warring nations, and those looking on from the sidelines. Understood in this way the conduct of battle is a semiotic process—a way of sending messages about moral statuses. Following the end of the diplomatic phase of activity—itself a performative elaboration of the concept of "last resort"—many of the more demonstrable opportunities to display allied fidelity to the Discourse of Liberty involved the use of weapons. There is an irony in the fact that the use of force can be a token of one's peaceful inner nature. Yet in the initial days of the war there was an unparalleled degree of adulation in Britain for technologically advanced equipment—not because it represented scientific achievement, but rather because it was read as permitting suitably civilized destruction. When complemented by organized and rational decision making and a polished diplomatic performance the resulting sustained aerial and missile bombardment could be a sort of aesthetic celebration of precision akin to ballet. As the *Times* (editorial, January 18, 1991) wrote: "Modern technology enables targets to be selected which have so far minimized the loss of life whilst maximizing pressure on the enemy to surrender. Commanders exude the disciplined projection of vast power. Considerations of Middle Eastern politics move in delicate tandem with the needs of war to contain the conflict whilst hastening its conclusion." At the tactical level this tour de force was claimed to be remarkable. Although it involved unprecedented destructive force, the bombardment of Iraq could be blithely contrasted with unrestrained and polluted acts such as those that had retrospectively come to mar the allied memory of World War II. The *Times* continued: "The firepower unleashed was far greater than that which destroyed Dresden, roughly equivalent to the atomic bomb dropped on Hiroshima. There the comparison ends. This operation bore no resemblance to the morally and militarily controversial bombing of German cities in the 1940s."[5]

Contrasting with the merciful and civilized allied attacks that conformed in some way to the norms of a postmilitary society was Iraq's "illegal" use of Scud missiles against civilian populations. Despite being totally ineffectual on a military level, these could be mobilized on the cultural plane as exhibits of reckless indifference to civilian life. Although "indiscriminate bombing" was "now more or less out of the question on the allied side . . . Saddam has happily used it against Saudi Arabia and Israel," wrote the *Daily Telegraph* (February 4, 1991). By the second week of the conflict the Scud and Patriot had become shorthand icons for the differences between the allies and Iraq: The one aggressive and indiscriminate, the other defensive and selective. This pattern was made visible yet again in Saddam Hussein's orientation toward the environment. When a giant oil slick appeared in the Gulf this was quickly understood as an attack on a vulnerable and defenseless natural world that had no place in the conflict. It was "an act of unparalleled environmental terrorism" (*Sunday Times*, January 27, 1991). Responsibility for this, perhaps not surprisingly, could be given to only one man. As the veteran British politician Michael Heseltine put it: "Words are inadequate to condemn the callousness and irresponsibility of the action of Saddam Hussein in deliberately unleashing the environmental catastrophe" (quoted in *Independent*, January 29, 1991).

The binary oppositions we have been exploring could not be easily countered. Whether inability or failure or choice was responsible, the British Labour Party did not step forward and articulate an antiwar policy as it had done at the time of Suez. This left protesters without an institutionally central political voice. Although opposition to war had some support among Labour MPs, they were constrained by their popular base. On January 9, 1991, some 88 percent of Conservative voters favored the use of force—as did 66 percent of Labour voters. Conservative voters were slightly more inclined to countenance the use of chemical and nuclear weapons against Iraq, but only slightly more so (Hastings and Hastings 1992, 217–18). Saddam Hussein was almost universally condemned as dangerous and evil. Nasser, it should be remembered, had started off this way but began to look more reasonable to the British as the Suez Crisis lumbered through the summer of 1956. This character shift had given nonviolent options some credibility and enabled the Labour Party to switch genre. History has yet to provide an easy solution to the problem of how to argue for peace when simultaneously claiming that your opponent is a dangerous madman at the head of a powerful army. It was against the weight of this cultural and institutional handicap that positions against war had to be fashioned. Insofar as any coherent or influential counterclaims were made, these focused on eliminating simple binarisms and reproducing a more tragic sensibility. We can quickly review the three most important arenas of challenge here and explain how each was neutralized in turn by further counterdiscourses in the ongoing dialogic activity of civil society.

One of the more visible efforts to bring about a genre shift out of apocalypticism and into tragedy hinged around the expression "No blood for oil." Some analysis is required of the implicit polysemic qualities at play. The phrase "No blood for oil" draws attention to the violation of symbolic boundaries. Blood is a both a common and sacred human substance (Durkheim 1965), oil is a common, but also profane, commodity. The underlying theme being invoked by the protesters here is that each belongs to its own sphere of exchange (see Bohannan and Bohannan 1968). Items from one realm of value are not considered to be exchangeable for items from another no matter what the quantity involved.[6] The slogan further explains why military buildup toward an eventual war was happening. It does this by attributing a motivation to prowar parties and hinting that shadowy interests are behind conflict. The implicit narrative is a tragic one—that lives are being sacrificed unnecessarily by larger powers and industrial organizations. These are again implicitly aligned with the Discourse of Repression. Our common sense leads us to think of evil capitalists, faceless bureaucracies, and cynical politicians.

As the peace movement and its various constituencies worked hard to redescribe the origins of the war, its arguments were confronted in turn. The "no blood for oil" argument was itself dealt with by introducing narrative complexity and sophistication. For example, oil could be acknowledged as an important but not decisive factor. It was one component in a matrix of pragmatic and normative concerns that made fighting morally appropriate. The Bishop of Oxford captured this logic succinctly, asking, "if there was no oil interest, would the war still be morally worth fighting? I believe it would. Respect for the integrity of national boundaries, the observance of international law, the crucial importance of resolving border disputes by peaceful means and not allowing bullies to take over small countries, the authority of the United Nations—all this is at stake" (*Observer,* January 20, 1991). If the allied forces represented universalism and the rule of law, oil was needed to keep them strong and independent in their cause. This being the case, the argument that "the influence of oil compromises the cause of the allied coalition" was nonsense. The issue of control over oil "merely reinforces moral with practical arguments. The industrialized world has a vital economic interest in preventing a megalomaniac dictator from gaining control of a substantial share of the world oil supplies" (editorial, *Daily Telegraph,* February 25, 1991).

The rejection by Western leaders of a Soviet peace plan in the closing stages of the conflict opened up another arena through which a critique of the dominant codings and narrative could have taken root. Knocking back the plan might have damaged allied claims that they were of peaceful intent and engaged in a war of last resort. These possibilities were compounded by the fact that the author of the plan was the (then) charismatic and Nobel Peace Prize—winning Soviet leader Mikhail Gorbachev, and that the proposal had been accepted by Iraq. Perhaps surprisingly the blackballing of the plan created few ideological or political problems. In order to understand why it is necessary step out of our immediate context and look at the ways that Gorbachev and the Soviet Union had themselves become narrated over the preceding few years.

During the mid- to late 1980s, Gorbachev and the Soviet Union had enjoyed an unprecedented symbolic transformation from the negative to the positive side of the Discourse of Civil Society (Sherwood 1994). The Soviet

Union had long been understood in terms of the Discourse of Repression as secretive, hierarchical, irrational, and antidemocratic. It was a land of grim apparatchiks, gulags, and the KGB and was locked into a pattern of slavish conformity to Marxist dogma. In the space of a few short years this image changed as the charming Gorbachev implemented his trendy policies of "glasnost" and "perestroika," initiated structural reforms, and allowed the velvet revolutions to proceed in Eastern Europe without military intervention. This romantic narrative was to be repudiated. A tarnish formed on Gorbachev's halo when he seemingly permitted a Soviet crackdown on independence movements in the Baltic republics. Gorbachev entered into a symbolic purgatory in which his actions were increasingly seen as either self-interested or as constrained by his domestic circumstances. So, on the one hand we find the idea circulating that Gorbachev "desperately needs a foreign policy success," and that his peace plan for the Gulf was simply an effort to "ward off hysterical attacks from inside the Soviet establishment" (*Sunday Times*, February 24, 1991). On the other hand the understanding existed that he had been a Machiavellian entrepreneur who had been "feigning to support American action" only so as to be able to "grab all the money on offer and to ensure that the Americans were caught on the hook, while the Russians ran free . . . even if Gorbachev's intervention fails to conclude a peace, the fact that he has tried will still win the approval of his neighbors in the Gulf, including the post-Saddam regime in Baghdad. The Americans, in contrast, can reap little but hatred" (*Daily Telegraph*, February 20, 1991). Whether he was constrained or just playing games, Gorbachev's move could be easily discounted.

Allegations of opportunism that could be used to discredit the peace plan were further manifested in what was described as a cavalier attitude toward the United Nations by the Soviet leader. It was "hard to take seriously Mr. Gorbachev's protestations of loyalty to UN resolutions when he was helping broker a plan that lifted all those resolutions immediately after an Iraqi withdrawal, and removed economic sanctions even earlier—after only 2/3 of Iraqi forces had left" (editorial, *Independent*, February 23, 1991). The ability of the peace proposal to derail Britain's narratively encoded self-image was further mitigated by descriptions of Iraqi diplomatic activity as insincere. "Saddam is simply playing for time, seeking to split the allies, embarrassing everybody available to be embarrassed," wrote the *Times* (February 21, 1991) in an editorial. "There could be no clearer indication of his reckless cynicism," it concluded (see also editorials in *Times*, February 22, 1991 and *Independent*, February 27, 1991). Saddam Hussein's meddling with the prospect of peace of course turned out to be as big a mistake as his other ploys. If he had "hoped the Soviet peace plan would be a vehicle to break up the coalition against him. . . . He was wrong" (*Independent*, February 22, 1991). When he "vowed to fight on in rhetoric suggesting a dark obsession with violent death" this had merely "made life a great deal easier for the Americans" (editorial, *Independent*, February 22, 1991) by providing evidence of his underlying insanity and belligerence.

During the war, injunctions were voiced for Britain to remain calm, reasonable, and restrained. Immediately after the war, rather self-satisfied readings could now be completed confirming that this had indeed been the case: "There was no sense of jingoism in this country in the weeks preceding the Gulf War. Nor is the nation triumphalist in the aftermath of victory. The popular mood can best be described as a feeling that a necessary job was performed with courage and professionalism. . . . Only a very limited and unrepresentative group of people felt shamed by British participation in the Gulf conflict, and—even among their number—almost nobody questioned the conduct of our forces in the air or on the ground once battle was joined" (editorial, *Independent*, March 5, 1991). However, the semiotic and performative challenge was not quite over, for the vexing matter of appropriate celebration conjured up once again in a very concrete way the problem of enacting proportionality, decorum, and rationality. Something had to be done as failing to offer a procession or ceremony of some kind would demean the exemplary contributions of the British troops. So when the British prime minister authorized the Ministry of Defence to hold a "victory parade," those in favor had to be careful to argue for a restrained and contemplative affair that would not be an "orgy of triumphalism" (editorial, *Independent*, March 5, 1991). Even so, many objected to the proposed event. This perspective originated in an understanding of the war as a tragic affair—a reading that seemed to gain ground in the final days of the conflict. For many the victory had become tainted by the one-sided nature of the fighting, and in particular by aggressive combat against fleeing Iraqi troops on the road from Kuwait to Basra. "The fact that so many Iraqis were killed and wounded, many on a hiding to nothing is surely to be regretted," wrote one correspondent to the *Independent*, "In these circumstances a victory parade is, as the Bishop of Durham has said, obscene" (letter, March 6, 1990). In the end, then, the allied military superiority that had made war politically acceptable had come at a cost. It had enabled allied casualties to be minimized and the war to be presented as a clinical affair. But it had also come to undermine the heroic narrative with its predictions of a grim apocalyptic struggle. The satisfactions of victory could only be diluted, the victory parade a problematic and half-hearted two cheers event.

FRANCE AND THE GULF WAR

In France, popular support for war against Iraq lay somewhere between its moderately high levels in the United States and the United Kingdom and, as we will see, its very low levels in Spain. Its legitimacy was in general slightly higher on the Right than on the Left, despite the presence of a socialist government under the tutelage of President Mitterrand. In many ways the narratives we find in the French context are identical to those we have already reviewed. Where major discourses and debates closely follow those we have already looked at in other contexts, I treat them only very briefly. Greater emphasis is given here and in the discussion of Spain that follows to "national" themes. By exploring these we can see how particular instantiations of universal codes and narratives are inflected by a country's visions of itself, by its historical experiences and anxieties, and in concerns over its identity. We will see that if our deep culture structures are shared, this does not mean their thematic or rhetorical resonances are identical in each country. To the contrary, abstract structures are made relevant through intersections with these local and contingent environments of meaning. Indeed the odds of a particular genre becoming dominant can be influenced as decisively by such contextualizing idioms as by the immediate events of any given crisis.

Moral principles can hardly be considered a major factor in France's policies regarding the sales of arms and technology to emergent nations. That said, the extensive aid that France extended to Iraq's nuclear program in the late 1970s and early 1980s indicates the Baghdad regime was accorded a certain credibility. Following Israel's 1981 raid on the Osirak nuclear reactor the French media spent a lot of time debating whether or not Iraq had the intention of destroying Israel and of obtaining a nuclear capability (*Point*, June 15, 1981; June 22, 1981). This was despite the fact that Iraq's aggressive intentions were relatively clear to some French analysts (see Amsel et al. 1981). They also debated the impact of Israel's forthcoming election on Begin's decision to bomb the reactor. Curiously absent from the discussion was any sustained consideration of Iraq's regime. The official reaction was to reveal secret clauses that "proved" that the reactor could not be converted for military uses and to demand that the United Nations condemn the Israeli aggression (*Le Monde*, June 17, 1981). All things considered this event suggested France viewed Iraq in an ambivalent way and could give somewhat more than just the benefit of the doubt.

The Iraqi invasion of Kuwait changed this climate of uncertainty. An apocalyptic frame fell into place that should by now be instantly replicable by readers of this book. As if cut and pasting from its Suez coverage *Paris Match* wrote: "Saddam Hussein now appears as that which he has always been: a dictator without scruples who wants to impose himself by force on the entire Middle East. He has applied the method that Hitler, in his time, applied to Europe. . . . The Iraqi President only believes in the balance of force. Therefore, unfortunately, one must reason with him in terms of force. . . . The stakes are vital . . . the dignity of the civilized world" (August 9, 1990). No longer a merely local problem, Saddam Hussein was a man "who makes the Gulf tremble and who defies the planet" with weapons of mass destruction. This man was a "Caligula or Pol Pot" (*Nouvelle Observateur*, August 23, 1990) who had not "hesitated to use gas to massacre entire villages of people in Kurdistan," and had "triumphantly announced the imminent production of an atomic bomb" (*Paris-Match*, August 16, 1990). The minister of foreign affairs insisted that the situation in Kuwait would not mimic that of the Sudetenland because "we have refused a Munich meeting. The international community has taken its lessons from history" (interview in *Nouvelle Observateur*, August 23, 1990). Poll data suggest such a vision of a new Hitler was widely shared if not dominant (Hastings and Hastings 1992, 579–80) and that there was a level of eagerness for war situated between that of Britain and Spain. Some 75 percent of the French surveyed supported the use of military force to free Kuwait, 82 percent to free hostages, and 72 percent to protect oil supplies (UK = 86 percent, 86 percent, 78 percent; Spain = 66 percent, 63 percent, 64 percent). Other measures confirm this status. For example, 48 percent of French people ranked the restoration of independence to Kuwait as the most important explanation why there was as "international force in the Gulf," as opposed to 24 percent who cited oil. We find the ratio of idealistic (free Kuwait) to material (oil) explanations reversed in Spain (29 percent to 46 percent) and heightened in Britain (57 percent to 24 percent). In October of 1990 some 62 percent supported sending French ground troops to fight Iraq (Spain = 33 percent; Britain = 77 percent) and in January 1991, 61 percent said that they would approve of French military intervention (ibid.; also *Le Monde*, January 15, 1991). The popularity of national leaders climbed. By mid-February Mitterrand had a support rating of 77 percent and George Bush some 70 percent (*Le Monde*, February 19, 1991, see also Hastings and Hastings 1992, 207).

This support base was underpinned by military and diplomatic events and also by an unrelenting application of the Discourse of Repression to Saddam Hussein that was sharpened by France's own historical experiences in the twentieth century. *Le Monde* (editorial, January 23, 1991) voiced its outrage at the use of human shields, writing that, "With the sending of these men to

strategic sites, he commits a crime . . . with cynicism, sadism and premedita-
tion . . . after Nazism this is almost in first place in the list . . . of the horrors
of war." Likewise, Saddam's August treaty with Iran was the product of a "cynicism without limits." It was "a little as if France, a few months after 1918, had
returned Alsace and Lorraine to Germany in order to better threaten a new
war against Britain" (editorial, *Le Monde*, August 16, 1990). As elsewhere,
Orientalist discourse accounted for Saddam Hussein's popularity. His followers were either dominated by him or else attracted by irrational and perverse
sentiments. They were "seeking primitive compensation for their humilia-
tions . . . we can call this the Saladin complex" (*Le Monde*, February 3, 1991).

Those looking for peace were confronted with powerful arguments that
mobilized France's history in insisting on the need for forceful actions faithful to national values and the search for honor, as much as on any national
interest more narrowly defined. For France the failure to combat the Nazi
menace had led to the national humiliation of occupation and a sense of
partial responsibility for the horrors of World War II. The prime minister,
Michel Rocard, alluded to the policies of appeasement that had failed: "None
can forget, and certainly not the French who have had the experience, that
there are some situations where to pretend to save the peace at the price of
a withdrawal leads usually to a greater shame and to war despite everything"
(Press conference, in *Le Monde*, January 10, 1991). President Mitterrand himself took care to drive home the comparison with the Hitler years. In his
New Year's message he demanded: "Understand me: if we leave the right of
people to self-determination violated, nothing will stop it . . . the strong will
wipe out the weak and impose their violence. I knew this when I was twenty
and I don't want it to begin again" (in *Le Monde*, January 2, 1991). Gerard
Fuchs of the Socialist Party also used history to assert that values were worth
fighting for: "I believe that the France of 1792 did well to fight for the values of the Republic. I believe that the France of the '30s is at fault for not
understanding soon enough that to fight was the price of liberty" (*Le Monde*,
January 15, 1991). Alain Touraine, the leading intellectual, asserted that Iraq
"comports itself like a Prussia which will call for a new pan-Germanism and
is even more militaristic" (*Le Monde*, January 2, 1991), and took care to cut
off alternative, more tragic historical parallels in stating that "those who seek
to re-live their reactions to the war in Algeria and even that of Vietnam are
completely mistaken in their analysis of the present situation."

Haunted by the memory of their failure to stop Hitler, the French had been
at last presented with a chance for redemption—a redemption that could only
be attained by accepting the moral and political burdens of a great nation—
burdens that it had avoided in the past. The theme that France should be a

nation in the first rank (*premier rang*) was a pivotal ambition of Gaullism. It provided an important adjunct to this theme of stepping up to assume historical responsibilities. Thus Mitterrand pointed out that national honor would grow with engagement rather than retreatism in an unfolding postcommunist era. When for the "first time in the history of nations a possibility is offered to construct a world order founded on the common law of the right of peoples to self-determination, it appears inconceivable that she [France] will neglect to provide help and support" (message to *Assemblée National*, in *Le Monde*, January 17, 1991). This participation would in turn "testify to the rank [*rang*] which our country occupies in the world and its ability to take part in the regulation of the important affairs of the world, to the place which we have inherited from the Second World War . . . she is there, living, active and strong at this end of the twentieth century, in the forefront of the ideas and initiative which will model that which follows" (New Year's message, in *Le Monde*, January 2, 1991).

Such references to France's moral strength and political autonomy made clever use of the Discourse of Civil Society. Only by becoming involved in the war in a substantial way could France stand up for what was right and also become a truly independent nation alignable with the Discourse of Liberty rather than passive and dependent, shamed by her history. This position, with its emphasis on national destiny and power, more obviously appealed to the Gaullist Right. However, there was also an attraction for the Left. A strong French involvement in a coalition could minimize the often symbolically polluted or dangerous impacts of American foreign policy. So the French Left could support engagement in the war without having to compromise its habitual negative coding of America. The theme of national autonomy and strength provided a leitmotif for a prowar alliance that could transcend the boundaries of Left and Right.

Indicative of the centrality of these tropes was the domestic response to Mitterrand's own last-minute diplomatic efforts to avoid a war. These raised ire in Britain and America as unilateral meddling, but were applauded in France as demonstrations of freedom of choice and action. Indeed the very fact that the British and Americans despised Mitterrand's peace-making efforts aided his movement to war. For the French they were not only a badly needed demonstration of French diplomatic independence, but also proof of the "last resort" nature of violence, much as the Baker/Aziz negotiations had been in the Anglophone nations.

As in Britain and the United States, discourses against the war attempted deflation toward low mimetic and tragic genres. The low mimetic genre guess could be found across the political spectrum and focused in rather unimaginative ways on the humdrum costs of battle. Some thought that France would pay for its participation by losing what they imagined was a privileged relationship with the Magreb. The mayor of Paris, Jacques Chirac (a former prime minister and later president), warned of likely consequences such as a reaction against the West in Arab public opinion, price increases for energy, and economic recession. In effect Chirac was crying jeopardy and suggesting the quantifiable downside risks of confrontation outweighed any possible upside. Many critics were no doubt surprised to find as their bedfellow Le Pen's notorious National Front Party. At times straying into a more value-driven discourse, especially on the need to maintain national autonomy, the National Front's perspective for the most part emphasized the importance of calculating the "national interest." In an official Policy Statement it explicitly talked down Manichean cultural logics and argued (much like Dulles at the time of Suez, or Pat Buchanan in the United States) for common sense and prudence. Calling in effect for genre deflation it proclaimed, "The National Front has a realist vision of international relations. For it, politics does not consist in a struggle of good and evil, but in a regulation, if possible peaceful, of conflicts of interest and aspirations between peoples and nations . . . in brief the conception of the National Front of foreign relations is a conception national, realist, founded on the search for the balance of powers." The outcome of all this "realism" was the assertion that "the national interest does not recommend the participation of France in the war" (Policy statement, in *Le Monde,* January 25, 1991).

By the time it launched this policy statement in late January the National Front had already missed the boat. As the long period of buildup of the fall of 1990 became transformed into the aerial war of January 1991, the terms of debate had decisively shifted toward value-rational grounds for legitimation and away from actuarial logics. Antiwar scripts increasingly had to engage in a more polarized deployment of the Discourse of Civil Society. As might be expected, a tragic narrative underpinned this new strategy. Events were understood to have switched onto a downward track that could have been avoided. France had wrongly elected to become the helpless puppet of an imperialistic United States. Letter writers to *Le Monde* bemoaned the "spectacle of a west enfeoffed to American decisions," and cried that France that was "in the course of losing its soul" (January 24, 1991) in a war that "imposes the American law" (January 12, 1991). In this tragic vision, not only was America repressive and particularistic, but also Kuwait was transformed into a victim unworthy of salvation. Human lives and resources would be needlessly lost in a war in which there was no good side. America, Kuwait, and Iraq were birds of a feather. Why should France itself be polluted by this sordid business?

While the evil of Saddam Hussein was acknowledged in this tawdry scenario, his world-historical significance was denied. The danger he posed, it was argued, had been inflated to an unrealistic degree. The situation in the Gulf could be likened to Suez, and thereby debunked: "In 1956, one remembers, Nasser was Hitler and accepting the nationalization of the Suez Canal was Munich" (*Le Monde*, January 19, 1991).

A final avenue in which the critique was expressed was in recasting the relationships internal to French politics in terms of the Discourse of Repression. The assertion here was that internal autonomy had been sacrificed to political authority in much the same manner as external autonomy had been ceded to U.S. hegemony. Mitterrand's call for France to assume her *rang* was seductive so long as France—and more particularly its leaders and institutions—could be trusted. Yet a crucial parliamentary vote for the military engagement produced a result that was out of proportion with wider public opinion. This led to claims that the war had seen national democratic institutions threatened by the growth of increasingly repressive social and political relationships based on coercion and submission: "The vote of 92 percent of the voices, in the *Assemblée National*, in favor of the military engagement of French forces against Iraq makes us ask ourselves some questions about the true nature of our political regime. . . . Are the people and their representatives only to listen to M. Rocard and to lower their heads like naughty children if they don't agree with him? Don't we already hear talk of sanctions against socialists who have the courage to express a divergent opinion?" (letter, *Le Monde*, 16/1/1991). Whereas the vote even in America had been "left to the conscience of each parliamentarian . . . in Paris this isn't an affair of conscience but of discipline, or of tactics" protested Didier Motchane of the Socialist Party Executive Committee (*Le Monde*, January 17, 1991).

Despite the force and commitment of these sentiments, as the war progressed, those advocating a peaceful policy continued to lose ground. France's much-vaunted intellectuals could not find traction for their antiwar messages—even among themselves. The writer Gilles Perrault led a call for "desertion" and "sabotage," which was supported by numerous leading thinkers and artists, including the ecologist René Dumont, and the psychoanalyst Félix Guattari. Yet there was no uprising. The powerful street level antiwar protest movements involving coalitions of intellectuals, students, the Communist Party, and trades unions, which had been a Gallic tradition for decades, did not eventuate. Likewise, the leadership of both the Communist Party and the National Front, were "not followed" by their supporters (*Le Monde*, February 20, 1991) who increasingly rallied behind President Mitterrand's call to confront aggression and assert France's autonomy and power. Among Communist

Party voters Mitterrand's support rating rose from 44 percent to 67 percent between January 12 and February 17, while that of George Bush ascended from 17 percent to an incredible 57 percent. Among the National Front it is clear that the party leadership's strategy was more unpopular from the start, with Bush's rating falling slightly from 79 percent to 73 percent and that of Mitterrand rising from an initial 60 percent to 75 percent (ibid.).

In France, more so than in most other countries, America's response to internal repression in Iraq became the pivotal issue and cause for angst in the weeks immediately after the war. Both sides stood to gain from playing upon this theme. The war's moral detractors could find evidence of America's mercenary, calculating policy. Meanwhile those who supported the war could demonstrate their humanitarian credentials and autonomy by professing outrage. In a series of editorials *Le Monde* switched from the pro-U.S. positions it had taken throughout the war and argued that in allowing the Kurds to be killed, American policy and its leader were becoming polluted. A tragic genre fell into place as *Le Monde* protested that the United States had moved out of value-rational politics too early. Bush had made "a sacrifice to *Realpolitik* only to help—even if it is by passivity—M. Saddam Hussein to re-establish his power" (editorial, *Le Monde*, April 3, 1991). The leading writer and historian Max Gallo likened the Kurdish affair to the biblical narrative of Pontius Pilate. In an article entitled "The White Hands," he writes, "Enough of hypocrisies and of boasts! The *après-guerre* is tragic. A crime is being committed against a people. We know the murderer, Saddam Hussein. And we've let it be for nearly two months . . . we are the accomplices of the assassin" (*Le Monde*, April 19, 1991). Or to put it more simply, "in waiting we wash our hands" (letter, *Le Monde*, April 12, 1991).

SPAIN AND THE GULF WAR

The story from France, then, is one in which visions of national autonomy, national redemption, and national status were folded into the genre politics of the Gulf War. We find something remarkably similar taking place in Spain, only here the empirical outcomes were rather different as discourses of the "national" collided with genre positions on the crisis in the Middle East.

Much had changed in Spain between 1956 and 1990. In the intervening years it had made a secure and successful transformation to democracy. It had developed a prosperous economy and a newfound international credibility. No longer an ossified anachronism of fascist underdevelopment, it had been selected as host nation for the Olympic Games and the World's Fair in 1992. In the course of the Gulf War the policies of the nominally socialist

Spanish government were tugged at by contradictory forces. Spain's credibility as an emergent world power (of the order of Britain or France) as well as its relationship with members of the G7 depended upon its taking an active and cooperative role in major world crises. It needed to show it was a player and no longer on the sidelines of global affairs. Yet its relationship with its neighbors in the Magreb (Algeria, Tunisia, Morocco) could have been damaged by a too-enthusiastic embrace of American initiatives.

Domestic constraints also beset Prime Minister Felipe González Márquez. Since the time of colonial wars, especially that in the Philippines, a strong tradition of anti-Americanism had been present in Spanish culture across all social classes. This was reinforced by political links and cultural exchanges between Spain and the Spanish speaking countries of South and Central America who wished to assert their cultural and political difference from the hegemonic power of the New World. Added to this anti-American streak was a strong pacifist/isolationist tradition that had been reinforced by the influence of the fratricidal Spanish Civil War of the 1930s. Notwithstanding General Franco's decades-long effort to institutionalize an understanding of this as a war of national salvation, by the 1990s it had become fixed in the collective memory as a futile and terrible moment in Spanish history in which everyone was to blame. It had brought neither glory nor prosperity nor democracy but quite simply tragedy, because a path to peaceful coexistence could not be found (Edles 1992). Most recently these antimilitarist, anti-American impulses had found their expression in a widespread campaign to pull Spain out of NATO. A referendum on the issue was narrowly defeated only through what many thought of as governmental duplicity and dirty tricks. The Spanish government, then, had to tread a careful path between these conflicting interests and impulses on both domestic and international fronts.

Given this cultural context it is hardly surprising that military solutions to the crisis in the Gulf had lower legitimacy in Spain than in any other major industrialized country. How widely was the war rejected? An extensive survey conducted by the *Newsweek*-style magazine *Cambio 16* (February 4, 1991) provides some indication. It revealed that in February 1991, only 18 percent of Spaniards considered the war "just." Some 27 percent thought that the best policy for Spain was to "stay out of a conflict amongst Arab countries," 25 percent favored a "strong diplomatic protest" against Iraq, and 21 percent wanted the blockade prolonged. Only 10 percent thought that war was the best policy.[7] The majority of Spaniards saw the war as led and orchestrated by the Americans in order to protect their petrol interests. Some 51 percent considered that the presence of "oil wells" had caused the war, 13 percent the "expansionist policies of Saddam Hussein," and only 3 percent considered that the "defense of democracy" was a key factor. Let's repeat that. Only 3 percent considered that the "defense of democracy" was a key factor. Behavioral data support this thesis of illegitimacy: A strike against the war, called on January 18, 1991, was supported by more than 2 million workers. Street demonstrations could also mobilize effectively. On January 13, 50,000 people turned out in the streets of Madrid and 50,000 in the streets of Barcelona to protest the war. This figure contrasts with only 40,000 in the much larger city of London on January 12.

This domestic discontent helps to explain why—in contrast to Britain, America, and even France—the diplomatic and military response of Spain to the Gulf War was limited. Three small ships were sent to the Persian Gulf. These provided a token military commitment but did not require the more substantial risks involved for ground troops. More important in practical if not symbolic terms was the quiet but effective logistical assistance provided for operations centered on the American air bases at Torrejon, near Madrid, and Moron near Seville. Contrasting with this half-hearted effort was an opposition to the war that was widespread and vocal and that enjoyed extensive institutional and social bases of support. Broadly speaking, the intellectuals, the Left, and the church united in condemning the war. Although the government, the Center, and the Right supported a military response to Iraq, for the most part they were able to do so only in a highly qualified manner. Center and Center-Left positions emphasized pragmatic reasons for aiding America and the war—a low mimetic position that could not sustain blood sacrifice but could perhaps allow the kind of logistical support activity that took place.

Before the summer of 1990, Spanish discourses on Iraq, as in the other countries we have examined, were almost nonexistent. Iraq was not really in the attention space. The readings that were made appear to have been slightly favorable. An early 1980s report on the Iran-Iraq war in *Cambio 16*, for example, does not mention political repression in Iraq but does talk in positive terms of the economic changes wrought by Saddam Hussein. As we have seen elsewhere, the romance of modernization offered a convenient frame: "The Ba'athist regime is transforming Iraq. Modern roads, new towns, overpasses, factories, hydro-electric projects, hotels, schools and hospitals surgeries everywhere. Baghdad is a city of construction work. The Spanish politician Alfonso Guerra said recently in the Iraqi capital: 'In this country there are more cranes than palm trees. The benefits of nationalized petrol are a blessing for this country'" (*Cambio 16*, May 10, 1982).

As elsewhere the invasion of Kuwait put a definitive end to such rosy understandings of Iraq and its leader. From August 1990 right through to the end of the war, Saddam Hussein was widely understood as an embodiment of the

Discourse of Repression. The specific content of these discourses concerning the Iraqi leader was very much the same as in the other countries in this study. There are even signs that the apocalyptic narrative just might have taken hold in August 1990. Although the story should by now be familiar, let us run through it one last time. Saddam Hussein was understood to be a tyrant and dictator in the worst tradition—he was not to be taken as a joke but rather was to be treated with the utmost seriousness. He was not a "picturesque dictator" like "Papa Doc or Idi Amin" but rather one of those "terrifying heads of state, such as Stalin, who consider just anything which furthers their true historical mission" (*Cambio 16*, August 28, 1990). Narrative parallels with Hitler's rise to power demanded that firm action be taken to stop him. His action had brought to mind "Austria, Poland, Czechoslovakia," and its philosophy was to use "pure aggression, force for its own sake, until nothing remains and a country disappears" (editorial, *Cambio 16*, August 13, 1990). It was a pattern that could be traced back to Iraq's war against Iran in the 1980s, which had its origins in Saddam's desire to "build his own glory, his longing for *Lebensraum*, for living space" (*Cambio 16*, August 13, 1990). The Iraqi leader's psyche was described as the familiar cocktail of cynical, calculating pragmatism and manic insanity. Saddam Hussein was a man of "paranoiac inclinations" (*Cambio 16*, August 28, 1990) whose "drug is power and his obsession to maintain it." He was "an astute politician, Machiavellian, implacable and insatiable" (*Cambio 16*, August 13, 1990). With the demonization of Saddam Hussein so well established from August onward some could even argue in January that there had been too much appeasement and delay; that "The present ministers and heads of state are following the same steps as their unfortunately celebrated ancestors, Chamberlain and Daladier—constantly fooled and humiliated" and that they should have "acted promptly, with a forceful and hard intervention of the democratic armed forces, so as to cut short a conflagration that would cause millions of victims" (letter, *El País*, January 7, 1991).

Yet if this apocalyptic position was discursively available it was to remain a minority view. When inserted into a different genre matrix the same clues thrown out by Iraq and Saddam Hussein were to have very different policy implications from those selected by the United States, Britain, and France. By January 1991 a shift toward narrative deflation had become dominant. The Center-Left newspaper *El País* (editorial, January 15, 1991) reflected the dominant national mood well. It argued that sanctions did not amount to appeasement (dependency) but to forceful action (autonomy), that what "the international community is doing already against the Iraqi aggressor is the furthest that can be imagined from an appeasement . . . the appeasement of the '30s didn't consist of not declaring war on Hitler until 1939, but rather in stimulating his aggression and in not taking steps against that which he was doing. Today the embargo against Iraq is having a significant effect."

Why did this pattern emerge and a strong anti–Saddam Hussein coding fail to engender an apocalyptic genre guess? Why was support for blockades and sanctions so strong in Spain when these were understood by the majority in the United States and the United Kingdom as a waste of time? More than any other factor it was the effective mobilization of the anti-American tradition that doomed all hopes of apocalypticism. As we discussed toward the start of this book, apocalypticism is a genre that demands strongly Manichean dualities. If neither side can don the mantle of the good, then war begins to look unnecessary, imprudent, without purpose. For the majority of Spaniards both the United States and Iraq were polluted. As Julio Anguita of the Izquierda Unida party put it, "both Hussein and Bush are criminals. Neither is squeaky clean" (quoted in El Sol, January 21, 1991). The present-day politics of America was "very distant from the ideals of its founding fathers" (op-ed, El Independiente, March 23, 1991) and could be thought of as part of a pattern of American international domination—the "new world disorder" (editorial, El Independiente, February 26, 1991). Difference collapsed and antisolidaristic sentiments favorable to isolationism emerged. The details of this deflation can be traced, for example, in letters published in El País. America's ideologically problematic history was mobilized through mininarratives that drew upon the Discourse of Repression. It had been "born massacring Indians," had "filled [its] flag by taking lands from the Mexicans," and "converted Latin America into an enormous puppet theater" (February 12, 1991). It was remarked that "Our guiding light of today invaded Panama yesterday, got rid of the democratically elected Allende government in Chile and invaded Nicaragua with its armies," (January 31, 1991) and that on the "100th anniversary of the slaughter of Wounded Knee" the heirs of the 7th Cavalry "ride out again sowing the earth with corpses" (January 15, 1991). Cutting irony was used to reconfigure American claims as hypocritical and irrational. America was profaned as self-interested, amoral, misguided, and antidemocratic. It believed that its "military and economic power" gave it the right to be the "Sheriff of the whole world" (February 8, 1991). The war was about "two mad men, each one defending his own interests and attempting to bring the world to war in order to justify his madness" (January 31, 1991). Consequently, "words such as democracy, liberty, justice, peace" had been "prostituted" (January 15, 1991). Parallels to the origins of World War II were taken up and reworked in creative ways that debunked heroic accounts and emphasized a tragic history of complicity with evil: "We must remember that Hitler was allowed to remilitarize the Rhineland (March 1936) annex Austria (March 1938) and to occupy Czechoslovakia (March 1939). It was only when Hitler made a pact with the Soviet Union (August 1939) that the Western powers decided to stop him. . . . History repeats itself (the first time as tragedy, the second as farce, said Karl Marx). Saddam Hussein was allowed to arm himself to the teeth, was allowed to launch a criminal aggression against Iran, he was allowed to gas the Kurds . . . and to wipe out internal opposition. It was only when he moved against our interests invading Kuwait that we changed our clothes and discovered the monstrous character of the Iraqi dictator" (January 18, 1991).

The powerful anti-American discourse was not restricted to a critique of alleged instrumental, power-seeking motives. From the Spanish perspective America's actions could also be read as irrational, unrealistic, and expressive. We have already seen how an Orientalist discourse was used to account for popular support for Saddam Hussein in Iraq and the Arab world. A remarkably similar frame was used to explain what was going on in America as signifiers from the Discourse of Repression were mobilized. The result was an onslaught of psychobabble that was every bit as patronizing and stereotyping as that deployed in the United States to describe the Arab hordes. "The present crisis of identity of the North American people," wrote the psychiatrist Luis Marcos, "is the result of a clash between the 'invincible America' of the Second World War and the 'vulnerable America' which arose from the Vietnam conflict . . . like a child who had to see the world in simple terms of the good and the bad, North America was obsessed with communism . . . the surprising collapse of communism has displaced the basic scheme of good and bad . . . the conflict in the Gulf . . . is a challenge for that young nation to face up to itself and to resolve its crisis of identity" (op-ed, El País, January 8, 1991). The average American citizen was said to have "fanatical patriotism combined with a mental block towards different opinions." They were guided by the simplistic logic that "if Saddam is the bad guy, then Bush has to be the good guy of the movie, following from this that all disagreement with the war is identified with the influence of the Devil" (letter, El País, April 6, 1991).

While opposition to the war was targeted for the most part on George Bush and America, the Spanish government was itself to become tainted in the later stages of the fighting. The expansion of a discourse of pollution to domestic arenas was facilitated by a concurrent wave of political scandals. Yet it was the revelation that Iraq had been bombed by B-52s flying directly from Moron, near Seville—and this without the knowledge of the people—that formed a more proximate catalyst. The Discourse of Repression was activated as themes of dishonesty, hierarchy, and dependence came to the fore. A survey of prominent intellectuals and politicians in *Cambio 16* (February 11, 1991) produced comments that Spain had been "converted into an appendage of empire" or an "immense aircraft carrier" and had "surrendered to the interests of Bush." The war had been "justified with all kinds of cover-ups and lies." The magazine's editorial concluded that the government had perverted the "very essence of the democratic system." Even *El País* (editorial, February 3, 1991), usually an advocate of the government, was moved to criticize such actions, remarking that although the administration had done well to fulfill international obligations now that Spain was "no longer isolated by Francoism," it had failed to respect its promises "with its own citizens."

We have seen that Saddam Hussein and his actions were broadly condemned in terms of the Discourse of Repression. However, with America and the Spanish government also on the ropes, anyone wishing to advocate war was faced with a vast legitimation problem. The long and the short of it is that there simply was not enough binarism around. For the majority in Spain, Saddam Hussein was different from the coalition forces only in degree, not in kind. Unable to summon a convincing theodicy at the symbolic level, and perhaps unconvinced themselves of the validity of American claims to universalism, the war's supporters were forced to explain Spain's involvement in terms of *zweckrational* criteria. These half-hearted and rather apologetic low mimetic justifications typically revolved around the legalistic themes of "responsibility" and "obligation" and attempted to imply that Spain's involvement in the war was an inevitable, and indeed ironic, consequence of its involvement in the modern, democratic, world system. Although this discourse was by and large prosaic, we can detect within it some latent symbolic leverage. Because internationalism and involvement are associated with Spain's new democratic status, isolationism and neutrality were liable to become tainted beliefs summoning the ghost of Francoism. In the fifteen years prior to the Gulf War, Spain's image and attitudes had changed. It had become a "member of the European Community, with obligations that cannot be liked" but that had to be met (*Cambio 16*, September 3, 1990). Spain had developed a "politics of support consistent with the resolutions of the United Nations, assuming in the light of its international responsibilities and promises the role which it must carry out" (Speech by Raimon Obiols, PSOE politician in *Leviathan*, Winter 1991, 42). It was "satisfying to see that the Government is aware of all its responsibilities and is prepared to assume them" (editorial, *El País*, February 15, 1991). This meant that now the "Spanish foreign and defense policy" was "inseparable from the foreign and defense policies of the

European Community and the Western world (*El País*, February 25, 1991). In short, Spain had to "fulfill the obligations of both a member of the UN and the European Community" (editorial, *El País*, February 17, 1991). The overall picture here is that participation in war was required as the price of growing up and being accepted by peers. This uninspiring discourse left the government severely hamstrung in terms of the practical aid it could render to the allied war effort. Contractual obligations do not offer a theodicy for death. Spanish troops could not be placed in the line of fire. The three small boats that were sent to the Gulf had orders to "only use force in the case of legitimate self-defense" (*El País*, August 23, 1990). The secrecy regarding the use of Spanish bases for American long distance air raids testifies to some reflexive awareness of this lack of cultural legitimacy. It was further refracted in the open reaction of the Spanish government to the bombing of civilian targets in general and the Amiriya bunker in particular. Perhaps anxious not to isolate themselves too far from the mainstream of opinion Felipe González's government sent a strong message to President Bush asking for the bombardment of Iraqi cities to stop, and for an immediate investigation into the targeting of the bunker. Whether or not he really meant what he said is something we cannot know. What is clear is that the message served to demonstrate the Spanish government's moral and political autonomy from the United States.

As might be expected, the unfolding postwar Kurdish problem was grist to the mill of a cultural system organized around suspicion of the United States. This new set of clues seemingly vindicated the anti-American suspicions held by the war's critics and confirmed their tragic genre guess had been the correct one. The Kurds were primarily described as innocent victims of U.S. indifference rather than as targets of Saddam Hussein's evil. It was observed that "the suffering of the Kurds can wait in contrast to the petrol of Kuwait" (op-ed, *El Mundo*, April 16, 1991), and the international community was putting its "strategic, economic and military interests before acting unanimously in the defense of the Kurds" (letter, *El País*, April 8, 1991). As if to atone for their role in the war the Spanish government took part openly and forcefully in the rescue of Kurdish refugees. Considered as a proportion, the six hundred soldiers they sent demonstrated a far stronger practical and symbolic commitment than any that had been shown for the Gulf War proper. The atonement could work in two directions. To Spain's international allies the "frontline" contribution served to confirm Spain's willingness to shoulder some of the collective burden. Simultaneously, the perceived universalism of the humanitarian mission helped to repair relations between the government and those at home who had not supported its war efforts. As *El País* (editorial,

April 24, 1991) put it, "the action of the government and popular sentiment seem to have coincided . . . the humanitarian dimension overcomes in this case any suspicion of hidden intentions and interests at play."

The story from Spain, then, was one very different from the other countries we have looked at and well exemplifies what can happen when a violence-averse narrative becomes strongly institutionalized. Opposition to war was widespread and mobilized tragic themes. Justifications for the war were half-hearted, defensive and couched in a low mimetic genre. Participation was minimal and without risk of blood sacrifice. The Spanish case provides important clues as to what might have happened if minority positions in the other three countries had taken root. In its elaboration of discourses of cynicism and tragedy it also foreshadows in important ways some of the narrative patterns pivotal to the next conflict—the far more controversial 2003 War in Iraq.

At the end of the previous chapter we itemized some lessons from the Suez case study. We have seen these repeated and reinforced here: Events are seen through genres, disputes over the legitimacy of war involve debates over genre and moral coding, discourse follows familiar and predictable patterns. Another theme has emerged quite strongly in these concluding pages. This relates to the way that genres and narratives about a current war become filtered, channeled, and made relevant through specific national narratives, visions of the nation's place in the world, and collective memories of events that might be long distant. Atoning for past national wrongs, asserting national autonomy and strength, living up to a heroic national tradition, avoiding past national mistakes, confirming a new national identity—these are all concerns that became woven into the genre wars over what to do about Saddam Hussein's invasion of Kuwait. So although we have identified invariant cultural structures that cut across the familiar ideological boundaries of Left and Right and transcend national borders, there is space for specificity. Genre choices are related to political cultures both more broadly and more narrowly conceived. This further lesson is one we will see repeated even more emphatically in the next chapter.

THE WAR IN IRAQ OF 2003

Our next conflict, the War in Iraq of 2003 emerged out of the Gulf War, although just how it did so remains a complex and contested issue. The shell of a narrative can be related as follows. At the end of the Gulf War, Saddam Hussein remained in power. Iraq was subject, however, to United Nations sanctions and also to inspections intended to prevent rearmament. These focused, in particular, on weapons of mass destruction or WMD—an acronym used with increasing frequency during the buildup to war to refer in a generic way to chemical, biological, and nuclear technologies. In April 1991, Iraq had been forced to accept a UN resolution that required it to abandon its WMD programs, destroy stockpiles, and allow regular inspections by international teams that would attempt to verify compliance. Over the following years a scenario repeatedly emerged in which Iraq would first allow and then deny access to inspectors, or try to impose restrictive conditions on when, where and who could inspect, or attempt to negotiate on inspections in order to have an oil-for-food trade policy lifted. After each standoff and its associated diplomatic activity Iraq would back down and the inspections would resume. At one point President Clinton considered the use of force to be necessary. December 1998 saw Operation Desert Fox in which British and American air strikes were made against what were thought to be weapons programs. Although the presence of practicable ongoing WMD programs and/or capabilities was never conclusively demonstrated it was widely believed that Saddam Hussein was up to something. Certainly he was understood to be an irritation, thumbing his nose at the UN and making life difficult for the victorious powers of the Gulf War.

This pattern might have continued for another decade but for the terrorist attacks on the United States of America on September 11, 2001. Carried out by the radical Islamic al-Qaeda organization, these provided the mandate for a more proactive American foreign policy against potential threats. President George W. Bush (son of the George Bush of the previous chapter) initiated U.S. military actions in Afghanistan that destroyed al-Qaeda bases and removed the Islamic fundamentalist Taliban regime from power. Next came a shift of agendas to one that could encompass the elimination of Saddam Hussein. It was a policy move announced and justified by President Bush in his famous "Axis of Evil" State of the Union address on January 30, 2002 (we analyze this below). Over the next year military and diplomatic preparations for conflict took place in Britain and America. However, many felt that the case for war against Iraq was never properly made, that links between Iraq and al-Qaeda were never demonstrated, and the dossiers of evidence concerning Iraq's WMD programs were vague, inconclusive, and contestable. In short, many considered that there was no clear and immediate danger and that sanctions and inspections should continue. France, alongside Germany, China, and Russia refused to support the United States in the United Nations. On March 5, 2003, France, Russia, and Germany announced they would block any effort to push a resolution authorizing war through the Security Council. The United States and the United Kingdom pressed on regardless of now-uncertain international legitimacy.

By March 19, 2003, there were 170,000 troops, almost entirely American and British, on the Iraqi/Kuwaiti border. From March 20 onward there followed aerial bombardments and a steady but modestly contested military advance on the ground toward Baghdad. On April 9 a giant statue of Saddam Hussein was torn from its pedestal. The war it seemed was over. There followed sporadic, then more persistent resistance to the occupation as guerilla attacks were made on U.S. and British troops. Words like "Vietnam" came to be bandied about as a period of very expensive reconstruction got underway. Efforts to find WMD proved futile, links to terrorism were not substantiated by any new information, and the justifications for the war that had been advanced came under renewed scrutiny. Several months later Saddam Hussein was found hiding in a hole in the ground. Yet the disorder in Iraq did not go away; nor did critique of the move to war by Bush and Tony Blair, the British prime minister. Soon the point was reached where more troops had died after the end of major hostilities than in the advance on Baghdad. Relentless uprisings against American occupation, executions of Western hostages, and photographic evidence of American torture of Iraqi prisoners provided yet more fuel for debate. Official reports on intelligence failures over Iraq's WMD continued to emerge on a regular basis, all of them indicating grave errors of interpretation.

Two dimensions of this war deserve our analytical attention. First, there is the question of how the conflict could have domestic legitimacy when it did not have a UN mandate and was intended to be preemptive. As an article in *Time* magazine (April 21, 2003) put it, "this war was optional." In contrast to Suez (where a canal was nationalized) or the Gulf War (where a sovereign country was invaded) there had been no obviously threatening triggering act or violation of international law by Iraq. If President Bush had "ignored Iraq . . . the price would have been a few disappointed Administration hawks and one or two grumpy Op-Eds" (ibid.). Yet millions of Americans agreed with the president when he put Iraq on the agenda and sent troops to die there. How could this have happened? If support for the war raises one set of questions, then the widespread opposition to the War in Iraq raises another. What was it about this war, in contrast to the Gulf War, that led to France removing its assistance and to growing opposition and legitimation crisis in the United Kingdom and eventually the United States? Both conflicts had involved the "evil" Saddam Hussein and both were dealing with a possible threat to world security. Something happened to make the threat posed by Saddam Hussein in 2003 qualitatively different for many people than that of 1990. What was this?

For readers who have made it this far there are no prizes for guessing that the answers to such questions lie in the genre guess and its derivative narratives. These were used to fill in the blanks and to allow confident inferences to be made from weak information. Many of these readers might also argue that the War in Iraq was a cynical exercise driven from the top down by political elites who had little concern for public opinion, whether domestic or international. Certainly it seems as if George Bush set his course for war months before combat started. Does this mean that public opinion and civil discourse were peripheral to the main event, a talkfest on the political margins that could be ignored by the decision makers? Looking closely we find that civil codes and narratives were absolutely central to political and diplomatic agendas from September 11 onward. They were repeatedly and reflexively invoked in struggles to explain why war was necessary and also informed a broader worldview that could guide American foreign policy. Readers should not confuse the fact that they find the justifications for the war incredible or manufactured with the theoretical claim that culture is irrelevant. To the contrary, the very effort that went into constructing a meaningful ground-work for conflict confirms the centrality of storytelling to legitimacy, as does the fact that leaders were asked *post facto* to explain the genre choices and interpretations they had made *ante bellum*.

THE WAR IN IRAQ AND THE UNITED STATES

The American perspective on Iraq during the 1990s was something like the following: Saddam Hussein was evil, the Iraqi people oppressed, the Gulf War perhaps a little too inconclusive. We have seen already that Saddam had been more or less ignorable in the 1980s and that when attention was paid to him this was broadly favorable. He seemed then to be the kind of person who should be given the benefit of the doubt. During the 1990s he was understood very differently. He was a known violator of human rights and a persistent thorn in the side who sent out pricking reminders of his presence whenever he started squabbles over weapons inspections. He was not, however, linked to any apocalyptic scenarios of world domination. Saddam's armies and weapons programs were thought to have been emasculated. His aggression seemed limited to predictable tirades against the United States. Saddam Hussein was simply bad and full of hot air. This spirit is captured in the title of chapter seventeen of U.S. Secretary of State Madeleine Albright's (2003) autobiography: "Migraine Hussein." Albright's book makes it clear that during the Clinton era, Saddam was defined primarily as an intractable problem and not as a global threat (see e.g., Albright 2003, 273). The idea of invading Iraq to eliminate any WMD programs once and for all was never seriously entertained. Even the hawkish Dick Cheney, as vice president to Bush a vigorous future advocate of the war, stated as late as August 2000 that "we want to maintain our current posture vis-à-vis Iraq" (quoted in Albright 2003, 277). Likewise a perusal of the index to Bill Clinton's (2004) autobiography shows scattered references to Iraq and Saddam Hussein—there is no sustained discussion or coherent narrative elaboration suggesting that this was a front burner issue in his administration.

Saddam Hussein, then, was a pain in the ass that could be dealt with through Preparation H remedies like inspections and resolutions, no-fly zones, and the odd bombing of his weapons facilities when he refused to comply. Containment and regulation were the shibboleths of this low mimetic reading of the situation. U.S. policy was to push for compliance on WMD issues through UN sanctions. As the decade wore on, Albright (2003, 275) reports there was even "a general sense of sanctions fatigue and the feeling in some quarters that Baghdad no longer posed a serious threat." Protests and negative media coverage of the impact of sanctions took hold, with the United States—and not Saddam Hussein's intransigence—seen by many even at home as the cause of starving children and economic chaos (Albright 2003). Such tragic narratives began to confront the Clinton administration's efforts at hardheaded regulation.

Iraq's failure to comply with inspection protocols led to the Operation Desert Fox air strikes of December 1998. The action, authorized by President Clinton, was approved of by 78 percent of the American people, although only 51 percent at that time thought Saddam Hussein worth assassinating (Fox News/Opinion Dynamics Poll Dec/1998, PollingReport.com). This disparity is consistent with the idea that a genre shift had fallen into place toward low mimesis. Saddam Hussein needed to be spanked for failure to meet the technicalities of UN resolutions. He did not need to be killed—after all that would be illegal. So it seems that the deflationary genre shift in thinking about Iraq that George Bush had tried to initiate too early at the immediate end of the Gulf War had eventually come to pass. Sitting comfortably in power, Saddam Hussein could have done without 9/11 for it enabled a further genre shift to take place and with it stories that translated him once again into a global menace.

The September 11 terrorist attacks on the World Trade Center and the Pentagon that indirectly triggered the War in Iraq set off an episode of collective effervescence, patriotic solidarity, and righteous anger that has not been equaled in America in recent years (Alexander 2004a; Tiryakian 2004). They unleashed discourses of conspiracy and narratives of doom to suggest that civilization, and in particular a tolerant, reasoning, democratic American civilization, was under attack from unreasoning, intolerant, totalitarian fanatics possessed of who knows what cunning and weapons. As we know, the move to apocalypticism enables conventional barriers to vigorous action to be pushed to the side. The legal and bureaucratic procedures of business-as-usual were now to be read as impediments to efficiency. Legislation on what came rather winsomely to be called Homeland Security gave arguably unprecedented powers to state agencies, funds were released to fight terrorism, and decisions were made quickly and with less accountability.

I have often reiterated that events do not determine their own interpretation. Skeptics of this view might be persuaded by thinking on how previous al-Qaeda attacks had failed to spark a shift out of low mimesis and thereby to set alarm bells ringing. These had been in far off places like Africa and seemed related only to the internal squabbles of distant nations rather than plots for worldwide chaos. On August 7, 1998, American embassies in Kenya and Tanzania were bombed. Over two hundred people died including twelve

Americans. Around 5,000 were injured—most of them Africans. Limited retaliatory cruise missile strikes were organized against al-Qaeda bases in Afghanistan and Sudan. There was no use of ground troops and substantial levels of demand for further revenge did not eventuate in civil discourse. Critics even suggested that the strikes had been simply a ruse to distract attention from President Clinton's ongoing sex scandal and his problems with the aggressive special prosecutor Kenneth Starr (Albright 2003, 368). Efforts continued to *negotiate* with the Taliban for the handover of Osama bin Laden, the al-Qaeda *supremo*, who was believed to be in hiding in Afghanistan. In other words it was believed that diplomacy could save the day even if this involved working with a radical Islamic regime. Once this strategy failed, sanctions were imposed on the Taliban in October 1999, after U.S. lobbying of the UN Security Council. Bob Woodward (2003, 6–7) suggests that the CIA did not plan to assassinate bin Laden due to the force of a presidential assassination ban that had a history extending back to the era of Gerald Ford's presidency. The rule of law, then, was still in place and extreme measures were not required. Likewise, the military were lukewarm when the president asked them about sending Special Forces in to eliminate al-Qaeda training bases (Clinton 2004, 804). The option to invade Afghanistan and deal with the problem head on was never seriously entertained. There was no sustained will to risk American lives to avoid some potential future catastrophe. Why not? Albright suggests that there would have been insufficient domestic or international support without the "megashock of September 11" (2003, 375). This explanation places weight on the event but not its interpretation. The fact is that the embassy bombings, like the al-Qaeda engineered attack on the USS *Cole* on October 12, 2000 that cost seventeen sailors their lives *could* have been inserted into a different narrative. This would have ramped up these events as evidence of a pattern of escalating malice and capability, fanatical resolve, and boundless ambition extending back to the 1980s and attacks on the American presence in Beirut. Such a big-picture, genre inflated culture structure would have allowed the bureaucratic constraints on assassination and invasion to have been lifted as they were to be after 9/11. That they were not testifies to the stranglehold of the low mimetic genre in place and its tacit implication that negotiations and UN sanctions could save the day.

Albright complains it was difficult to get the public interested in the terror issue although it was taken seriously by the administration. She is probably right. Clinton's statement after the attacks did indeed signal a modest effort toward genre inflation. Using words remarkably similar to those of Bush a few years later he remarked, "These acts of terrorist violence are abhorrent; they are inhuman. We will use all means at our disposal to bring those responsible to justice, no matter what or how long it takes" (quoted in *New York Times*, August 8, 1998). The discourse, however, was one of lawlessness, not of global threat. In his autobiography Clinton tells us that after the embassy bombings he was "intently focused on capturing or killing him [bin Laden] and with destroying al Qaeda" (2004, 798). Perhaps this was so. However, the public mood was less genre inflated and low mimetic critique of Clinton's policies abounded. The *New York Times* (editorial, August 8, 1998) wrote that "modest progress" had already been made in curbing terrorism. The missile strikes on Sudan and Afghanistan were treated with suspicion. It sniffed that "Mr. Clinton and his aides provided no real details of the evidence," and that the "credibility of the Administration's case against Mr. bin Laden was difficult to assess, both for the African bombings specifically and for terrorist activities in general." It also ran speculative stories on the "Wag the Dog" hypothesis. This referred to a recently released satirical movie in which a president had initiated a war in order to distract attention from his sexual transgressions. "In real life was the Clinton administration doing something similar?" asked the feature (August 21, 1998). The *Washington Post* (August 21, 1998) also put up the headline "US Action Conjures up Scenarios from 'Wag the Dog'" and remarked that it was "only a matter of moments before questions arose: were the attacks on what the Pentagon said were terrorist camps and operations in Sudan and Afghanistan a case of life imitating art?" The climate for apocalypticism was weak. This made strong character polarization between protagonists and antagonists difficult to establish. Bin Laden had yet to be excommunicated; we have just seen that he could still be called "Mr." and given the benefit of doubt by the *New York Times*. Clinton looked shifty. Although 73 percent approved of his decision to bomb terrorist targets overseas, 40 percent believed that political diversion had a place somewhere in the decision (*Newsweek*, August 31, 1998). It would seem al-Qaeda was viewed as a threat—but not a large enough one to allow the strikes to be universally popular or to allow doubts about the sincerity of Clinton's motives to be expunged. This was not the kind of cultural environment in which America could send in the troops.

THE APOCALYPTIC IMPACTS OF 9/11

The September 11 attacks allowed a new sensibility to fall into place not only because of the objective death and destruction they caused but also because of their properties as a cultural performance (Alexander 2004b). As the terrorists well knew in designing the event, the point was not simply to kill some 3,000 people, wreck some aircraft, and destroy some expensive Manhattan real estate. The terrorist incursion was intended to suggest that American hegemony was weak, that the social order was unstable, and that havoc and fear could and should exist at the very heart of the American empire. This message came through loud and clear and became keyed in turn to iconic visual images of jet airplanes smashing into the twin towers, the twin towers burning, the twin towers collapsing. Collective representations eventuated that sustained a rapid shift into the apocalyptic genre. There was a doomsday sensibility to the raging inferno and the clouds of gray fall-out looking ash that billowed through the streets of downtown Manhattan. It was an event of Hiroshima-like resonance with "pillars of smoke and dust" and "streets snowed under with the atomized debris of the skyline" (editorial, *New York Times*, September 12, 2001). Themes of conspiracy conjured up the image of unknown others, so-called sleeper cells lurking unnoticed in motels and garden apartments throughout America, just as the 9/11 terrorists had done, and driven by the same kamikaze beliefs. There were caves and training camps overseas when yet more faceless warriors were lurking, preparing yet more unspeakable evil. Whereas previous al-Qaeda terrorism had been ignorable the menace was now immeasurable. If al-Qaeda guilt and al-Qaeda intentions had been in doubt after the embassy bombings, now the case was supported by clues closer to home, by a trail of boarding passes and money and finally a tape of Osama bin Laden seemingly claiming responsibility. They belonged in the story. Binaries were set in place between the good Americans—firefighters, police, and the ordinary family people who had died—and the evil terrorists with their plans for world domination. This was an epochal moment (another "hinge of history"), one of those points in time where "history splits and we define the world as 'before' and 'after,'" a world in which "everything has changed" (editorial, *New York Times*, September 12, 2001), a "turn in history" that would impact upon "the way the US will look at the world for a long time to come" (Morton Abramovitz, former Head of Intelligence and Research at the State Department, in *New York Times*, September 12, 2001). The cultural foundations for the War against Terror were starting to be dug.

It is instructive to trace this new narrative being progressively entrenched and concretized in the pivotal speeches and addresses of George W. Bush. Importantly, these headed off fatalistic interpretations of the apocalypse (that this was a fight against evil that had already been lost or could not be won) with activist ones that gave America a heroic role in fighting back and destroying evil. In a session in the cabinet room after the attacks, Bush stated that the attacks were an act of war, that America would rally the world and that there would be a "monumental struggle between good and evil" (Woodward 1993, 45). In a televised address to the nation on the night of September 11 he spoke of "evil, despicable acts of terror," "evil acts" and the need to "go forward to defend freedom and all that is good and just in our world" (Bush 2003, 2–3). In an address at a memorial service at the National Cathedral on September 14 the same motif came up (Bush 2003, 5–7). There was a need to "answer these attacks and rid the world of evil."

A more elaborated scenario was unfolded from this imagery a week later in the address to a joint session of Congress on Thursday, September 20, 2001. Here we see the American leader more clearly specifying players, objectives, and stakes. In effect Bush (2003, 11–18) takes up the signifiers and smaller-scale narratives that had been ejected into public circulation with the collapse of the twin towers and connects them in a coherent pattern by invoking a new master narrative. Using the Discourses of Liberty and Repression Bush identifies heroes and villains, gives them motivations, and allocates them to roles in a new American drama of world-historical proportions. It is a vision built upon the strongest possible binaries, and so its only possible narrative form is the apocalyptic. The first set of contrasts involves marking out good and bad agents and consists, at the crudest level, of ordinary people and inhuman terrorists. The former group includes "passengers who rushed terrorists to save others on the ground"; "rescuers working past exhaustion"; "loving decent people who have made the grief of strangers their own"; and decent folk in other nations such as "South Korean children gathering to pray outside our embassy in Seoul," or those who offered "prayers of sympathy" at "a mosque in Cairo"; the Police Officer George Howard who "died at the World Trade Center trying to save others." America's antagonists included, at this stage, only al-Qaeda and the Taliban regime in Afghanistan. The terrorist groups could be defined by their methods and values as exemplifiers of the Discourse of Repression. In "camps in places like Afghanistan they are trained in the tactics of terror" before returning home or hiding out to "plot evil and destruction." They are "enemies of freedom" who "hate our freedoms: our freedom of religion, our freedom of speech; our freedom to vote and to assemble and to disagree with each other." In order to tell what such an unfree society might look like we can turn to Afghanistan where the "people have been brutalized, many are starving and many have fled. Women are not allowed to attend school. You can be jailed for owning a television. Religion can be practiced only as their leaders dictate."

The evil-other was further defined in terms of its mission. In the television address of September 11, Bush had spoken of the attacks largely as an assault on America. The attacks "were intended to frighten our *nation* into chaos and retreat" (my italics). Now a full-blown apocalypticism emerges in which the object of struggle is not America but the world. The aim of al-Qaeda is to "overthrow existing governments in many Muslim countries" and to "drive Christians and Jews out of vast regions of Asia and Africa." This, however, is simply the thin end of the wedge, for these are steps in a scheme of world-historical proportions and not just a series of local struggles. The terrorists have "*global* reach" and al-Qaeda's ultimate goal is "remaking the *world* and imposing its radical beliefs on people everywhere" (my italics). Although shocking this was not without precedent for they are "heirs of all the murderous ideologies of the twentieth century . . . by abandoning every value except the will to power, they follow in the path of fascism, Nazism and totalitarianism." Consequently "what is at stake is not just America's freedom." Indeed this could be seen as "the world's fight . . . civilization's fight" where "freedom itself is under attack." The mission of the United States was to ensure that this "will not be an age of terror but an age of liberty" because "the advance of human freedom, the great achievement of our time and the great hope of every time, now depends on us." And so there was to be a "War on Terror," a war dedicated to "the destruction and defeat of the global terror network."

In this speech Bush scripted out a classic apocalyptic scenario, one reminiscent of that of Eden at the time of Suez, or that which dominated America just after Saddam Hussein's invasion of Kuwait in 1990. There is an evil and unscrupulous enemy and a bold hero; there is a struggle for world domination; there are attacks upon and efforts to protect those most sacred of values, freedom and democracy. The events that have been already witnessed are simply the tip of the iceberg of dangers. We have been warned about what will occur in future installments of this unfolding drama. We are at a hinge of history, something needs to be done and that something will probably be violent as the enemy is not interested in reason or peace. The speech was well received. Congress voted 420 to 1 to give the president new and arguably unprecedented powers to combat terrorism.

The core message was repeated just a few days later, on October 7 in a televised address to the nation concerning America's military activity in Afghanistan, where troops were to be sent ostensibly to root out bin Laden and his followers (Bush 2003, 33–35). Put simply, an unscrupulous enemy was killing innocents and hated freedom, the terrorists of September 11 were supported by rogue states, and the Taliban needed to be removed from power. As Bruce Lincoln (2002) perceptively points out, Bush's speech-making here was not only constructed from binaries but also carried a coded allusion to the myth of the biblical Apocalypse: "the terrorists may burrow deeper into caves and other entrenched hiding places." This image replicates the passage in Revelations 6: 15–17 where sinners try to hide from the Lamb of God on Judgment Day: "Then the kings of the earth and the great men and the generals and the rich and the strong, and every one, slave and free, hid in the caves and among the rocks of the mountains, calling to the mountains and rocks, 'Fall on us and hide us from the face of him who is seated on the throne, and from the wrath of the Lamb; for the great day of their wrath has come, and who can stand before it.' " Lincoln comments that this "Biblical subtext" brings about a "qualitative transformation" and "invests otherwise merely human events with transcendent significance." In this he is partly right and partly wrong. To be sure the biblical allusion adds depth and resonance. But Bush's discourse was never purely secular. It had already engaged the sacred and profane codes of civil discourse in identifying evil, mobilized a civil religion that spoke of national duty and destiny, and conjured into being an apocalyptic vision of the Armageddonic final showdown. It is possible to imagine this speech being perceived as blinkered or bombastic or bellicose, as mawkish or as scare-mongering, and certainly many on the American Left thought this way. They were, however, at this stage a minority and a small one at that. In the wake of 9/11 Bush had offered a narrative road map that seemed to make sense of a world where a bolt could come from the blue and challenge certainties. U.S. military actions in Afghanistan went ahead soon after, and suspected al-Qaeda members captured there were transported to Guantánamo Bay, Cuba and held without trial or legal counsel. Of course the usual bureaucratic and legal restraints on international policy could be ignored—this after all was a struggle of world-historical proportions, not a diplomatic garden party.

A few months later Bush further elaborated his narrative in ways that pointed more explicitly to the undoing of Saddam Hussein. The fact that he was able to do so depended in part upon the existence of a new U.S. security ideology that had gained a toehold, then a foothold, and next, some would argue, a stranglehold on the Bush presidency. This intellectual incursion offered the programmatic groundwork for policy that was thematically consistent with the orientation of this worldly activism generated by the War on Terror. The "Project for a New American Century" had been forged during the Clinton era by right-wing intellectuals and think tanks and was deeply implicated in shaping the worldview of influential figures for the Bush administration such as Donald Rumsfeld, Richard Perle, Robert Kagan, and Paul Wolfowitz. These men were often referred to as the neoconservatives or simply "neocons." The self-proclaimed aim of the Project was to devise a strategy for American military power in the era since the end of the cold war. The new agenda was for America to move beyond containment and to engage in preemptive assaults. Using its overwhelming military superiority the

United States could engage in aggressive policies toward those rogue states that were believed to now offer the greatest threat to U.S. security. Such action was to be unilateral if need be, for the UN with its mantras about cooperation was an increasingly toothless obstacle to the imposition of peace. Such unofficial doctrines, however well or ill we might think of them, cannot become widely legitimate policy unless connected to the broader narratives and codes that define their validity, necessity, and morality. They also needed to be linked to power and office lest they be simply howling in the wilderness. Largely ignored by Clinton, the neocons did manage to have regime change in Iraq endorsed as official U.S. policy in 1998. They obtained more substantial leverage after Bush was elected over Gore and attained political office. Now they had influence in the White House and the Pentagon and persuaded the president to attach their ideas to the antiterrorism initiative in the first few days and weeks after 9/11. Wolfowitz apparently initially raised the question of removing Saddam Hussein at Camp David over coffee (*Time*, December 21, 2003). In Bush's subsequent speeches we see efforts to validate the neocon doctrine with reference to the broader myths and agendas with which we are familiar: the dramas of democracy and liberty, of terror and Armageddon.

And so it was that by the end of the State of the Union address of January 29, 2002, the writing began to appear on the wall for Saddam Hussein. Bush (2003, 105–12) begins by reminding his audience of the recently successful missions that had "liberated Afghanistan" from enemies who "laugh at the loss of innocent life" and whose hatred was "equaled by the madness of the destruction they design." The triumph, however, was only the prelude to a much larger conflict to come. Evidence had been found in Afghanistan of diabolical schemes: "diagrams of American nuclear power plants and public water facilities, detailed instructions for making chemical weapons, surveillance maps of American cities"; a "terrorist underworld" that viewed "the entire world as a battlefield" operated in "remote jungles and deserts, and hides in the centers of large cities." Now Bush brings new players onto the stage. There were not only terrorists in this drama of good and evil but also "regimes that sponsor terror" and who, when joined with "their terrorist allies, constitute an axis of evil." The great danger was that these states would develop WMD and either use these themselves or give them to terrorists. There was a murky web of shadowy ties in a conspiracy of evil whose exact extent could only be approximated but whose intent was clear. Consequently, the president argued, history had "called America and its allies to action." There was a need for proactive intervention and WMD programs had to be shut down, stopping short would lead to only a false sense of security. Iraq is singled out as part of the Axis of Evil. It supported terror and had "plotted to develop anthrax, and nerve gas, and nuclear weapons for over a decade," it had "something to hide from the civilized world." This was to be a "decisive decade in the history of liberty" in which America had been called "to a unique role in human events." Ideas of manifest destiny, it seems, had found a new home. Here, then, we find the fibers of the narrative that would be used for the justification of the War in Iraq that was to start some thirteen months later. Bush had stitched the case for war into the fabric of apocalypticism that had been established more or less unchallenged by 9/11 just four months before. Iraq was no longer a pain in the butt, but rather had returned to its previous status as a danger to civilization.

APOCALYPTICISM CONTESTED

The threads of this story that wove together Saddam Hussein, WMD, and terrorism, were to be relentlessly picked at by critics of the war in accord with the genre laws we have been outlining throughout this book. The various arguments against the war diverged in their particulars but followed the standard recipes in the structural poetic cookbook for genre deflation. They flattened moral divergence between characters and suggested similarities. They pointed to the ironies and inconsistencies of patterns of action and so deflated heroic pretensions. They flagged missed opportunities and the opportunity costs of lines of action in a kind of actuarial exercise. They talked down risks and dangers by attributing limited powers to the central characters in the unfolding drama. Like Ronald Reagan before him, Bush's own vulnerability to counternarration as a "cowboy President" rather than as an intellectual or pragmatist was to count against his efforts to ramp up threats. The Left in particular saw him as overreacting, driven by a crusading and simplistic worldview and as seriously underestimating the military difficulties, diplomatic complexities, and geopolitical repercussions of his stance. In short, as the Discourse of Repression would have it, that he was deficient in reason, was unrealistic in approach and favored force over law.

Narrowing the moral gap in the cultural coding of the players in this way could allow tragic and low mimetic themes to be expressed. Thus it was also indicated how bin Laden had become rich from American contracts; that the American response to Palestine had not shown sensitivity to Arab interests; that the FBI and CIA had bungled intelligence, and so forth. In this tragic telling of needless suffering and lost opportunities there was moral equivalence. America had reaped what it had sowed. Dialogue and a constructive reworking of American foreign policy were needed. Hope could only exist if America switched toward a romantic engagement with difference. The

Christian theologian Stanley Hauerwas, for example, spoke of the need for nonviolent solutions and the requirement to abandon the language of "evil" that "threatens to turn war into a crusade" (op-ed, *Time*, March 3, 2003). Susan Sontag gained few friends in Manhattan when she wrote controversially in the *New Yorker* (September 24, 2001) that the 9/11 attacks had been the result of "American alliances and actions"; that America was replete with a non-rational discourse of mutual consolation and psychotherapy and that a "historical awareness might help us understand what has just happened, and what may continue to happen." The eminent historian Arthur Schlesinger Jr. (*Newsweek*, March 22, 2003) argued the White House was probably well intentioned but it wanted for a "sense of history. They lack a respect for the views of other countries." This was Pearl Harbor in reverse because America had become the aggressor. When the United States declared itself "judge, jury and executioner" this was "a tragically mistaken notion." Moreover, for Schlesinger there was no real threat. Containment had worked against Saddam Hussein for ten years. War would bring new anti-American sentiment and encourage nuclear proliferation. Bob Woodward tells how within the Bush administration the now Secretary of State Colin Powell had tried to make similar arguments to Schlesinger's over a period of months. In a meeting with the president on August 5, 2002, for example, he pointed out the broader diplomatic and economic implications of any war with Iraq and argued for multilateralism and suggested that containment was practicable (Woodward 2003, 332–33). During the buildup to war there was a constant tension among Bush's advisors between Powell's multilateralism grounded in a more low mimetic understanding and the more aggressive approach of the administration engaged in an apocalyptic struggle with global evil.

There was a faint echo of such views in the major press responses to each of the key speeches. Questions about genre choices and their consequences were aired but Bush generally received the benefit of the doubt each time. The *New York Times* (editorial, September 20, 2001) admired Bush's "firm and forceful speech" to the joint session of Congress, but argued that the country was "understandably wary and realistic about achieving a victory over an enemy that is so diffuse and difficult to locate" and remarked that some Americans found the president's characterization of a struggle between good and evil, freedom, and fear "overly simplistic" (September 20, 2001). Its editorial on the "Axis of Evil" speech noted that "power and intimidation has returned to the forefront of American foreign policy" (editorial, January 31, 2002), and an opinion item by Kevin Phillips in the same edition noted that for a Bush who had "become transcendental," references to evil blurred the boundary between "justifiable retaliation" and a "wider crusade."

Undaunted by such commentaries Bush steadfastly maintained the apocalyptic reading of world events. In a speech in Cincinnati delivered on October 7, 2002, Bush spoke of the fact that we should not wait for "the final proof—the smoking gun—that could come in the form of a mushroom cloud" (quoted in *Vanity Fair*, May 2004, 282). On the eve of the War in Iraq, on March 17, 2003, Bush once again brings up the theme of weapons of mass destruction. In a Presidential Address to the Nation he gave Saddam Hussein an ultimatum to leave Iraq and announced that military operations were imminent (Bush 2003, 231–35). He lays out his stall thus: In the period since the Gulf War, Iraq had refused to reveal and destroy its WMD, had not acted in good faith with the UN or its inspectors. Intelligence had shown that "the Iraq regime continues to possess and conceal some of the most lethal weapons ever devised" and it was known to have used these in its past. It had a history of "reckless aggression" and harboring terrorists including those from al-Qaeda. In this speech Bush conjures images of an Armageddon even more explicitly than in those prior: "Using chemical, biological or, one day, nuclear weapons obtained with the help of Iraq, the terrorists could fulfill their stated ambitions and kill thousands or hundreds of thousands of innocent people"; "Destruction of a kind never before seen on this earth"; a threat that might "appear suddenly in our skies and cities." America's role was to act decisively and autonomously as any passivity would only increase danger. Hence "instead of drifting along toward tragedy, we will set a course toward safety" that would "overcome hatred and violence" and lead to "a new Iraq that is prosperous and free." The narrative established by Bush is one of high stakes where good and evil fight for dominion and where a better future can be won only through taking tough choices. War is unavoidable not because of our qualities, but rather those of our enemies who inhabit the Discourse of Repression so deeply that they can never be trusted, can never limit their ambitions, can never become open, honest, or rational. With them diplomacy and sanctions will always be a waste of time.

From the platform of this inflated genre, low mimetic arguments for an alternative, more multilateral and conciliatory path could be dismissed as unrealistic, as failing to recognize an imminent threat. The neocon Richard Perle pointed out that by passing one resolution after another and not enforcing them the UN was becoming meaningless—in effect it was worthy of satire. It was dismantling itself resolution by resolution and shirking responsibilities. In any case, the United States had a right to self-defense that did not require it to consult the UN. If weapons inspectors had found nothing, this was because Saddam Hussein had duped them. As for the antiwar stance of the French (we review this later), commercial interests and pipeline contracts motivated this. Preemption was needed as it was "possible to wait too long to deal with a known threat" as September 11 had shown (public comments reproduced in www.newamericancentury.org, February 24, 2003). Vice President Dick Cheney weighed into the fray, declaring in an August 26 speech that UN inspections could provide a false sense of security and that Saddam Hussein's WMD provided "as grave a threat as can be imagined" (quoted in Woodward 2003, 344). Condoleezza Rice spoke of the "nightmare" of an "aggressive tyrant" who was "armed with a nuclear weapon" (quoted in Woodward 2003, 350) and, like the president, invoked the imagery of a nuclear holocaust when interviewed by CNN's Wolf Blitzer in September 2002: "We don't want the smoking gun to be a mushroom cloud" (quoted in *Vanity Fair*, May 2004, 282). In the same month former Clinton national security official Kenneth Pollack's (2002) book *The Threatening Storm: The Case for Invading Iraq* was published suggesting that Saddam Hussein was on the verge of acquiring nuclear weapons. A climate of fear and urgency was established.

Curiously, many intellectuals and commentators on the Left defected to the Bush camp. William Shawcross, Christopher Hitchens, and Paul Berman for example, considered the War in Iraq to be a justified strike against intolerance and repression as much as a blow against terror. Shawcross (2003) endorses Bush's understanding of dangerous ties between dictatorships and terrorists and understands Saddam Hussein's regime as offering a Hitler-style threat. Hitchens modified his cynical stance toward the earlier Gulf War (Hitchens 1991). Now he claims that the United States owed the Iraqi people for its previous support of the thuggish Saddam Hussein, and another intervention to remove him could cancel the moral debt. Hitchens (e.g., *The Nation*, August 19, 2002; October 14, 2002) also believed that there really was strong evidence of ties between Iraq and al-Qaeda and that we had entered a point in history where neutrality in the face of dangerous "theocratic and absolutist" versions of Islam was not an option given that the war had now been exported to the United States. For Hitchens a global struggle had been going on for years between jihadist fascists and fanatics and carriers of more universalistic and democratic values including many in the Islamic world. The United States needed to intervene on behalf of the liberal and tolerant good guys. Berman (e.g., op-ed, *Dissent*, Winter 2004) likewise insisted that the spirit of universalism was afoot. Fellow liberals had been blinded by their hostility to George Bush and suspicion of Israel and did not understand that a wider moral issue was at stake. The West needed to liberate Arab people from oppression rather than apply a double standard. This was a crisis situation in which "it is

1943 right now in huge portions of the world and people don't see it . . . war against the radical Islamist and Ba'athist movement, in Afghanistan exactly as in Iraq, is war against fascism."

A substantial portion of the American people believed in the truth of this general vision. Yet efforts to gain international and liberal support required some more clues to be given out that could substantiate the president's reading of Iraq's character and trajectory. Driven in part by Colin Powell's own desire for multilateralism, Bush sent Powell himself into the UN on February 5, 2003. The secretary of state's performance, in which he talked through a number of items of "evidence" of Iraqi WMD including surveillance intercepts, photos, and defector testimony, was narrated in a broadly positive way. Some liberals then moved to support the war, although whether this was due to Powell's reputation or the information he presented is not clear. Like John Major and George Bush at the time of the Gulf War, the moderate Powell was seen as prudent, sane, and realistic. Just as John Major had been praised for eschewing "ersatz Churchilliana," the *New York Times* (editorial, February 6, 2003) noted that Powell had "focused on shaping a sober, factual case" against Iraq. Under the heading "Irrefutable," the *Washington Post* (editorial, February 6, 2003) declared it "hard to imagine how anyone could doubt that Iraq possessed WMD" in the light of the presentation; spoke of the way that Powell's presentation had avoided "histrionics" and would "change all minds open to evidence"; and reported a senior Democrat on the Foreign Relations Committee calling it "powerful and irrefutable" evidence.

Powell's speech was a tipping point for many people. It showed that a respected statesman and so-called reluctant warrior was prepared to endorse the president. Moreover, it provided to the public more clues that WMD, al-Qaeda, and Iraq were all in the same plot. This allowed many to revise their genre guess about Iraq from low mimesis toward apocalypticism. It increased support for an invasion of Iraq perhaps more than the president's own speeches. An ABC News Poll showed that 56 percent of Americans who had watched, considered Powell had presented "hard evidence proving" Iraq had WMD. Support for an invasion of Iraq increased to 63 percent, whereas it had been only 52 percent at the time of Bush's State of the Union a couple of weeks before (*USA Today*, February 10, 2002). By the start of military action on the ground, 54 percent were in favor of using force to remove Saddam Hussein. This was a higher figure than on the eve of Operation Desert Storm, where the nation was divided. This can be attributed to a more strongly endorsed apocalyptic genre. Citizens seemed to believe the scenario of an Iraq/al-Qaeda link that the president had been propagating. Some 53 percent thought that "Saddam Hussein was personally involved in the September 11,

2001, terrorist attacks on the World Trade Center and Pentagon" (CBS/New York Times Poll, April 2003, PollingReport.com) and 88 percent that he was "involved in supporting terrorist groups that have plans to attack the United States" (CNN/USA Today/Gallup Poll, March 2003). Saddam Hussein increasingly seemed to belong in the story and G. W. Bush Jr. enjoyed a 67 percent approval rating (*Time*, March 3, 2003). The crucial votes in Congress were far more emphatic than those on the eve of the internationally legitimate, UN endorsed Gulf War. In the House the vote was 296 to 133, and in the Senate 77 to 23, for a unilateral attack on Iraq.

FROM APOCALYPSE TO TRAGEDY

As in the case of the 1991 Gulf War, Iraq was able to offer little by way of resistance to the overwhelming force arrayed against it. Air and missile attacks were followed by a rolling advance over land that reached Baghdad in a matter of days. Despite this cruise to efficient victory, in the period after hostilities had ceased questions about the legitimacy of the war stayed current—in fact they simply would not go away. Eden and Mollet had gotten into trouble at the time of their invasion of Egypt. After they had pulled out, Suez was a more or less dead issue—politics moved on to new hunting grounds. Nasser was in control, ships kept moving, Britain and France became good world citizens again. With the Gulf War, postconflict questioning and critique eventuated briefly over the abandonment of the repressed Kurds. Once their protection zone had been established this controversy too fizzled out. By and large the Gulf War was seen as a positive achievement. It had removed Saddam Hussein's forces from Kuwait and demonstrated the continuing relevance of the United Nations and international law. In the case of the War in Iraq the debate over events lingered in multiple contexts for months and months. It had been a "good war" only in the sense that Saddam Hussein was removed from power. Yet the UN had not sanctioned the war, it had split the West, WMD that might have confirmed the apocalyptic reading remained elusive. Moreover, troops from the United States, Britain, and a few other countries remained as an occupying force. This military presence kept the issue on the front pages as soldiers continued to die.

Fixing a date for the end of the conflict is a rather arbitrary exercise. Arguably the war never ended. The Iraqi regime did not stick around to surrender but rather melted away. We can suggest some time around April 9, when statues of Saddam were toppled in Baghdad, or April 11 when Iraq's 5th army corps surrendered in Mosul. Or we can point to the final chapter of George Bush's book *We Will Prevail*—the "Top Gun" speech (Bush 2003, 259–63), so called because it was delivered on the USS *Abraham Lincoln*, an aircraft carrier. Bush had arrived by military jet dressed in Navy pilot gear, just like Tom Cruise in the hit movie. Designed to mark the end of large-scale hostilities, the speech provides a heroic account of what had happened and why. American troops had fought "for the cause of liberty and the peace of the world" just as they had done in World War II. Iraq was free of a tyrant and as "images of celebrating Iraqis had shown, its people had chosen liberty." The war had been against a regime and not the nation. Like the Battle of Afghanistan this had been another step in the ongoing fight against terror, with America engaged in "hunting down" enemies of freedom, making a response that had been "focused and deliberate and proportionate to the offense." Now events were on an upswing. There had been a "turning of the tide" in this war, Iraq was being rebuilt, its people were beginning to experience freedom, and democracy was on its way. Bush repeated the story in a speech given at London's banqueting house on November 19, 2003 (in *New York Times*, November 20, 2003). He alluded to World War II and its origins in the appeasement of "aggressive evil," conjured the image terrorists who would "kill by the millions" if they could obtain WMD, and argued that "duty sometimes requires the violent restraint of violent men" with the measured use of force. The positive benefits of this could now be seen. Iraq was on a narrative trajectory toward the Discourse of Liberty as Bush made clear with a series of binary contrasts showing a movement from repression to freedom: "A new Iraqi police force protects the people instead of bullying them. More than 150 Iraqi newspapers are now in circulation, printing what they choose, not what they are ordered. Schools are open with textbooks free of propaganda."

This is a story with several key claims about major characters. America was an avenger and a liberator acting as an agent of the good, bringing perpetrators of evil to justice. The Iraqi people had moved from slavery to freedom and had welcomed their liberation and their liberators. The Iraqi regime had been evil and tied to terrorism and WMD programs. Those who endorsed this view applauded. For them Bush was the man who had played a Big Inning strategy in his "momentous decision to take out Saddam" bolstered by his religious faith and unwavering determination (*Newsweek*, April 9, 2003). He had demonstrated his autonomy by becoming the man who had pushed his agenda and had displayed "real leadership." He was a "wizard . . . waving his wand over history" (*Time*, April 21, 2003). As for the Iraqis they had greeted the arrival of U.S. troops by "chanting anti-Saddam slogans" and "dancing in the streets" (*Newsweek*, April 9, 2003) thus endorsing the magician's vision.

Many considered that the reality was otherwise on each of these points and that Bush and his supporters had made a seriously erroneous genre guess. From June 2003 onward we find rapidly growing levels of comment on inconsistencies between "facts" and the official narrative of the war. First up, "Saddam's weapons of mass destruction and his ties to the terrorists of Al-Qaeda" were "proving elusive" and justifications had "evaporated like water in the desert sun" (Salon.com, July 31, 2003). Bush had established a climate of expectation before the war when hints about secret intelligence reports had been made. After the liberation of Iraq all would be able to review the classified evidence. WMD would be found, the secret intelligence would be made public, and we would see that Bush had been right all along. Nothing materialized. Week after week they searched and day after day the seekers could only confirm the story that UN inspectors had been telling during the buildup to the war: there was nothing to report. The apocalyptic scenario started to look like a convenient lie and many critics noted the Bush administration shifting the goalposts to talk about WMD "programs" (which could be little more than wish lists and calculations on scraps of paper) rather than clear and present dangers.

Although this WMD question was to prove a central theme in the genre wars of the United Kingdom (reviewed below), it was less important in the United States than motifs relating to the war's more concrete aftermath in occupied Iraq. Pivotal to the worldview of the true believer in liberty is an understanding that a liberated people will welcome their liberators. If love of liberty is a natural law, then all people should celebrate freedom spontaneously. If America was indeed the bringer of liberty, then the Iraqi people should welcome American troops. Such unprompted actions of the Iraqis could be taken as evidence that two of the identities pivotal to George W. Bush's narrative, those of the "liberators" and the "oppressed," really were the ones we should be using to think through what was going on. As Bush himself had put it in the Top Gun speech: "everywhere that freedom arrives, humanity rejoices." Bush's problem was that such activity was patchy and that other responses to liberty seemed to prevail. The high-water mark for Bush's story was the combined efforts of crowds and U.S. Marines to topple a statue of Saddam Hussein. There was also some celebration in the streets on and around April 9, 2003. Little else fit the picture. Looting broke out in Baghdad and other cities, including theft and destruction of archaeological treasures. Sporadic firefights continued throughout Iraq. As early as April 18, 2003, thousands of Iraqis protested at the U.S. occupation. Efforts were made to interpret such actions as a collective effervescence arising from liberation. When challenged over who was in control in Iraq, White House spokesman Ari Fleischer replied, "The taste of freedom" (quoted in *Time*, April 21, 2003). A few days later such a response might have looked glib. On April 28, U.S. troops killed thirteen angry demonstrators and wounded seventy-five others.

As the summer of 2003 dragged on and one negative event followed another, civil discourse organized around a familiar and unsettling narrative. Scattered insurgencies and ambushes were killing American troops every day, their names and photographs displayed in silence at the end of the PBS news broadcast each evening. By November more had died after the end of major hostilities than in the war proper. In this new scenario America was an occupying power in a place where it was not wanted, a place that did not really matter for its strategic interests, a place full of ungrateful fanatics that was costing American lives and dollars—a place a lot like Vietnam. America had won the war but was losing the peace. Its soldiers were trying hard but were let down by incompetent politicians. The political leaders in Washington seemed to have no real plans for getting American troops out of a country where perhaps they should never have gone in the first place. How and when could they be brought home and out of danger? This new narrative was in the tragic genre. Themes of descent abounded. There was empathic pathos for the soldiers and a sense that poor choices that were avoidable had been made. This new, tragic narrative had appeal across the spectrum from so-called peaceniks to Wilsonian moralists to isolationists of the Right although each had their own understanding of just what was tragic about the situation.

We find this vision of disillusion taking center stage, for example, in *Newsweek*, the magazine that we saw in April 2003 pointing to dancing in the streets and heralding President Bush's leadership skills. By July there was a different mood in its pages. "As the death toll for Americans goes up day by day and folks back home are having to think about what it means to fight what's by now acknowledged to be a guerilla war," wrote their columnist Christopher Dickey, "you're starting to hear comparisons with the long, soul-destroying counterinsurgency in Vietnam. Well Iraq could be even worse" (*Newsweek*, July 24, 2003). He goes on to talk of "blunders and indecisiveness," which had led to a country with no indigenous army, police, or bureaucracy and a power vacuum that made the United States look like an army of occupation seeking to dismember the Iraqi state. Writing in the same magazine just after back-to-back tours had been announced Colonel Mike Turner, former assistant to Gulf War hero General Norman Schwarzkopf, drew a series of parallels between the War in Iraq and in Indochina. In both cases there had been "overblown and distorted threat assessments," unilateral actions without international backing, politicians with their "tragically simplistic and naïve view." Turner's vision is of soldiers being used by incompetent politicians and an unnecessary invasion that would only foster terrorism (*Newsweek*, September 12, 2003).

The *New York Times Magazine* cover story of November 2 pushed this line of thinking in a more analytic and forensic direction. According to the author, David Rieff, there had only been a "blueprint for a mess" that had originated in "blinkered vision and overoptimistic assumptions" among Bush's advisors that had led them to reject more negative scenarios out of hand. These included thinking that Ahmad Chalabi, the leader of the exiled Iraqi National Congress, would be a popular figure in a liberated Iraq, underestimating the amount of looting, and having no contingency plans for dealing with widespread civil disorder. One is reminded here of Colin Powell's (1995, 527) comment that it was naive to think that "if Saddam had fallen" in 1991, he "would have been replaced by a Jeffersonian in some sort of desert democracy where people read *The Federalist Papers* along with the Koran." Such wishful thinking was said to be the product of the unrealistic neocon worldview with its dualistic vision of freedom and constraint, and its illusory belief that Saddam Hussein's evil and America's bona fides would be perceived as such by the ordinary people of Iraq. The image here, then, is an ironic one of incompetence and faulty reason. In terms of the discourse of civil society this theme of incompetence was a mild rebuke—but a rebuke all the same that chipped away at the *post facto* legitimacy of the war.

For critics even further to the Left, the tragic narrative was intensified into a melodramatic form in which the United States had done more than simply let down its soldiers—it had also betrayed the ordinary decent people of Iraq and the Middle East and been an active villain rather than a misguided idiot. The justification for the war had been phony, President Bush deceitful. The war had been about oil and political hegemony. Such a strategy had derailed the peace process in Israel and jeopardized future peace by generating ill will and resentment that would boomerang into future support for al-Qaeda and other groups like it. Evidence for the truth of this counternarration could be seen in Iraqi resistance to the U.S. occupation, America's interminably slow handover to the UN or Iraqi self-rule, and the fact that fat contracts had been handed out to U.S. corporations for rebuilding Iraq. The Leftist commentator Columbia University professor Edward Said neatly captures this logic for our purposes (op-ed, *The Observer*, April 20, 2003). Here Said spins a Chomskyesque narrative in which it is America that is the world's biggest villain, who threatens world peace, and is engaged in terrorism. This is the strategy of inversion (P. Smith 1991) that we have already seen used to undermine war. Said argues that America's War in Afghanistan had used high-altitude bombing, a technique that resembled "ordinary terrorism in its effects and structure"; that it had tried to "push" the UN into compliance; that "dissent disappeared" from the media; that treatments of Saddam Hussein had overlooked U.S. complicity in the 1980s with his regime; and that he had been accused of having WMD "without proof or with fraudulent information." This had been a "failure in democracy" masterminded by "reactionary Washington institutions" and a president who "looks like a cowboy." The victims of this were the ordinary people of Afghanistan, Iraq, Palestine, and the United States—the very people, we remember, that Bush had sworn to protect from the Axis of Evil. They had been betrayed by leaders who could be typified in terms of the Discourse of Repression as nonrational, motivated by a desire for power, and governing through deceit and force and not consent. Bush, in effect, was like Saddam Hussein and the war therefore pointless and irresponsible. These more radical criticisms did not propagate with much success. Conservative critics counterattacked with the Discourse of Repression suggesting that the "blame America first crowd" was back in town. It had an essentially nonrational, unrealistic understanding of events. Superficial reasoning masked a "perplexing animosity toward the United States" and "an atavistic reflex that jerks the knees of too many on the Left" (Richard Cohen, *Washington Post*, May 8, 2003).

As in the Gulf War those on the far Right also had objections. These centered on a narrow noninterventionist vision of America's interests. They did not "blame America first" but rather suggested that America had been hijacked. Paramount once again was Pat Buchanan and a magazine titled *The American Conservative*. Buchanan's argument was that American policy had been captured by neocons with strong ties to Israel. The war was being fought to further Israel's needs, not those of the United States. Buchanan asserted that a "cabal of polemicists and public officials seek to ensnare our country in a series of wars that are not in America's interests"; that President Bush had been "lured into a trap" baited by these neocons; that these people had exploited September 11 to "steer America's rage into an all-out war to destroy their despised enemies," most of whom had nothing to do with al-Qaeda but a lot to do with hostility to Israel, they wanted to "conscript American blood to make the world safe for Israel" (*The American Conservative*, March 24, 2003). Buchanan's vision is one of well-intentioned people being dragged by underhand conspirators into an unnecessary and incendiary war. In Buchanan's reading what was needed was a more cautious, low mimesis driven foreign policy based on prudent and close calculation of the national interest and not "endless wars on the Islamic world."

Pat Buchanan was not the only person to point the finger at the neoconservative elite using motifs of conspiracy. At the Web site Antiwar.com we find columnist and intellectual Paul Craig Roberts working hard to identify good and bad politicians in accounting for and critiquing the war. Colin Powell had been "deceived into lying to the United Nations" and "ruthlessly used by neocon administration officials"; Bush had been "deceived and trapped in a war of attrition"; "Fear created by neocon lies caused Congress to emasculate itself"; and the media had been manipulated into spreading war propaganda. Roberts sees the war as an unnecessary act that had been waged for false reasons. Its costs included $200 billion wasted, Iraqi and American lives lost, damage to American alliances, and a new wave of recruits for bin Laden (Antiwar.com, November 17, 2003). He envisages a truly apocalyptic scenario will eventuate *only if* the neocons cannot be stopped. This will involve a "jihad against Islam" using small nuclear bombs against Damascus, Tehran, Baghdad, Mecca, Cairo, and Mogadishu in a "final solution to their Muslim problem" (Antiwar.com, October 27, 2003).

THE NARRATIVE CRISIS OF 2004

In 2003, efforts to undermine Bush's vision of apocalyptic struggle and heroic liberation had been creative and determined but had not gotten too far. This was to change in 2004. By the start of that year the failure of the search for Iran's WMD became finally and decisively evident. A pivotal moment came when David Kay, who had been leading the Iraq Survey Group hunt resigned and told the U.S. Senate Armed Services Committee that Iraq seemed to have no stockpiles or credible WMD programs. It now seemed clear to many that the Bush administration had indeed got the genre wrong. It had been a mistake to insert Iraq into the apocalyptic drama when al-Qaeda was the lone villain. Although "undeniably eager to make Iraq a threatening world power" the Iraqi leader was toothless (editorial, *New York Times*, January 11, 2004). His rocket plans existed only on two compact disks, his biological weapons appeared to have been destroyed in 1991, and he had almost no nuclear program. The *New York Times* (editorial, January 11, 2004) concluded that inspections and multilateralism could have done the job. Drawing on the Discourse of Repression it asserted that the "Bush administration's obsession with the Iraqi dictator" had "warped the American intelligence reports that did so much to convince Congress and the public that the attack was justified," and that there had been a "reckless rush to invade Iraq." Whereas Bush Sr. had once been on the ropes because he had switched genres too early from apocalypse to a hardheaded but mean-spirited worldview, Bush Jr. seemed to have gotten it wrong all along in interpreting Iraq. This, of course, is the danger of apocalypticism. When prophecy fails one looks like a scaremonger and hysteric. One can also look like the bully who tried to force incorrect views on others. The *Carnegie Endowment for International Peace* (2003) for example, issued a report in which it claimed the administration had put pressure on intelligence to remove caveats and doubts and to focus on higher-end estimates of danger.

If others saw Bush as the advocate of a misleading genre, the president's discursive response was to try to position himself as the fact finder. In this new narrative he was the person who had been misled by poor intelligence and given the wrong clues, and not the overeager leader who had pushed weak data into preconceived molds. Taking a bet each way he called for an independent and bipartisan inquiry into the failures of prewar intelligence, and simultaneously reiterated how bad Saddam Hussein had been: "I want all the facts . . . Saddam Hussein had the intent and capabilities to cause great harm . . . he slaughtered thousands of people" (reported in *Times*, February 2, 2004). The inquiry bought him time and Bush got off lightly. In Britain similar concerns over evidence and interpretation created a political life and death struggle for Tony Blair.

As the year of 2004 wore on uprisings in the cities of Fallujah and Najaaf and resistance led by the Islamic cleric Muqtada al-Sadr suggested that peace and democracy were a long way off and that the foreign liberators were not welcome. Photographs of U.S. soldiers torturing and humiliating Iraqi prisoners in Saddam Hussein's former jail were released, providing fuel for the claim that there was little moral distance between America and Iraq— the liberators were just a new set of oppressors. A bestselling book by former "counter-terrorism Czar" Dick Clarke (2004) suggested that the Bush administration's fixation on Iraq had led it to ignore and underestimate the danger of al-Qaeda and that it had been asleep at the wheel on the day of 9/11. This perception was reinforced by the hearings of the Senate 9/11 Commission, which sustained the impression that the White House had gone needlessly apocalyptic over Iraq but had failed to read al-Qaeda correctly, treating it as a routine, manageable threat before 9/11 and failing to implement the radical structural reforms needed to track this new form of danger. In effect it had been wrongly low mimetic over al-Qaeda and should have inflated that danger earlier.

It would be misleading to say that in the United States the once-prevalent apocalyptic reading came to be falsified in any clear sense. Advocates remained for this position, insisting that sooner or later Iraq and terror would have gotten together—or contending that they already had in secret—and pointing to missing quantities of WMD from the early 1990s. For an increasing majority of people, however, it came to look as if Bush had made the wrong reading. Al-Qaeda remained a threat of immeasurable proportions, but Saddam Hussein did not seem to belong in the same story frame. The clues had been wrongly assembled. The result was a nation torn between two genre choices over Iraq. We see this pattern playing out toward the end of 2004 in the presidential election. Although voting patterns closely mirrored those of 2000 and exit polls suggested that so-called moral values had played a decisive role in voter choice, the dominant issues in the election campaigning were the War on Terror and the War in Iraq and in particular whether these were separable. In two of the three nationally televised presidential debates, President George W. Bush and his challenger Senator John Kerry hammered away at each other on this theme, question after question. The candidates differed on whether Iraq and Saddam Hussein belonged as characters in the same story as the terrorist group, on the genre that should have been applied to Iraq in the period before the war, on which genre should be used to narrate ongoing events in postwar Iraq, and they further competed to be the most apocalyptic interpreter al-Qaeda. The result was a layered discursive field of surprising complexity. An analysis of the transcripts (Commission on Presidential Debates 2004) shows Kerry's genre politics involving the following claims: (1) Bush had failed to be sufficiently and consistently apocalyptic about the al-Qaeda threat. In effect he had not inflated his genre and consequent policies enough when it came to reading these evils, even after 9/11. Kerry told the studio and television audience that the president had even stated that he was "not that concerned" about bin Laden (debate, October 13, 2004). When Osama bin Laden was surrounded in the mountains of Tora Bora, Afghanistan, the president had "outsourced the job" to "Afghan warlords" rather than committing American troops—the "best trained in the world"— to the task (debate, September 30, 2004). Bin Laden had escaped. This kind of "colossal error of judgment" showed that Bush was not the kind of leader we could trust to deal with apocalyptic dangers and so protect the American people. (2) Moreover, the president had brought the wrong players into the storyline and onto the stage. Consequently, he had made the grave error of diverting "attention from the real war on terror in Afghanistan against Osama bin Laden and taking it off to Iraq where the 9/11 Commission confirms there was no connection to 9/11 itself" (debate, September 30, 2004). The president had taken his "eye off the ball" (debate, October 8, 2004) and so there were "10 times the numbers of forces in Iraq than we have in Afghanistan chasing Osama bin Laden" (debate, October 8, 2004). Thinking back to an analogy in the first chapter, Kerry's claim is in effect that Bush had wrongly put the waterlogged scraps of paper with the words Saddam Hussein into the same pile as those with al-Qaeda on them. Yet in reality "Iraq was not even close to the center of the war on terror" (debate, September 30, 2004). (3) There was no immediate danger from Iraq itself for "we had Saddam Hussein trapped" (debate, September 30, 2004), yet the president had "rushed to war" (debate, October 8, 2004). The correct reading of the Iraqi situation in 2002 or 2003 should have been low mimetic. This would have meant working with the United Nations, building an international coalition, and using inspections and sanctions to enforce compliance. Because Iraq was not part of any apocalyptic script this was not a war of last resort. (4) The upshot of all this was an ongoing scenario in Iraq that needed to be narrated in the tragic voice. Here was a lamentable story where wrong and avoidable choices—"the President didn't make the right judgments" (debate, October 8, 2004)—had led to negative outcomes. Some $200 billion had been spent on Iraq that could have been used for "health care, for schools, for construction, for prescription drugs for seniors" (debate, September 30, 2004). American troops were dying: "More in July than June. More in August than July. More in September than August," and yet still there were "terrorists pouring over the border" and into Iraq (debate, September 30, 2004). Prime Minister Allawi was "like a puppet" (debate, September 30, 2004), and the world was "more dangerous" (debate, September 30, 2004). America had ended up carrying the major burden of responsibility in Iraq due its violation of the Pottery Barn principle (You break it, you own it), and its failure to work with other countries and thus share the costs. In summary, Kerry's claim was that the president was unfit to rule because he had been too genre deflated in his orientation toward al-Qaeda, overly inflated toward Iraq, and had therefore generated a situation of ongoing tragedy.

As might be expected, President Bush's counterinterpretation was simple in its message but also robust in its structure. Iraq belonged in the apocalyptic scenario because "the war on terror is to make sure that these terrorist organizations do not end up with weapons of mass destruction" (debate, October 8, 2004). In other words all potential helpers of terrorism belonged in the plot. Kerry's belief that "resolutions and failed inspections would make this world a more peaceful place" was a "pre-September 10th mentality" (debate, September 30, 2004) that was "naïve and dangerous" (debate, October 8, 2004). The president referred to a statement by Kerry that "terrorism could be reduced to a nuisance." This was also "dangerous" (debate, October 13, 2004). In short the challenger was being unrealistic because he was insufficiently aware of the apocalyptic threats of terror and thought they could be managed in routine ways. Further, he could not lead in a situation of impending doom because he was a poor interpreter of the world. A flip-flopper without deep convictions to guide his thinking, Kerry was unable to decide how to read events. As a result he would "send mixed signals to our troops, our friends, the Iraqi citizens," and this would weaken resolve in the face of danger (debate, September 30, 2004). As for Iraq and Afghanistan, we were seeing clues that could be assembled into a romantic genre guess not a tragic one. Iraq was "going from tyranny to elections" and reconstruction efforts were "beginning to take hold" (debate October 8, 2004). Saddam Hussein now "sits in a prison cell" (debate, September 30, 2004), while Iraqi forces were being retrained to "fight for their own freedom" (debate, September 30, 2004). The Taliban were "no longer in power" (debate, September 30, 2004). "Ten million people" had "registered to vote in Afghanistan" (debate, September 30, 2004), and the "first voter was a 19 year old woman" (debate, October 13, 2004).

Bush and Kerry were going head to head over the interpretation of the War in Iraq a year and a half after its end had been rather prematurely called. After a slow start dissent had finally moved from the periphery to the absolute center of the attention space.

These contending narrative visions were to appear again and again over the following months. Iraqi elections were held at the end of January 2005. President Bush was buoyed by the strong turnout and evoked themes of ascent when he spoke in a White House press release (January 30, 2005) of the "brave patriots" who had stepped forward as candidates and of the Iraqi people who had "rejected the anti-democratic ideology of the terrorists." Yet his critics continued to point to evidence of more problematic and negative outcomes rather than making an optimistic prognosis. Themes of descent could still be conjured into relevance because by this point in time around 1,500 Americans had died in Iraq, there were an estimated 200,000 rebels against the occupation in a widespread insurgency, suicide bombings were an almost daily occurrence and an eventual civil war was a possibility if Shiites and Sunnis were unable to cooperate in the new state or if Iran were to stir the pot. So in the United States the year 2005 brought more questions than answers in the matter of how to interpret the War in Iraq. In Britain, as we are about to see, such intense and widespread genre contestation could be found much earlier than it had in the United States, with boiling point attained in the middle of 2003.

BRITAIN AND THE WAR IN IRAQ

Britain's policy with respect to the War in Iraq depended to a great extent on the decisions of Tony Blair, the prime minister. He was confronted with the difficult choice of following the United States as a loyal ally or joining with Britain's European neighbors. His decision to team up with America and push the apocalyptic wheelbarrow was to cause perhaps the greatest crises and embarrassments of his lengthy administration. Separated from the events of 9/11 by the Atlantic Ocean, the case against Iraq was to be a tougher sell than it was for Bush. I have suggested that the momentum of the terrorist attacks on September 11, refracted through narrative embellishments and magnified by collective effervescence, gave President Bush's visions of impending Armageddon visceral resonance and immediacy. In the United Kingdom, in contrast, Blair had to confront to the full the inertial weight of a low mimetic genre that was well entrenched in the civil discourse even of his own party. There eventuated relentless questioning, calls for hard evidence and common sense, and talk of war as a last resort. Trying to bring about a decisive genre shift to apocalypticism became the major goal of Blair's discourse. These ponderous efforts became the millstone that burdened this usually confident swimmer of political waters and left him struggling to stay afloat. To understand exactly why this outcome resulted we need to turn back the clock and look at Tony Blair's rise to power.

Elected in 1997 against a Tory force led by the "grey" John Major, the youthful and modestly charismatic Tony Blair had been the savior of the British Labour Party. Dubbed "New Labour" and guided by the "Third Way" philosophies of sociologist Anthony Giddens that claimed to put pragmatics before ideology, Blair's party retained only a vestigial attachment to the state redistributive mechanisms it had historically championed. The lesson had been taken from Margaret Thatcher that market friendly policies encouraging capitalist investment and rewarding individual choice, achievement, and effort were the route to economic prosperity and electoral success. Taking this path had required Blair to engage in some momentous policy decisions that amounted, in effect, to a U-turn in the identity of his own party. During the Thatcher years Labour had been kept out of power partly by the efficient Conservative machine and partly by its own rifts and vulnerabilities. The traditional Left wing, what was often referred to in the press as a "Loony Left," had continued to advocate unilateral nuclear disarmament, nationalized industries, tax hikes, and close alliances with so-called militant trades unions. It had also opposed all wars, including a broadly popular one against an Argentine military dictatorship over the Falkland Islands (see P. Smith 1991). These were not electable policies. The Labour Party lost the support of the upwardly mobile working and lower middle classes as Thatcher transformed them into homeowners and shareholders, winners and investors in the game of life rather than losers and grumblers—a much more attractive subject position.

Considerable blame for this electoral failure could also be placed on the press, which had crucified the 1980s Labour leaders. The intellectually gifted but politically rather inept Michael Foot was lampooned as a feckless, absent-minded, donkey-jacket wearing, Campaign for Nuclear Disarmament—loving, head in the sand, disheveled professor type. His successor, the simultaneously affable and earnest Neil Kinnock, was dismissed as an anorak-wearing, pompous Welsh windbag. Neither was understood as having the strength of character needed to tame the Loony Left. Looking disciplined and professional like the Tories, with their pinstripe suits and Saatchi groomed profile came to be seen as equally important for retaining power as having low-tax, pro-achievement policies. Building on the work of his immediate predecessor (the potentially electable John Smith who had died while leader of the opposition) Blair moved the party to the Right. He endorsed the Third Way and gave top priority to relations with the media and image control.

For a time this approach seemed to work. A romantic narrative gave Blair an extended political honeymoon. An upbeat Britain became, for a brief spell, a "Cool Britannia" of energy and chic. Blair and his Third Way policies were touted as the fresh face of socialism throughout Europe. This early Blair was seen as an ethical man. He was understood as a Christian who was guided by principles in contrast to John Major's Tories whose "Back to Basics" morality politics had been exposed as hypocritical in a wave of partly amusing, partly just sleazy scandals.

This romance started to falter around 2000. Critics noted that Blair had failed to deliver on basic promises with respect to improving efficiency in public services and that his administration was seemingly more concerned with style than substance. This view found its analogue in two collective representations. The first was the Millennium Dome, a white elephant project designed to celebrate the arrival of the year 2000 that looked good from a distance but whose exhibits were universally derided as vacuous and patronizing when scrutinized. Opportunities for parallels with New Labour were too tempting for commentators to resist. The second icon was Peter Mandelson, a shadowy figure and so-called master of spin said to have great influence with the prime minister but little public accountability. Mandelson was deeply unpopular with the electorate and eventually resigned after a scandal. As Blair entered his second term these kinds of accusations grew and symbolic pollution in terms of the Discourse of Repression started to set in. Many came to see him as too presidential and too slick. "Phony Tony" had surrounded himself with a kitchen cabinet of deferential advisors and spin-doctors who ruthlessly enforced party discipline. Number 10 was said to trash party dissidents in underhanded ways and to disdain Labour's grassroots support. There was a growing tide of feeling that the still popular Blair and his Third Way philosophies had less to do with the stated agendas of New Labour and more to do with retaining personal power at all costs (Begg 2003). It was against this background that Tony Blair had to justify Britain's involvement in a war against Iraq. It was a cultural environment that saw his claims microscopically examined for both spin and sincerity.

So far as Blair's decision to attack Iraq goes, the die were probably cast quite early. We find him sitting in Congress as an honored guest at George W. Bush's September 20, 2001, address. This was the very moment when the U.S. administration's apocalyptic genre choice is formally announced to the world. Blair's allegiance to the United States locked him into advocacy of a series of claims as the buildup to the War in Iraq progressed that he might perhaps not have made of his own volition: that WMD existed, that terrorists had ties to Saddam Hussein and, most controversial of all, that there was an imminent threat of attack. Blair repeatedly made claims on these only to see them repeatedly disputed. Events during 2002 and 2003 took the following form. Blair or one of his ministers would make a statement, which they would say was based on intelligence that was a little murky but which generally indicated evil doings and bad intent. They would call for trust given that all the intelligence could not be revealed and ask for support for war given the Pascalian wager at hand. Not convinced, skeptics asked for a smoking gun showing irrefutable proof of an immediate danger. Blair's government would then produce a public intelligence document that contained only circumstantial evidence, much of it more relevant to the past evils of Saddam Hussein than his present activities. This would be attacked as inadequate and the cycle would continue.

And so it was that with the all the brio of a farmer walking over a wet clay field in Wellington boots, Blair plugged on with efforts to spread a message of truly apocalyptic gloom and an associated clarion call to arms. This is most clearly stated in a section of his speech to the House of Commons of March 18, 2003. The "threat is chaos," he said, that originates in "tyrannical regimes with WMD and extreme terrorist groups who profess a perverted and false view of Islam" (Hansard, March 18, 2003). These were expanding. There were already "terrorist cells now operating in most major countries," and "countries or groups within countries that are proliferating and trading in WMD, especially nuclear weapons technology." According to Blair, "the possibility of the two coming together—of terrorist groups in possession of WMD" is "a real and present danger." The true shock of September 11 was the knowledge that "had the terrorists been able to, there would have been not 3,000 innocent dead but 30,000 or 300,000." Blair goes on: "Three kilograms of VX from a rocket launcher would contaminate a quarter of a square kilometer of a city. Millions of lethal doses are contained in one liter of Anthrax. 10,000 liters are unaccounted for." The vision is of shady enemies and corrupt regimes and the destruction of cities by those who are opposed to freedom, order, and pluralism. There was a need to act decisively against "tyrannies and dictatorships and terrorists," to stand firm, to transform the UN into something more than a "talking shop" and to liberate the Iraqi people.

BLAIR UNDER SIEGE

If widely accepted this vision was never truly hegemonic. To the contrary, it was vigorously contested even (perhaps especially) by Labour's own supporters. On February 15, 2003, over a million people marched in London against the war. On February 26, 2003, 121 Labour MPs went against their leader after a heated debate on the war. A total of 198 MPs voted for an amendment that the case for war was "as yet unproven." A humiliated Blair was able to survive only thanks to the support of the rival Conservative Party. The situation became worse for the prime minister. Following a Bush/Blair summit in the Azores in March 2003, where it became clear that war was inevitable, he was hit by mass dissent in his party. Although a motion for war passed in the Commons by 412 to 149, some 139 Labour MPs voted against their party. Three ministers resigned, including the Leader of the House, Robin Cook. Familiar Labour mavericks (survivors of the "loony left") made their mark. George Galloway spoke of imperialism and Anglo-American aggression and called British arms workers to acts of sabotage. The charismatic veteran Tony Benn flew to Baghdad and conducted a television interview with Saddam Hussein. Cabinet Minister Clare Short threatened to resign and suggested that a war without UN sanction was "reckless." Further notable opposition came from Britain's political Cinderella, the Liberal Democrat Party whose leader Charles Kennedy spoke out against unilateralism and drew telling, widely quoted analogies to the blunders of Suez.

What was the narrative genre of these critics? Operating from a low mimetic perspective they were concerned about the United Kingdom following international law, about the availability of evidence and information, about the proper consultation of parliamentary and military opinion, and about the need to take measured and prudent steps. This is the bank manager's worldview, not that of John of Patmos, albeit one tinged with the worry that Blair was slipping toward the Discourse of Repression and that events might eventually turn tragic. It is neatly captured in the Commons debate of February 26

(Hansard). There was disquiet expressed at the seeming inevitability of the conflict. Donald Anderson, Labour MP and Chairman of the Foreign Affairs Committee, voiced his apprehension that Britain was in a "phony peace. War drums are rolling and I approach the next few weeks with a deep sense of foreboding." Likewise, former Minister John Gummer claimed that it was a "war by timetable and the timetable was laid down long before the US had any intention of going to the UN," and MP Alan Simpson (Labour) that the government seemed to be "looking for a pretext for war rather than an avoidance of one." Several found it problematic to be following a "born-again, Right wing, fundamentalist Republican administration" (George Galloway, Labour), an "unappetizing US administration" that was a "bad world citizen, bad on global warming, bad on international criminal courts, bad on steel tariffs" (Gerald Kaufman, Labour).

Some even understood Blair in a more satiric mode. He was the well-intentioned man who was a little out of touch with the harsher realities of life. This line of thinking was a relic of earlier discourses that had dogged Blair's Third Way platform as a set of empty mantras, hopelessly unrealistic, and dodging difficult choices with the kind of wishful thinking that suggested you could have your cake and eat it on any difficult issue: taxation versus growth, public education versus private schools, rewarding achievement versus preventing inequality, and so forth. In this collective representation Blair was depicted as confused and bumbling. As an editor of the *Washington Post* put it in the *Daily Telegraph,* his problem "isn't that he can't make up his mind between Europe and America, or between multilateralism and the transatlantic alliance. The problem is that he still doesn't believe he will ever really have to make a choice" (*Daily Telegraph,* March 30, 2003). In some ways this discourse worked to Blair's advantage. As he was not deeply polluted, most of Blair's critics were prepared to give him the benefit of the doubt as to his intentions if not his actions. Symptomatic here is an article in the *Guardian* that contrasted a potential war in Iraq with Suez and noted a key difference: "Eden was dishonest, while Mr Blair is not. The Tory Prime Minister's 72-hour war was based on a lie" (*Guardian,* January 15, 2003). A year later a different story would be told.

Despite such critique in early 2003, many supported Blair—some of them outside his own party. The *Daily Telegraph,* a reliable index of right-of-center opinion, went along with the case for war, quibbling only over the blunders of Blair's management of this and ready and willing to introduce a broader range of factors into the mix. "Ridding the world of Saddam Hussein would be an act of humanity. It is leaving him there that is inhumane," it wrote (February 16, 2003). The Conservative MP Sir Patrick Cormack echoed this pattern so familiar from Suez and the Gulf War of the need to uphold the "credibility of the international order" and to "stand up against evil" (Hansard, February 26, 2003).

The war itself was an easy victory and one can imagine an alternate history in which Blair basked in glory. It had been a comparative cakewalk without costly military engagements. The doomsayers had been seemingly proven wrong. Indeed poll data showed Blair enjoying a brief "Baghdad Bounce." The cut-price removal of the unpopular Iraqi dictator started to look like a smart move. Blair had a 49 percent approval rating in April 2003—a significant gain from frosty lows in the 30s he had endured in February—and 64 percent of respondents said that it had been right to take military action (*Times*, April 14, 2003). So Blair might have been understood as making the right call and averting an eventual apocalypse at very low cost. This did not happen. Here is the irony: the very ease of the victory suggested that his genre guess had been wrong. There had been no evidence of WMD, no sign of a powerful military or desperate Baathist regime. Saddam Hussein had kept a low profile and then disappeared. Opposition had, for the most part, melted away. When the hunt for WMD turned up nothing, Blair had to endure a horribly bumpy ride. This can be understood as a kind of postmortem asking how an avoidable war had happened and why an incorrect interpretation had been made and then so enthusiastically endorsed.

From as early as April 2003 onward Blair's retrospective justifications and statements were beset by the most withering scrutiny. In America Bush could still be emphatic about the apocalypse around the corner and was permitted by public opinion to continue to tell scary stories. Blair by contrast had to make concessions to the entrenched low mimetic genre because he was playing off the back foot to a rather skeptical audience who knew well his reputation for spin management. His defensive posture required him to add the weight of facts to his discourse of crisis, in effect to painstakingly explain what clues he had had and how he had interpreted them. Blair revealed more openly than Bush that the picture was not fully transparent and that he had taken a measured genre guess or wager rather than made a definitive reading. Bush did not tell us he was interpreting what was happening, he told us what was happening. So Blair told us he had to guess in order to do his job, albeit in a way informed by clues of sorts. As Robert Reich, the U.S. Secretary of Labor under Clinton, perceptively observed (op-ed, *The Observer*, August 3, 2003), these differences were revealed in press conferences delivered at the end of July 2003. Bush spoke of fighting tyranny, hunting down Saddam Hussein, and the fact that the war would be vindicated by history. Only two of the following questions concerned the accuracy of prewar intelligence. Blair's presentation was about domestic policy. He talked to charts about results in economic and schooling spheres but was hit "with a barrage of questions about whether he's quitting because of the flare up over intelligence." Reich observes the Americans did not "care much about the details of Bush's strategy" so long as he was acting decisively.

Blair's confessional voice got him into trouble. Consider his speech at the Labour Party Conference, held that year in the genteel seaside resort of Bournemouth. Here the prime minister tried to explain why he had taken the country to war. Engaging his fireside chat mode, he invites the listener to identify not with his vision of evil and redemption but with his uncertainty and his vision of war as risk aversion, he contrasts "intelligence" to "fact" and points to interpretative choices: "Imagine you are PM. And you receive this intelligence. And not just about Iraq. But about the whole murky trade in WMD. And one thing we know. Not from intelligence. But from historical fact. That Saddam's regime has not just developed but used such weapons gassing thousands of his own people. . . . So what do I do? Say 'I've got the intelligence but I've a hunch its wrong?'" (quoted in *Observer*, October 5, 2003). The recognition that the facts required interpretive leaps of faith led in turn not to applause for honesty but to discussions of spin and authorship that generated unsympathetic resonance from Blair's ongoing reputation as a master of image control and public relations. Had the evidence been hyped up? Who had written vital briefing documents—was it the Ministry of Defense or Downing Street? The murky information came to be seen as managed rather than honestly and openly interpreted and debated. And so Blair was to become bogged down in mind-numbingly detailed discussions of dossiers and briefings, of who said what to whom, on who had written what and where and when. This was to continue long after the end of large-scale conflict in Iraq (see for example the interview of Blair in *Observer*, July 6, 2003). Certain emblems became iconic collective representations or totems in this discourse. One of these was the so-called Dodgy Dossier on Iraq released by Downing Street in February 2003 to help make the case for war. It was quickly discovered that members of Alastair Campbell's Downing Street communications team had plagiarized large parts from an academic source. The government conceded that the production of the document had been a "Horlicks"—a public school kind of term roughly equivalent to "dog's breakfast"—and that the academic sources should have been credited. The *Daily Telegraph* (editorial, February 8, 2003) commented sadly: "Once again the No. 10 culture of spin is undermining a perfectly good case." Questions persisted. These asked whether Blair had misled the house with the document and his claims to have had "fresh intelligence" were false given that much of the material presented was already in the public domain.

As WMD still failed to materialize and links to terrorism proved elusive the scrutiny of claims intensified. When the government started to shift the goalposts in May and June 2003 and talk about evidence of weapons "programs" and the moral evil of Saddam Hussein's regime, critics instantly noticed the disjunction between this set of justifications and those that had led to the war. Blair faced increasing pressure for a judicial inquiry into the case for the war and how it had been made.

As this hullabaloo died down critics zeroed in on a claim in a government document of September 24, 2002, that WMD could be launched within forty-five minutes. To be precise the claim in the document had been: "Iraq's military forces are able to use chemical and biological weapons. . . . The Iraqi military are able to deploy these weapons within 45 minutes of a decision to do so" (British Government 2002, 18). This claim was not attributed to a source but was inserted along with other, less controversial statements about Iraq's ballistic missile programs and read in the context of a foreword from Tony Blair hinting that the government held more cards than it could reveal for "we cannot publish everything we know . . . the detailed raw intelligence" (ibid., 4). The picture was of an Iraq that could strike against a major city at the whim of Saddam Hussein, the implicit but not stated claim of an imminent and apocalyptic threat to Britain requiring immediate action. On March 17, 2003, Robin Cook resigned from his post as Leader of the House in protest at the government's policy, stating that "Iraq probably has no weapons of mass destruction in the commonly understood sense of the term—namely a credible device capable of being delivered against a strategic city target."

On May 29, a BBC journalist, Andrew Gilligan, drawing on a secret Ministry of Defence source, suggested on a radio program that the forty-five-minute claim had been inserted by Blair's press secretary, Alastair Campbell, in order to "sex up" the dossier and make a more convincing case for war from vague intelligence reports. By early June this row intensified. Suspicions grew that the claims were spin and lies and that the prime minister had misled Parliament when presenting the dossier and explicitly flagging the forty-five-minute claim. Some seventy-three MPs signed a petition demanding the government reveal the full evidence on which the claim had been made, and the Conservatives hinted that they might call for an independent inquiry if the previously secret information was not forthcoming. Weary of all the carping and sniping, Tony Blair started to snap at his critics.

Labour MP Malcolm Savage suggested that the situation might be more serious than Watergate. The foreign secretary, Jack Straw, was evasive when asked in a radio interview on June 2 if Iraq's threat was really less imminent than the dossier had suggested, switching the subject to talk about Saddam Hussein's "weapons program," and his failure to comply with UN inspectors. The *Times* (June 3, 2003) summed up the situation in the banner: "Criticism, Contradictions, Confusion and Concern." At the same time Clare Short, a senior Labour politician, launched a claim that Blair had made a secret war pact with Bush at Camp David as early as September 2002. This had established a timetable that locked Britain into conflict with Iraq.

So in the summer of 2003, Blair was caught up in a genre war that was really a form of retrospective accounting activity. It was not about what was going on in Iraq at that time, or what to do next, but rather about why in the past Blair had made what more and more people thought was the wrong reading of Iraq. Moreover, had he propagated this false interpretation of dangers knowingly in the lead-up to the war? Should he be understood in terms of the Discourse of Repression as the deceitful promulgator of incorrect interpretations? Or was he well intentioned but foolish?

Ongoing disputes about the minute facts of the case were components of this much larger game of accounting for the wrong genre guess and its implications. In early July the House of Commons Foreign Affairs Committee (2003) reported on the government's use of intelligence with respect to the case against Iraq. This inevitably came to focus on the government's published dossiers. Although Alastair Campbell was exonerated and the government was cleared of lying, the report made the government look as if they had been playing tricks with spin. The "45 minutes claim did not warrant the prominence given it in the dossier, because it was based on intelligence from a single, uncorroborated source" (paragraph 70), and the language used in the September dossier had been "more assertive than that traditionally used in intelligence documents." The Committee called for an approach that retained "the measured and cautious tones" that were customary (paragraph 100) rather than "undue emphases" (paragraph 186). Moreover, the media guru Campbell and his Iraqi Communications Group seemed to have enjoyed too much influence (paragraphs 79, 122). The Committee also suggested that the government had been less than fully helpful in providing it with "access to intelligence papers and personnel" and was "hampering it in the work which parliament has asked it to carry out" (paragraph 170). The overall picture, then, was of a Blair regime that was economical with the truth, that had stretched its case, and that did not trust its own Parliament. The Discourse of Repression was gaining more traction.

A few days later things became yet worse. Through June a scrap had en-sued between the BBC and Downing Street over Andrew Gilligan's allega-tions about the "sexed up" dossier. Just who was lying? Then the name of the source was leaked. He was a Ministry of Defence scientist, Dr. David Kelly, who was an expert on WMD. On July 18, 2003, he was found dead in an Ox-fordshire forest having apparently killed himself. A formal inquiry was called, to be headed by Lord Hutton. This was to look into the circumstances of the death, and so it inevitably came to touch on the dossiers and the ways that intelligence had been treated. Equally pivotal was the question of who had authorized the leaking of Kelly's name, an act that might have driven him to his death. Gilligan? The BBC? Campbell? The Ministry of Defence? Blair himself? Over several weeks the Hutton inquiry heard evidence of Byzantine complexity.

The upshot of this activity was that even more mud stuck. A new narrative started to form in which No. 10 was looking as if it was at the heart of a fiendish conspiracy and cover-up involving phony justifications for war, dirty tricks, and spin. Campbell resigned, publicly stating that this was for reasons unconnected to Hutton, Kelly, or the dossiers—a claim nobody really took se-riously given his increasingly Mandelsonian image and the need for Downing Street to be buffered from this. Campbell's situation had been compounded by the fact that Kelly was narrated as a man of honor. He was a quiet man, a scientist who was above politics and wished to serve his country. He was a man who had gotten out of his depth and been betrayed by politicians and bureaucrats. The government's treatment of Dr. Kelly had been "callous and cynical." It had "cut him adrift, dropping a series of hints about his identity and inviting journalists to guess his name." It was a game of "nudge-nudge, wink-wink" that had been "initiated on the direct instructions of the Prime Minister" (*Daily Telegraph*, January 11, 2004). The inquisition led to diverse visions of Blair molding him in terms of the Discourse of Repression. Had he become an irrational actor who saw what he wanted to see; a dependent puppet of Bush unable articulate his own vision; or a control freak hell bent on war, lying to the English people through his apparatus of spin and infor-mation control and cruelly sacrificing the life of the saintly scientist Kelly?

Blair could be lampooned as a blithering idiot who acted on the basis of in-stincts and impressions not reason: "Tony sees terrorism, he sees WMD and he sees Saddam's brutality and hey presto! Without troubling to make any other connection between them he decides to invade Iraq" (*Observer*, October 5, 2003). With Bush he had engaged in a "game of fantasy Middle East Poli-tics" (*Guardian*, November 21, 2003) and had indulged in the naive belief that Iraq would become a progressive role model. Another Blair was nobly well intentioned but misguided. "Nobody will be able to trust Tony Blair's judg-ment again," wrote one veteran columnist in the *Observer* (April 6, 2003), "He gambled on being able to restrain Bush and he failed." The perspective here is not only one of irony. His was "a political tragedy, Shakespearean in the cruelty of its denouement" (*Observer*, March 30, 2003) in which Blair, the pro-European, had abandoned Europe, assisted in the breakup of the UN, and turned his back on his own party. In joining with the conservatives of the United States and "fighting a barely legitimate war that is already a military and diplomatic quagmire" Blair had made a "historic political misjudgment" that had "increased the threat of global terrorism," not reduced it, and had "replaced the repression of Saddam Hussein with lawlessness and chaos" (*Guardian*, October 5, 2003).

A yet stronger position of critique identified a more sinister and gothic Blair and most strongly emerged out of readings of the disclosures to the Hutton Inquiry (discussed shortly). Here Number 10 is converted into something akin to Goebbels's propaganda ministry. It had "outed" the politically naive but truth-driven Dr. Kelly in order to destroy him. It had initiated a campaign against the BBC that diverted attention to points of fact when the BBC had been "correct in essence, if not in every detail." It had produced deliberately misleading dossiers in which "caveats and facts that might have revealed just how sketchy the real intelligence picture was were systematically filtered out and replaced with words of resounding certainty" such as the PM's claim in a foreword that there was a "serious and current" threat (*Daily Telegraph*, January 11, 2004).

Poll data suggest the rising importance of these new genres as the dom-inant resources for retrospective understandings of the war. The Baghdad Bounce of April seems to have worn off by June 2003. In April, public sup-port for the war had stood at 63 percent. As the long, unusually hot summer of 2003 wore on and Kellygate thickened and curdled like milk left in the sun, Blair's symbolic pollution intensified. People moved to distance themselves from him. By June polls showed that most believed Blair had been in breach of the Discourse of Liberty—63 percent thought he had not been "honest and trustworthy" (*Times*, June 27, 2003). By September his approval rating was down to just 29 percent, with more than 50 percent feeling it was time for him to resign (*Financial Times*, September 27, 2003). Only 38 percent believed that the invasion of Iraq was justified (*Guardian*, September 23, 2003). This mood was to spill over into the contentious Labour Party conference of late September. Delegates called for a vote on the War in Iraq but this was blocked. In November, Blair hosted a state visit by Bush to Britain that was marked by massive protests against the now unpopular American leader. A poll for the

Times (November 10, 2003) found that 60 percent of Britons disapproved of his handling of Iraq and only 40 percent thought Britain benefited from the close ties between the two leaders. For many the symbolic contamination seemed mutually reinforcing. By December a haggard looking Blair was identified as Britain's least trustworthy politician and as a potential electoral liability (*Guardian*, December 27, 2003). Politics had finally turned full circle—the fresh-faced critic of Tory sleaze, the energetic new broom of 1997 had become a Nixon-like figure holed up with his cronies in Number 10 and mired in allegations and suspicions.

The most dramatic evidence for this casting can be seen by fast forwarding to late January 2004 and the release of Lord Hutton's report into the circumstances of the death of the scientist and BBC informant Dr. Kelly. This exonerated Mr. Blair and Downing Street of wrongdoing. They had not "outed" the scientist or "sexed up" the dossier as the BBC journalist Andrew Gilligan had claimed. To the contrary it was the BBC who had run false reports and failed to check its facts. Heads rolled as BBC director general Greg Dyke, the chair of the board of governors Gavyn Davies, and Andrew Gilligan himself resigned. This finding should have been a triumph for a vindicated prime minister. But as so often happens in times of crisis an official inquiry failed to resolve what Victor Turner (1969) has called a phase of "breach," in which schism and factionalism prevailed. However accurate or inaccurate the report, its attempts to find closure through a detailed scrutiny of the facts did not change the wider reading that was made of Blair. As I have been arguing throughout this book, "facts" and "reasons" are subordinate to genres and narratives. And so the report was narrated in turn as an establishment whitewash and as having terms of inquiry that were too narrow to address the real issues.

Critics alleged Hutton had failed to consider the broader implications of the "sexed up" claim. Namely whether Number 10 had subtly altered words and phrases in the published case for war to make vague intelligence seem more certain and to make threats appear more imminent. Writing in the *Guardian* (February 2, 2004), David Clark, a former Foreign Office advisor, embodies this position for our purposes. He argued that Downing Street had "transformed the dossier to confect a threat that was serious and current" in order to put UN inspectors out of business and allow Britain to enter into a war alongside the United States. A sentence was deleted that indicated Saddam Hussein could not attack Britain; Blair should have indicated that the forty-five-minute claim referred to battlefield weapons only and came from a single source, the words "programmes for" were deleted from the title of the document: "Iraq's Programmes for Weapons of Mass Destruction." If Blair had not openly lied, neither had he been open, honest, or straightforward as demanded by the Discourse of Liberty. He remained tainted by the Discourse of Repression. Likewise an unrepentant Gilligan asserted that the spirit of his claims was true and that Hutton had become obsessed with irrelevant points of detail. Angry BBC staff posted a full-page newspaper advertisement. Poll data suggest that the report did little to cleanse Blair's reputation. Some 36 percent of those surveyed on behalf of the *Times* took a "less favorable" view of Blair as a result of "issues surrounding the Hutton report," and only 11 percent had a "more favorable view" (*Times,* January 30, 2004). Another poll suggested that 44 percent thought that Blair was not telling the truth and that he had in some way, authorized the "outing" of Dr. Kelly (*Washington Post,* January 31, 2004). The bulk of the media sided with the BBC and negative metaphors abounded. Far from absolving Blair, the Hutton report had been deeply flawed. Hutton had suffered from "blindness of Nelsonian proportions" in refusing to see what he did not want to see and had sprayed Blair's inner circle with "more whitewash than a Costa Brava timeshare" (op-ed, *Daily Telegraph,* January 28, 2004). Similar sentiments could be found in papers from across the political spectrum: the *Independent, Daily Mail, Mirror, Express,* and *Guardian* all expressed dismay.

Blair's case was dogged yet further at this juncture by the still ongoing, high profile failure of efforts to locate WMD. The Commons Intelligence and Security Committee reported in early February 2004, and once again latched on to the forty-five-minute claim made by the government as misleading. At the same time the Commons Foreign Affairs Committee reported that the "continued failure of the coalition to find weapons of mass destruction in Iraq has damaged the credibility of the US and the United Kingdom in their conduct of the war against terrorism" (quoted in *Times,* February 2, 2004). Like Bush, Blair responded by calling for an independent inquiry into prewar intelligence. To be headed by Lord Butler this was to explore why the *intelligence organizations* had got it so wrong. Blair was to have a harder time than Bush in playing this finesse. Opposing parties within the parliamentary game attempted to open up the inquiry to wider issues of how intelligence had been *used by the government* as well as its accuracy. The Liberal Democrats rejected the remit as Blair attempted to shut out the issue of whether the war had been right or wrong. Then at the start of March 2004, the Conservatives bailed out as well, their leader Michael Howard complaining that the Butler Inquiry would be looking only at "structures, systems and processes" and not at "the acts or omissions of individuals" (quoted in *Guardian,* March 1, 2004). The credibility of the Inquiry took a nosedive. Blair was understood to have picked his own judge and to have set up a process that would not ask the critical questions.

Only in America did Blair remain for the most part positively coded in the war's aftermath. Here he could indulge more poetically and less apologetically in spreading the apocalyptic message. Receiving the Congressional Gold Medal in July 2003, he sounded like Bush as he spoke of a battle against a "new and deadly virus" called terrorism and received nineteen standing ovations. Replicating the kind of discourses we find in medieval diatribes against witches such as the *Malleus Malificarum* he invokes this evil's ability to turn "upside down our concepts of how we should act and when," that it "crosses frontiers," and "can spread like contagion" although it "isn't obvious." According to Blair the "new world rests on order" and the goal of the terrorists is to disrupt this by spreading global "chaos" (from *Guardian*, July 18, 2003).

The case in Britain, then, differed from that in America. A more dispersed and widely accepted apocalyptic reading of world events had facilitated Bush's military agenda. Blair endorsed apocalypticism in the effort to justify a war and remain loyal to his ally. Although there was substantial support for this view that should not be underestimated, Blair was powerfully constrained by the narrative divisions and dialogical activities in the wider British civil society. Dogged by calls for evidence from those still firmly in the low mimetic mode and haunted by his reputation as a spinmeister, Blair was to become caught up in a complex debate about facts and interpretations. This was to intensify, not abate, once the fighting appeared to be over. It is a debate that would have been pedantic if the stakes had not been so high. France illustrates yet another national outcome in the genre politics of the War in Iraq. Here we see the political fate that might have befallen Blair had he taken the low mimetic track himself.

FRANCE AND THE WAR IN IRAQ

France had participated in the Gulf War with modest enthusiasm. It wished to have no part of the War in Iraq. Indeed the situation we find here is a reversal of Suez. In that conflict America had been low mimetic and unflappable and France apocalyptic. Mollet and Eden, it will be remembered, had insisted that the nationalization of the Suez Canal might set in motion a series of events that would bring the Western world to its knees when the ambitious Nasser and the Soviet Bear took control of oil, Africa, and the Middle East. Eisenhower and Dulles had mumbled incantations about international law, tried to broker compromise, and had insisted that there could be practical and technical solutions. Now it was France's turn to harp on about evidence, prudence, and international law and America's turn to experience frustration and betrayal. France's stated objective was the disarmament of Saddam Hussein through the agency of the UN, if possible peacefully. The majority opinion was that the case for war had not been made, that the war would destabilize the Middle East, that diplomatic efforts could be expanded, and that if there was to be war then France should be present in reconstruction efforts.

Consistent with the thesis of this book that genres tend to squeeze political analysis into a handful of familiar positions, we find that in the run-up to war the low mimetic narrative in France took the form that it did with Britain's Left. Saddam Hussein was evil, and of course he needed to be monitored and watched closely, but there was no evidence of an impending apocalyptic threat from Iraq, the United Nations needed to be respected, and the war required a legal sanction. This vision was supported from the very top by the president, Jacques Chirac, a former protégé of Charles de Gaulle and Valéry Giscard d' Estaing. Chirac had been elected president in 1995 after previous spells as premier and as mayor of Paris. Reading through interviews with the French leader we find a very different understanding of events from that of George Bush. There are concerns for multilateralism and the authority of the UN, for timelines and inspection reports. This is the world of low mimesis where crises can be "managed" and steps must be "prudent" and "diplomatic," even if forceful. Where Bush brushes these technical, legal-rational issues aside as impedimenta to a forceful response to impending doom, Chirac places them center stage and believes that world events are still under control. In his view the "inspections have proven their effectiveness" for reaching the goal of dis-arming Saddam Hussein: "We have also noticed, in listening to and reading the inspectors a lot of progress has been achieved, that weapons are being destroyed every day . . . the inspectors are telling us . . . that we are within reach of our goal, and that we can do without war." Chirac was confident from the International Atomic Energy Agency work that there were "no nuclear weapons or nuclear programs that would lead to the construction of nuclear weapons." He considered the inspectors needed more time to find out the truth about chemical and biological WMD and thought "rushing into battle" was not necessary (CNN interview, March 16, 2003, CNN.com). In Chirac's view the Western world was confronted by a problem for which a practical solution could be found. Indeed the very word "problem," like those relating to "management," appears repeatedly in his March 10 interview with French television when he refers to the Iraqi regime and possible WMD. As for vi-sions of the future, the wish Chirac expresses here is for a multipolar world characterized by "democracy and harmony," a world where "the inevitable crises—regional crises, or what we call proliferation crises—can be managed as effectively as possible" under the umbrella of the UN. Chirac vowed to do his utmost "to resolve the Iraq problem without waging war" not only to realize his positive vision but also to head off negative outcomes (TF1/France2 interview, March 10, 2003, ambafrance-au.org). For Chirac, war would bring "negative fallout" in Arab public opinion, would "give a big lift to terrorism" and create "a large number of little bin Ladens," and "destabilize the entire region." For the time being adherence to UN Security Council Resolution 1441 with its inspections programs was the most prudent policy (interview in *Time*, February 24, 2003). This line of thinking was amply reflected in the joint declaration of France, Russia, and Germany of March 6, 2003. It indicated "encouraging results" from the inspections policy such as the destruction of Iraq's long-range Samoud missiles and an improving flow of information on WMD, called for more inspections and detailed timelines, and vowed to block any proposed resolution in the Security Council that would authorize the use of force (text in *Guardian*, March 6, 2003).

Approval for leadership usually depends upon a genre alignment between leaders and civil society over important issues. This was the case in France with respect to the War in Iraq. Chirac was applauded for his stance against both the war and American policy. There was a certain Gaullist pride in the way he had "carried the interests of France conforming to its vocation of universality . . . and the idea of European Europe" (*Le Monde*, March 12, 2003). Whereas only 12 percent of those polled in America in March 2003 had a "favorable impression" of Chirac and 57 percent an unfavorable one (29 percent "not familiar," Time/CNN Poll, March 27, 2003, PollingReport.com) in France it was a very different story. Indeed Chirac's stance enabled him to turn around his reputation as a political opportunist dogged by scandals to become a man of principle representing the will of the French people. As the conflict started, 92 percent of respondents to a *Le Figaro* (March 21, 2003) poll supported their president's stand. Even after the fall of Baghdad in what had been an easy victory seemingly proving doomsayers wrong, a poll in *Le Figaro* (April 26, 2003) showed that some 84 percent agreed that Chirac had been correct in opposing the U.S. led military intervention. Of these, 77 percent were on the Right and 87 percent on the Left. His position had genuinely broad appeal and for the early part of 2003 gave him the highest presidential approval ratings in the history of the Fifth Republic. Here was a leader who could assert France's autonomy and its *rang*.

If orientations toward crisis management in Iraq had a low mimetic cast, those toward the United States made use of other narrative structures. Using the Discourse of Repression, America and its leaders were understood by many as deluded and irrational. This account could take two forms. In the tragic one an emphasis was on the War in Iraq as an error by a country with a noble history. Hence we find the following analysis on the eve of the war by columnist Jacques Julliard in *L'Express* (February 20, 2003): "It is a great mistake for a country so religious to only believe in the God of Armies, it is a great fault of a country imbued with juridicism to be in contempt of court, it's an immense fault on the part of a democratic country to neglect public opinion . . . under the direction of Bush, the US is in the process of losing its soul. This is much worse than losing the petroleum battle." Likewise, a letter writer to the same magazine (February 27, 2003) pointed out that "After the crimes of September 11 we were all Americans. Since then the capital of sympathy has been used up." The theme here, then, is of a history that has gone astray and of a country squandering its moral authority. A more negative view saw the American president as dangerous and malign, driven by ideology not reason. He was seen as having a "messianic program" driven by an "omnipresent faith" (*Le Monde*, March 8, 2003) that could lead to an *élan belliciste* as the *Nouvelle Observateur* (October 23, 2002) put it. Likewise, Paul Wolfowitz was seen as a "visionary and messianic hawk" (*Le Monde*, January 29, 2003). This kind of prophetic belief system could have disastrous consequences when the person behind it was tinkering with forces they could not understand. Although things were not apocalyptic now, they might become unnecessarily so. The veteran sociologist Edgar Morin commented that the war was a dangerous "intervention at the heart of the seismic zone of the planet. A war against Iraq cannot be circumscribed, it will be an operation of a sorcerer's apprentice which could set off a cataclysmic chain reaction." What might this lead to? Referring to a well-known post-apocalyptic movie he continues that we have a premonition "in the film *Mad Max* where an incredible barbarism of everyone against everyone is unleashed using the debris and detritus of technical civilization" (*Le Monde*, March 18, 2003).

The tragic understanding of the war as a horrible mistake originating in the erroneous genre readings of the United States was to underpin the influential analyses in *Le Monde Diplomatique* on the new global security environment and the failures of the United States to come to terms with this. The line here was that we live in an era of "asymmetric warfare" where conventional military power has to confront stateless organizations that use low-tech weapons, the Internet, the media, and deeply held grievances to further their cause. In this context direct military and diplomatic engagement become impossible—at least in their conventional form. A prolonged and bloody stalemate usually results. The United States had responded to September 11 through an "Israeli-style" politics that could only lead to "catastrophe." What was needed, according to the intellectual Marwan Bishara, were "public institutions and development" in the "world's grey areas created by war, globalization and impoverishment" (*Le Monde Diplomatique*, October 2001) not a politics of

repression that could lead only to a prolonged standoff with "alarming consequences for "fundamental human freedoms" (Ignacio Ramonet, Leader, *Le
Monde Diplomatique*, November 2001).

This broadly tragic vision of misunderstandings and missed opportunities was not inconsistent with a more negative characterization of the United
States as deeply and actively polluted. For many its politics were not simply
the misguided expression in actions of an inaccurate worldview but also a
cynical quest for power that had been furtively conducted by evil elites, decade
after decade. Such a vision can be traced right back to the early days after the
attacks of September 11. Writing his leaders for *Le Monde Diplomatique*, Ignacio Ramonet had repeatedly pointed to American imperialism during the
cold war. We have already noted that approaches that reject apocalypticism
narrow the gap between the characters, suggesting that we are all tainted by
some kind of sin. And so we find Ramonet itemizing the casualties of the
United States' "crusade against communism" during the cold war; the U.S.
support for terrorists in Cuba, Nicaragua, Chile, and Afghanistan; the way
that the United States has ignored the United Nations since 1991; and the
negative impact of its sanctions against Iraq. As for bin Laden, he could be
likened to Frankenstein's monster. Created to fight the Soviets in Afghanistan
he had "turned against his maker." According to Ramonet, Bush and his team
were excited to have a new enemy, radical Islam, that could justify a "modern
McCarthyism directed at the opponents of globalization" (*Le Monde Diplomatique*, October 2001).

This Saidesque/Chomskyesque picture of a hypocritical America hell bent
on global domination and driven by base motivations that could override principle continued through to the War in Iraq. Writing in *Le Monde* (February
18, 2003) the lawyer Jacques Verges suggested that the freedom the war was
bringing was "only the freedom to kneel down before Bush." Veteran politician Jean-Pierre Chevènement also argued it was a "war of recolonization"
disguised as a "war of liberation." This was "a war for global domination via
the occupation of Iraq and control of the Middle East" (in *Le Monde*, April 8,
2004). The left-wing newspaper *Liberation* spoke of an "American Blitzkrieg"
and of "nationalist hysteria" (editorial, February 11, 2003). This would lead
to "the unique superpower" dictating its "bellicose law," consulting its "messianic oracles," deciding the "axis of evil and axis of good" (editorial, February
16, 2003). Standing up to American power was a new hero. The "old Europe"
that Bush's administration had denounced for failing to come to the party
and invade Iraq took on for the French the mantle of the carrier of universalism. It "affirmed a conception of the world order where the use of force
must be a last resort, where multilateralism will be the rule and democratic

exchange at the heart of the UN must always prevail" (editorial, *Le Monde*, March 12, 2003).

As might be expected, for the minority in France in favor of the war these opponents of American policy were unrealistic and exhibited a confused rationality. The philosopher Pascal Bruckner was one of the more vocal spokespersons for this position. He suggested that the pacifists had "missed a good opportunity" to help the Iraqi people. They believed they could escape the "hardness of history in making a window dressing of good sentiments or recast a progressivist ideology in the demonization of the United States." According to Bruckner this was evidence that "we haven't made much intellectual progress since the fall of Hitler" (in *L'Express*, February 27, 2003). Teaming up with two other intellectuals, André Glucksmann and Romain Goupil, he continued his assault in *Le Monde* (March 4, 2003) a few days later suggesting that those who had demonstrated against war had become hopelessly confused over who was the real enemy: "In demonizing George W. Bush as 'new Satan,' 'new Hitler' and 'new bin-Laden' the protestors for peace of February 15 forgot Saddam Hussein . . . the great admirer of Stalin who has been crushing, torturing and strangling his people for 30 years." Elsewhere Glucksmann indicted Chirac for breaking up European unity, putting France under the Russian thumb and for "living in a cloud." A genre inflated approach made more sense as Saddam was "an ever-present powder keg in the heart of a fire zone . . . we must stop him playing with his apocalyptic matches" (*International Herald Tribune*, February 22, 2003).

We cannot tell exactly who bought into each of these narratives: The tragic narrative of a misguided America; the melodrama of an evil America; the counternarrative of a deluded French Left. However opinion polls indicate that 80 percent of French were opposed to the war (*Le Monde*, March 18, 2003) and 82 percent supported Chirac (*Liberation*, February 10, 2003) even though it was agreed by 46 percent that Chirac's diplomacy had isolated France (*Guardian*, April 16, 2003). For a brief period at the end of the war the idea was entertained that Chirac might have got it wrong. He began to look weak once excluded from the reconstruction of Iraq by the United States. Pictures of celebrating Iraqis suggested that the war had been a good thing and that he had been an unwitting ally of Saddam Hussein. Yet events a little later appeared to confirm that the French president's genre guess had been right all along. *Le Monde* gave center stage to the weak justifications and the WMD that had failed to materialize. In its headlines of July it spoke of "Lies and Manipulations" (July 17, 2003) and of "Lies of the State" (July 19, 2003), and over the next few days went on to give front-page attention to the death of British scientist David Kelly. As for America, it was "repugnant, arrogant, obtuse and criminal" and was responsible for "more innocent victims than September 11" (*L'Express*, May 8, 2003). By August attention turned to the crisis in the reconstruction of Iraq. Its patience finally worn thin, *Le Monde*'s editorial of September 11, 2003, lashed out against the United States in unequivocal terms: "Compassion for the US" had been replaced with "fear of ill considered actions," the war on terrorism was simply a "pretext for the extension of American hegemony," and Bush was engaged in a "crusade" driven by his simplistic belief that the civilized world was "engaged in a world war against a new totalitarianism." France could emerge from the War in Iraq with a clean conscience.

SPAIN AND THE WAR IN IRAQ

The most ardent antiwar positions in France, with their strongly negative coding of America and visions of tragic outcomes to military action were the dominant coin of discourse in Spain. The emphasis here is overwhelmingly on pathos, on the betrayals of leaders and the missed opportunities for peace. As with the Gulf War these fell into place early and did not substantially change, so we can deal with them briefly. A single editorial from *Cambio 16* (February 17, 2003) enables us to capture this spirit effectively. Here we find a different morality play from that of George W. Bush. This is the world of pacifist discourse, similar to that we find in antinuclear campaigns, where mad leaders are contrasted to ordinary people. Their irrational schemes and desire for power bring disaster to all: "The crazy and ambitious politics of the North American President, inherited from his father, will take this civilization to a huge catastrophe, to be the victim of his possessed impulses, to the visceral confrontation of two cultures that must coexist . . . the losers will not be the powerful leaders of whatever state, but the unprotected people who must flee from the battlefields as well as from disease and hunger." As the author Andrés Trapiello put it, "the only danger for world peace is Señor Bush" (*Cambio 16*, February 17, 2003) who, according to *Cambio 16* (March 10, 2003) had "dynamited the UN." Around 90 percent of Spaniards were opposed to the war (*Daily Telegraph*, May 24, 2003).

This situation was to create a minefield for Spain's prime minister José María Aznar. Leader of the right of center Partido Popular, Aznar had replaced the socialist Felipe González Márquez as prime minister in 1996. Like his predecessor he wanted Spain to take its place on the world stage and to be a player, putting an end to Franco-era isolationism. Like González at the time of the Gulf War his practical options were constrained by weak public support for his foreign policy—in effect by the tragic narratives that still dominated Spanish thinking about war. Featuring alongside Bush and Blair at a prewar summit in the Azores, Aznar tried to appear the statesman, the voice of reason. This had only very limited success. By failing to align with Chirac, Aznar was seen as the man who had betrayed the interests and beliefs of his own people and the dictates of morality. Rafael Estrella, a socialist spokesperson on the European Union asserted that he had "positioned Spain on the periphery of Europe and on the brink of a preventive war as unjustified and disproportionate as it was irresponsible" (*Cambio 16*, February 17, 2003). A peace march of February 15, organized in part by the left of center parties PSOE and IU and by unions was massively supported. Politicians of the Left, celebrities and personalities in the arts and culture industries such as film director Pedro Almodóvar, joined 1.5 million in Madrid and 1.4 million in Barcelona. Whereas the Conservative Party in Britain was by and large able to support Blair and critique had to emerge somewhat reluctantly from within his own ranks, Aznar was faced with a vocal PSOE opposition. Its leader José Luis Rodríguez Zapatero called for a "withdrawal of support for the conflict by Spanish soldiers and military bases on Spanish soil" and insisted that each bomb was an "attempted crime against the principles of democracy, against international law and against the Universal Declaration of Human Rights" (quoted in *Cambio 16*, March 31, 2003, 22). Perhaps not surprisingly we find the support offered by Spain matching that of the Gulf War. It was more or less symbolic: a hospital ship, a frigate, an oil tanker, 120 marines, and some nine hundred noncombat troops such as units with WMD and mine-clearing expertise. Not enough to make any real difference in battle, it was sufficient to enable President Bush to add Spain to his list of allies in the so-called Coalition of the Willing.

Spanish lives were safe. Yet even after the easy victory in Iraq the anger against Aznar remained. He was lampooned along with Blair and Bush as one of the "Three Amigos," and his popularity rating tanked to 31 percent. His friend and mentor Félix Pastor resigned from the Partido Popular citing the war. Terrorist attacks were to see him off. On March 11, 2004 (a date sometimes also known as 3/11), bombs exploded at the Atocha railroad station in Madrid killing around two hundred people. The nation entered into a phase of shock, mourning, and collective effervescence of the kind Durkheim (1965) termed a piacular rite. A general election was only three days away. Aznar and his party tried to deflect blame away from al-Qaeda and onto the Basque separatist group ETA. The prime minister personally phoned the editors of the leading four newspapers reinforcing this perception. If ETA were to blame then his rivals, the PSOE Party who were seen as soft on ETA, would lose votes. If it was al-Qaeda then Aznar's Partido Popular might suffer from a perception that it had attracted their attentions by supporting the war. As police leaks of evidence that Islamic extremists were involved increased, the government's efforts at spin began to look more and more duplicitous and anger grew at efforts to hide the truth. Aznar became caught up in a maelstrom of negative discourse about lies and conspiracy far more intense than any Blair had endured. The day before the election terrorists allegedly tied to al-Qaeda were arrested, and angry rumors of government cover-ups and misinformation circulated by cell phone and Internet (*Le Monde Diplomatique,* April 2004). Politicians on the Left began to publicly accuse Aznar of lying. Demonstrations eventuated in which the cries were "before voting, we want to know," "Aznar fascist," and "whoever votes for the Partido Popular votes for war" (*La Vanguardia,* March 14, 2004). The election was lost.

It would be simplistic to see Aznar's defeat as simply the result of his support for the War in Iraq or the Spanish people as voting for appeasement of terror by removing the prowar Aznar. Nevertheless his alliance with Bush formed the background for the interpretation of this sequence of events. Aznar had run with a foreign policy that was not supported by 90 percent of the Spanish people because of the entrenched low mimetic and tragic genres. The case for war he had laid out had not been confirmed by the discovery of WMD or Iraq/al-Qaeda connections so he had not been able to falsify this opposing interpretation in a convincing way. So when Aznar attempted to spin the meaning of the bombings he looked like a repeat offender of the worst kind, the kind of recidivist politician willing to play fast and loose with the truth again and again. "The growing probability that Islamic terrorism was the cause of the carnage" had served to "resuscitate the specter of the War in Iraq" (editorial, *La Vanguardia,* March 15, 2004). The bombings moved his unpopular war stance back into the attention space and allowed amplifying resonances to be set up. As the leader of the Basque nationalist Batasuna Party Arnaldo Otegi put it, when Aznar spoke about the origins of 3/11 he "lied just as he lied over Iraq and the WMD" (quoted in *El País,* March 14, 2004). Accounting for the subsequent massive pro-peace, anti-terror demonstration in Madrid in which 2.5 million people turned out in the rain, the magazine *Cambio 16* (March 22, 2004) agreed, suggesting that "indignation over Spain's participation in the war in Iraq became mixed with the suspicion that the Ministry of the Interior had not supplied all the available information." Aznar could now be described in terms of the Discourse of Repression as deceptive and arrogant, with the election lost as a result of a perception among the electorate of governmental "manipulation and trickery" (editorial, *El País,* March 15, 2004). His actions had "refreshed the memory of the war" with "one lie about WMD upon another about ETA."

Thinking counterfactually is one way to understand how the path of dependence established by prior genre choices influences the interpretation of subsequent events. The Atocha bombings could have confirmed the apocalyptic vision of an al-Qaeda threat with global implications and great powers of action, thus demonstrating the need for proactive military interventions rather than dialogue, inspections, and legal solutions. This alternative reading did not happen. Instead events only showed the Spanish that the wars in Afghanistan and Iraq had not been an effective way to deal with terror, that multilateralism and mutual understanding might provide a better solution, and that a culture of lies and cover-ups invariably accompanied war and led to violence.

The story of the War in Iraq is one of complex and overlapping genre wars. As with Suez and the Gulf War we found struggles within nations and between nations over how to interpret hazy events, evaluate uncertain threats, and arrive at appropriate lines of action. These debates and decisions were yet again shown to have been shaped by genre choices and cultural logics. In making this argument for the past several chapters we have been caught up in details about the cases. We have been exploring just how the activity of genre politics takes place, tracking the life history of events, and exploring the local idioms and concerns through which the universal is expressed with reference to the particular. In the next chapter we zoom out and open up some wider vistas: What are the implications of our findings for theorizing war, renewing cultural theory, and acknowledging ethical responsibilities?

WAR AND NARRATIVE

It is probably best to start this concluding chapter like a newspaper—with a few sentences that reduce the complexities of the story to their least elaborate summary formulation. This entails taking a sweeping and comparative if less nuanced turn. The material presented so far has, of course, expended a lot of energy unpacking the complexities and contingencies that accompany genre wars. For example, we have looked at how events are assembled into stories using the genre guess, explored the contestation around these, shown the centrality of the binary codes of civil discourse to storytelling, and documented the ways in which secondary elaborations are deployed in accounting for anomalies. Attention was also given to national histories and self-images and the ways that these are refracted in genre politics. Let us put this level of analysis to the side for the moment, don a positivist hat, focus our wide-angle lens, and engage with the comparative logic of concomitant variation. Are there systematic regularities over our cases when seen from afar? Table 1 presents the broad-brush findings from the three empirical chapters. It sets out the relationship between conflict legitimacy and genre within civil discourse for the four countries over the three wars. It also aligns this with the level of military involvement.

The findings are clear: genre choices align with war in ways that are regular and predictable over a large number of cases. When successfully institutionalized and widely shared the apocalyptic frame encourages war. Realist and tragic frames are associated with low levels of legitimacy and military intervention. Such a result has a number of significant implications. Adumbrating

Table 1   War legitimacy and narrative form

	Prevailing genre	Legitimacy	Military action
		Suez Crisis	
USA	Low mimetic	Very low	None
UK	Apocalyptic	Moderate	High
France	Apocalyptic	High	High
Spain	Low mimetic	Low	None
		Gulf War	
USA	Apocalyptic	Very high	High
UK	Apocalyptic	Very high	High
France	Apocalyptic	Moderate	Moderate
Spain	Tragic	Very low	Minimal
		War in Iraq	
USA	Apocalyptic	High	High
UK	Apocalyptic	Moderate	High
France	Low mimetic	Very low	None
Spain	Tragic	Very low	Minimal

these, batting away objections, and opening a normative door is the principal task of this final chapter.

THE PROMISE OF STRUCTURAL HERMENEUTICS

We can begin by indicating a methodological contribution. My belief is that the inability of cultural sociologists to define and catalogue the internal structures of culture has engendered negative methodological consequences. Clifford Geertz's injunction to interpret the world has led only to descriptions of varying degrees of thickness. Even when seasoned with the spices of continental theory, these proliferating accounts have not contributed to a science of social life, in Émile Durkheim's sense. That is to say there has been an accumulation of techniques and reflexive programs of ever-increasing complexity for reading culture but no corresponding effort toward the evolution of systematic, generalizable, causal theories. The result is, at best, an academic activity that operates according to the principles of the savage mind (Lévi-Strauss 1968). It is a way of investigating culture that sees us comparing and contrasting in ad hoc ways on the basis of the logic of appearances rather than essences, playing snap with the local and contingent rather than first ordering our cards into suits. What is needed is a more robust cultural sociology, one that understands meaning systems as social facts that are external and constraining and amenable to the formation of a more propositional kind of interpretative project. I believe this book has demonstrated the promise of such a strategy.

Endlessly reprising the keynote addresses of the *geisteswissenschaften* tradition, cultural sociology has traditionally defended its turf at the paradigm level. The result as Jonathan Turner (1989, 8) puts it has been that assertions are repeatedly made that "there are no invariant properties of the social universe, that problems of subjectivity and agency make sociological analysis interpretative and provisional, and hence that scientific sociology is impossible." The product has been a discourse that has spent more time talking about theory than actually building theory and that has been programmatically locked into a celebration of the particular. I have argued before that only if we return to an understanding where meaning is a property of relationships in cultural systems, what Jeffrey Alexander and I have called elsewhere a "strong program" of structuralist hermeneutics (Alexander and Smith 2001), can we bring the interpretive project to produce cumulative theory. With the detailed specification of finite cultural structures and the identification of the logics of their articulation we can engage in comparative cultural sociology that is systematic rather than ad hoc. The pay-off for this strategy can be astonishing: witness the fruitful paradigm revision in the discipline of anthropology during 1950s and 1960s following on the heels of Claude Lévi-Strauss's pioneering work on kinship systems, totemism, and myth (Lévi-Strauss 1964, 1969, 1983; cf. Needham 1962; Leach 1969), or the tradition of structuralist poetics established by figures like Vladimir Propp (1968) and Northrop Frye (1957) that has informed this work. A dividend bonus for such an approach to meaning is that the autonomy of culture, what we might think of as its structuring rather than structured quality, is established in a more robust manner (Kane 1991; Alexander and Smith 1993). When we speak of self-referential systems of difference and rule-driven cultural grammars the self-supporting architectural qualities of meaning become apparent and with this the realization that even the most reflexively ideological or artful of discourses must be constrained by the fixed repertoires through which humans are able to make their world meaningful. These templates are collective, shared, inescapable.

For these diverse reasons the "strong program" approach to culture should prove attractive even to systematic comparative sociologists such as Theda Skocpol (1979, 1985). She famously decried cultural work for its subjectivism, individualism, and relativism and lauds explanatory model construction in historical research, which entails clear understandings about relationships between autonomous, explanatory, structural variables, and hypothesis-testing research designs. This act of excommunicating meaning might have been mistaken. Here we have conducted cultural analysis that is not subjective or mysterious but involves the effort to understand publicly visible evidence, in this case public sphere discourses and dialogues that are structured in determinate, definable, and identifiable ways. The charge of individualism can be refuted by pointing to the fact that discourse structures were shown to be shared over publics and constituencies. Relativism starts to look problematic once we see—as we have in this book—that Skocpol's own methods can be used to engage with cultural materials in a positivistic way. Put simply, genre politics is a witnessable, reportable, measurable social fact that has determinate material consequences over multiple cases. Regrettably, the fact that culture is structured, public, and amenable to study in scientific as well as humanist ways does not allow us to easily dismiss the rather cheap objection that our causal arrows need to be reversed. I turn next to this issue.

FOR CULTURE, AGAINST IDEALISM

A commonplace of folk wisdom and political cynicism is to suggest that war involves the calculated demonization of the enemy. Interests, whether national and shared or simply those of elites and institutions, determine actions, and beliefs fall into place behind these. In this understanding the genres disseminated and the war stories told are simply rationalizations for policies driven by some other more material and usually sinister need. They are a form of ideological justification that tells why what is going to be done needs to be done, or why what has just happened needed to happen. Such a proposition is not only wrong but also dangerous if we wish to prevent unnecessary wars by understanding their origins. I have argued throughout this book that it is the image of the enemy and the narrative inflation of the precipitating crisis that leads to war. Negative symbolism does not arise simply because of interests, needs, or policies. It is far from being a cardboard prop that can be simply wheeled onto stage when required. Rather, as we have seen, agency, creativity, and struggle come into play as agents present and reject what Jürgen Habermas would call "good reasons" to others about the need to tether or let slip those Shakespearian dogs of war. This explains why long before military conflict takes place or becomes inevitable, storytelling activities and dialogical genre wars are taking place. Interested parties take this cultural groundwork seriously precisely because of their partly intuitive, partly studied understanding that a foundation of meaning is needed for a legitimate war to be waged. Culture I have also asserted becomes causal because it works as the dialogical filter through which perceptions of threats and outcomes are shaped. As machines for the reduction of complexity, narratives are markers of the terrains within which bounded rationalities are exercised. The image of an objectively identifiable "enemy" who is subsequently "demonized" by a *post facto* cultural process or "interests" that need "explanation" to the public is fundamentally mistaken. The "enemy" and "interests" require cultural patterns for their very recognition. In a sense they are talked into relevance—but not existence—through the storytelling, genre guessing dialogical activities of the public sphere. Likewise, any "threats" that need to be dealt with require identification, prioritizing, and evaluation. Here too we have seen that cultural resources are needed: frameworks that allow clues to be assembled and efforts made to guess likely costs and benefits to military action or inaction.

Making such an argument for cultural structures as a cause of war does not mean retreating toward an idealism where allegedly free-floating narratives single-handedly and in some mysterious way determine political and military actions. The cry of idealism itself requires specification, and when this is given we find that accusations fall out along four dimensions of neglect: *action, power, rationality,* and *resources.* To be absolutely clear on what has been suggested in this book we need to address these one at a time.

Although culture is a supraindividual structure whose systemic properties are not always recognized by agents it nevertheless requires situated practical *action* to make a difference. Discursive effort, what we might think of as interpretative and dialogical work, is what permits any cultural pattern to become institutionalized or dominant in any given historical sequence. Culture, in this context at least, can exert an impact only if it can be mobilized as a resource and made relevant by individual and collective actors. Consequently, the argument I have made in this book is one that can accommodate or elaborate an action theory rather than confront it. In a very real sense people with their visions, strategies, and difficult choices are the protagonists of the account given here, not narratives or codes. We have repeatedly seen how cultural resources are used by them in sense-making activity and claims-making work, or put another way, in cognition and justification. This reality suggests that the opposition, enshrined in the debate between Jean Paul Sartre and Claude Lévi-Strauss (Lévi-Strauss 1968) between the formalist treatment of culture as "system" and the humanistic explanation of culture as "project" is a false one. Far from diminishing the importance of human action and struggle, the structural approach to culture developed here enables us to see just why and how actors are able to act at all. Genres, codes, and narratives are resources that enable actions, even if at the same time they constrain action possibilities.

Power comes into the frame when we realize not only that claims-making activity can be used to construct coalitions and generate legitimacy by rational actors, but also that the means of symbolic production are themselves unevenly distributed. Media concentration, the party apparatus, holding state office, or having network centrality and thus controlling information flow, having expert knowledge or the status that allows one to be cited with authority in the public sphere—these are all forms of power that play out in the environments surrounding the generation of discourse. Although not determinate they can tip the odds of particular narratives or wider genre frames becoming accepted or discredited within a particular field of discursive contestation. Although I have suggested that genre mobilizations might be inspired by internalized value patterns or deeply cherished beliefs, hardheaded reasons for narrative position taking can also be accommodated to our explanation. As I suggested in the early pages of this book, a war without domestic legitimacy is a very poor bet. It is bad for morale, bad for diplomacy, bad for chances of re-election. This is why interested parties work with culture and try to use narratives to make and undermine claims. If such bids are successful they provide a mandate for action as well as affording more diffuse political or moral capital. So understanding culture structures in the way I have proposed here does not undercut claims about the centrality of power. To the contrary it provides us with more detailed resources for exploring how power works and for discovering how systems of ideas articulate as legitimating contexts for administration and policy.

The argument that wars often have a mythological underpinning, that they are predicated on storytelling that mobilizes powerful symbols and generates visceral emotions does not mean that human responses to situations of uncertainty or violence are inherently irrational or that *rationality* has no place in shaping human action. The extremism that bars rationality from cultural explanation leads to the dead ends that have confronted, for example, psychoanalytic understandings of conflict. The material presented here has not suggested that people are simply self-deluding mythmakers, but quite the contrary. Civil debate is relentlessly focused on the attempt to move beyond myth so as to construct accurate understandings of situations and options, to arrive at some kind of true diagnosis, and to offer good reasons to others backed up by facts and elaborated argumentation aimed at updating prior understandings. Civil discourse on war is in this sense a discourse oriented around norms of reason and the quest for mutual consensus among concrete and abstract others. It is a form of communicative reason that is not un-Habermasian in spirit even if the playing out of political life provides an agonistic rather than solidaristic context for this activity. It is equally clear that the conduct of war and diplomacy by politicians and the military remains an endeavor in which calculative rationality and the scientific evaluation of information play a substantial role. Yet even this activity does not take place in a cultural vacuum. At the risk of repeating myself I am going to say something very important again: no matter how perfect our reason, bits and pieces of information do not speak for themselves. Narratives, we have seen, provide the context within which the relevant facts are taken both as relevant and as facts and in which their wider significance is determined. Narrative horizons also provide a constraint on action—even (particularly) the most careful of military decisions will include some consideration of its own cultural repercussions. Genre choices, then, are a facilitating resource for the exercise of bounded rationalities in situations of uncertainty and a constraining environment with which political and military strategy must contend. In sum, the argument here is not so much that wars are irrational but rather that we need cultural theory to understand the concrete activity through which people try to arrive at fully rational opinions and decisions about them.

Postmodern mantras to the contrary, you cannot fight and win a war with words and images no matter how firm your beliefs or persuasive your simulation of reality. Adequate material *resources* are clearly a prerequisite for substantial military engagements on foreign soil. To meet the Saddam Husseins and, to be even handed, the George Bushes of the world on the conventional battlefield you need tanks, planes, ships, and equipped bodies, and the communications technologies and logistical structures to support these. This goes without saying—or at least it should. At the same time it has to be recognized that materiel simply opens up possibilities and policy options. Military power is a necessary but not sufficient cause for a military intervention. Politicians and other elites direct its use, and their policies, we have seen, are influenced by the narratives they hold or espouse and the distribution of support for these in a wider civil society. Moreover, the materiel of war is itself symbolically encoded. We have seen that it has a sign value as well as use value, becoming a signifying resource for the construction of narratives. Smart bombs and missiles, for example, are deployed not only because they can inflict damage to infrastructure, but also because they are more likely to be seen as consistent with legitimating stories. They symbolize the humane war and, if they work as touted, minimize opportunities for tragic counternarrations that speak of the suffering of innocents. Acknowledging this kind of a cultural landscape provides us with tools for better understanding why and how military power is used, not denying its efficacy.

So power, situated actions, rationality, and available resources all have an input into war policy. But so does culture even as it operates in and through these. As I said at the end of the first paragraph of this book wars are not *just about* culture but they are *all about* culture. This is so precisely because of its necessary intersection with the other environments of civil, political, and military action. Yet even if the approach taken here can be reconciled with or adapted to the position of wider social theory and popular common sense on the causes of war, questions may well linger over the broader empirical applicability of our model. Surely, the skeptic will say, we have been looking in this book at situations where war was optional, where information was weak, and where support for conflict had to be hyped into being. Were not the really major wars of our time predicated on a clear existential threat to national survival that could be understood without some cultural framing taking place? Does not culture come to the fore only when more solid practical or legal foundations for conflict are weak or when information is missing? Is the model presented in this book really just about runt wars, pseudo-wars, or television wars?

Before confronting such arguments let us recap the methodological advantages of the wars we selected and so justify our case selection. Comparability was enhanced and complexity reduced by looking at relatively small-scale conflicts with broadly similar parameters that were tightly bounded in space and time. To be sure the cases are not identical. In each of the three wars the broader geopolitical context differed. Suez was conducted at the height of the cold war, the Gulf War when it was on its very last gasp, and the War in Iraq within the context of American hegemony and an uncertain post-9/11 security environment. In addition, the rule of case independence has been violated— the earlier events had consequences for the later ones. Nasser provided an ideological template of sorts for Saddam Hussein, the weakened Iraqi regime that emerged from the Gulf War had to try to fight for its own survival a decade later, collective memories of the earlier conflicts were layered into discourses on those that followed. These problems are neither greater nor lesser in magnitude here than in other studies that have attempted to derive generalizable results from the messy stuff of history: to identify cases that conform to the requirement for deep analogy from a mire of unique, unfolding, but also interconnected events. Even Skocpol's (1979) much acclaimed study can be considered compromised: the French Revolution informed that in Russia, which influenced that in China. The revolutions were not really discrete events. Each is an exemplar for those that follow, providing templates of procedures and doctrines, role models for leaders and followers, and demonstrations of the possibility of radical change. Each generates lasting structural impacts too on the nature of the world system, shifting the balance of economic and political power and opening up and closing off windows of objective historical possibility. Short of having a machine to generate virtual universes or replays of history the identification of relatively discrete, broadly comparable sequences is probably the best we can do as comparative historical sociologists.

Notwithstanding these methodological advantages, it is perhaps more useful to go on the offensive here and apply the model we have developed to some wars of greater magnitude: conflicts that many feel had higher stakes or were characterized by equality of forces and hence greater potential for the loss of life by Western protagonists; wars where, some might say, it is not necessary to engage apocalyptic genres and gestures because the threat can speak for itself. The brief investigation of the major wars that follows suggests that the template outlined in this book remains valid. In all cases threats and risks had to be passed through a cultural filter and claims had to be made about global dangers and moral evils. No matter the objective events that took place, there were always narratively mediated disputes over what exactly was going on and what we should do next, over the extent of the real danger. It is a grave mistake to believe that only certain "optional" wars are culturally driven and that the rest can be explained as rational and sensible simply because we think the stakes were higher or the danger more clear-cut. To do so is to project retrospectively one's own sense of what is right and wrong or "clear-cut" onto events, to insert one's own judgments about "good" and "bad," "necessary" and "unnecessary" wars into causal explanation. A full treatment of discourses on these larger, arguably more necessary wars over the four countries would require another book or series of books. So here we limit ourselves to the American case, drawing for the most part on the secondary literature and providing a brief sketch indicating the prima facie plausibility of our cultural model to understand decisions and debates over World War I, World War II, and Vietnam.

FURTHER APPLICATIONS OF THE MODEL: WORLD WAR I, WORLD WAR II, VIETNAM

As Paul Fussell (1975) and others have documented, World War I decisively influenced the way we think about war. Its aftermath was a tragic narration of the consequences of modernity and militarism that exerted a cultural brake on war in the subsequent century. The prevailing imagery has been one of lost youth, disillusioned poets, mud and rotting bodies, clouds of mustard gas and shell shock, inept and uncaring commanders, and futile attempts at victory as initially enthusiastic but subsequently fatalistic or coerced men were mown down going "over the top." If the collective memory here is of a war that should not have been fought, its more proximate cultural causes correspond to the pattern outlined in this book. The last war of high militarism in the West, the Great War rolled into being on a wave of patriotic fervor, enemy stereotyping, and apocalyptic concerns for national survival in Britain, France, and Germany (Marwick 1965). Yet at the very same time a tradition of isolationism kept America out of the conflict until 1917. The story of this entry into war is one of a slow cultural shift. The isolationist position was founded on the low mimetic belief that America had no vital interests at stake, that this was a European squabble and that the protagonists had broadly similar moral qualities—they were all imperialists. American business reaped a profit from this noninterventionist stance, extending war loans to the allies and selling munitions, food, steel, and materiel. Meanwhile, Washington sponsored diplomatic efforts to end the fighting and President Woodrow Wilson was reelected with the slogan "He kept us out of the war."

This comfortable spectator position was slowly undermined by a new narration that inserted historically contingent "facts" into a moral matrix, and which played a part in the alignment of American sympathies with the Allies. This suggested in turn that an actuarial stance was not appropriate and that the players could in fact be morally polarized. The Central Powers looked authoritarian rather than democratic; they had invaded tiny neutral Belgium; France had helped America during the Revolutionary War; the Germans were cultural vandals burning the center of medieval Louvain and shelling the cathedral at Reims; they had executed the brave British nurse Edith Clavell; saboteurs and spies were discovered to have ringleaders in the German and Austrian embassies. The British were further advantaged in that they were more skilled at propaganda than the Germans and their control of the transatlantic cables allowed them greater control over news agendas in the United States. Moreover, notwithstanding his firm commitment to neutrality, President Wilson had great personal respect for British culture and politics and in particular the Gladstonian Liberal tradition. Only the ruthless British quashing of the Easter uprising in Dublin, and forceful British efforts to maintain a maritime blockade with stop-and-search policies on neutral shipping threatened a polarized coding. This increasingly situated the Allies in terms of the Discourse of Liberty and contrasted them to the morally polluted Central Powers (Lyons 1994).

Most pivotal of all in bringing about a move from neutrality in America was the sinking of transatlantic shipping including that of neutral nations by German U-boats. British blockading actions were a nuisance but did not cost lives. By contrast the U-boat attacks seemed indiscriminate and barbaric. The torpedoing of the *Lusitania* off Kinsale, Ireland, in 1915 saw the loss of over 1,400 lives, including 128 Americans. Stories circulated of mothers drowning with babes in arms. The *New York Times* spoke of German conduct as being like that of "savages drunk with blood." Following the resumption of unrestricted submarine warfare by Germany in February 1917, attacks on the Cunard liner *Laconia* and the USS *Housatonic* decisively influenced Congress at the very moment of debate. At the same time secret efforts by German foreign secretary Arthur Zimmerman to sound out a military alliance with Mexico against the United States became public and caused outrage, suggesting that the Germans were now clearly duplicitous, untrustworthy, and conspiratorial and that they were an evil who needed to be confronted. On April 2, 1917, Wilson appeared before Congress seeking a war that would "bring peace and safety to all nations and make the world itself at last free." On April 6, 1917, he signed a declaration taking the United States into the war. It was evident that the "quiet American" who sought isolation from the terrors of the world was misguided. "The wolf is at the door," wrote the *Chicago Tribune* (editorial, April 14, 1917), and the "comfortable home is resting on sand." All this said the apocalyptic reading was never hegemonically institutionalized in America. This assisted the rise of a tragic vision of war during the 1920s and 1930s that was to find an expression in America's delayed entry into the next truly global conflict of the twentieth century. We turn to this next.

World War II has developed its own mythology (Slotkin 2001). It is now seen through the myth of the good war as an event that was fully justified ending in an unequivocal victory. It also saw the greatest generation rise to their historical mission, defending democracy in the United States and abroad. This mythology was founded not simply on outcomes but also on the symbolic matrix that fell into place before and during the war as opposing frameworks slowly began to look implausible. Looking back at the 1930s from our liberal democratic perspective (of course if we were fascists the view would be different) we can see that the policies of appeasement and isolationism were based on a worldview that got the genre seriously wrong. There was a failure to narratively inflate the danger of Hitler and Japan to apocalyptic proportions early enough. This sustained the belief that dangers could be managed by the usual means of diplomacy and treaties, and that dictators could be trusted or at least were rational actors who could be bought off. This failure was a legacy of a now-dominant tragic understanding of the Great War as the kind of pitiable event to be avoided at all costs and a low mimetic reading of events as a series of isolated, containable, controllable crises rather than as a pattern or set that would cumulate in a global threat.

Although much has been made of the failures of Britain and France to stand up to or understand Hitler early enough, a perhaps more significant cause was American retreatism. As A. L. Rouse (1961, 18) put it, this "withdrawal of America out of the world-system" and "contracting out of responsibility" was an "enormous and irreparable mistake." We can account for America's position not simply as an expression of its interests, but rather as an outcome of the tinting of the cultural spectacles through which these were perceived. As America entered the 1930s anti-interventionism was the dominant theme in U.S. foreign policy. Figures such as Harry Elmer Barnes insisted that the Great War had served only the interests of bankers and industrialists, and such a view was widely aired during Senator Gerald P. Nye's inquiry into America's intervention that began in 1934 (Ekirch 1969). Acclaimed films like Carl Laemmle's 1930 feature *All Quiet on the Western Front* captured a vision of war as sordid and futile, not heroic or justified. For many Americans the Great War had been little more than an immoral struggle between greedy European empires. Secretary of State Cordell Hull observed that the press was unanimous that "we must not allow ourselves to be involved in European political developments" (quoted in Herzstein 1989, 76). In the early 1930s polls indicated that 95 percent of Americans wanted to sit on the sidelines come the next European conflict (Herzstein 1989, 77). A mélange of powerful organizations and constituencies within civil society gave voice to this perspective: Progressives with a belief in a Wilsonian liberal world order, Italian Americans, German Americans, and in particular the energetic and vocal pro-Hitler fascistic Bund, Charles Lindbergh's America First Party, the American Legion, student organizations, and the clergy (Ekirch 1969; Herzstein 1989). In 1937, when Roosevelt hinted in a vague way that a "quarantine" might be needed against aggressors there was uproar that this violated the neutral posture. Magazines such as the *Atlantic Monthly* and *Harpers* wrote about Hitler's economic policies and "went out of their way to be 'fair,'" thus giving the impression that the Nazi regime was simply unpredictable and unconventional rather than evil (Herzstein 1989, 113). Even the fall of France and Belgium to Nazi forces was greeted by statements from Lindbergh to the effect that this was a purely European conflict.

Consistent with this spirit we find a series of legislative and diplomatic foreign policy actions through the 1930s indicating a profound failure to come to terms with the nature of the gathering threat. These efforts to manage each crisis were consistent with the low mimetic genre guess. The Neutrality

Act of 1935 prevented the United States from shipping arms to nations engaged in conflict regardless of the rights or wrongs of the struggle. Mussolini's invasion of Abyssinia was met with feeble and ineffectual calls for a voluntary "moral embargo" on exports to Italy (Herzstein 1989, 80). Japanese aggression led to naval restrictions, tariffs, and trade sanctions as well as with concerted efforts at negotiation (Wray 1990). The Wilsonian and legalistic Secretary of State Hull seemingly believed that a negotiated settlement of differences in the Pacific was possible. When Japan occupied the north of French Indochina in late 1940, Hull responded most forcefully—with an embargo on the export of scrap metal. For a long time, even Roosevelt accepted "the almost universal prophecy that Japan would not fight the United States" and that the balance of rewards and sanctions could be used to contain Japanese aggression (Graebner 1990).

The story of the period from 1935 to 1941 is of the slow revision of this genre guess. Assisted by William Dodd, the ambassador to Germany, Roosevelt revised his estimate of Hitler somewhat earlier than most of contemporaries. His speeches and fireside chats demonstrate a subtle and progressively more concerted effort to implement a genre shift by suggesting that the object of struggle was the world and its destiny and not some local concern of the Europeans, and that the antagonist, Hitler, had unlimited evil ambitions. In effect, FDR spent six or seven years trying to accustom his citizens to the idea that war might be necessary, speaking in coded ways at first and focusing primarily on the need to protect the "Western Hemisphere" rather than becoming more actively involved in Europe's struggle. From his "I-hate-War" speech delivered in Chautauqua, New York, through to those of the eve of Pearl Harbor we find a transformation from the idea that war could be avoided with prudent policy and idealism through to the view that it was an unavoidable and necessary. By 1941 the Germans could be described in fireside chats and radio broadcasts as like a "rattlesnake poised to attack." They were looking to seize control of the oceans, they were building bridgeheads in the "Western Hemisphere" by means of shadowy Nazi saboteurs, they were seeking "world mastery" (Roosevelt 1950, 387). The "hard-headed, far-sighted and realistic American people," Roosevelt insisted, would come to see that appeasement and isolation were problematic. They would appreciate the "cruel, relentless facts" that the Germans were "unrestrained seekers of world conquest and permanent world domination," and that "the normal practices of diplomacy—note writing—are of no possible use in dealing with international outlaws" (Roosevelt 1950, 389). Americans, he said, faced a choice between "the kind of world we want to live in and the kind of world that Hitler and his hordes would impose on us" (Roosevelt 1950, 441). In such a context where "European conquest was but a step toward ultimate goals on other continents" there was a need to check "the advance of Hitlerism" before "the Western Hemisphere will be within the range of the Nazi weapons of destruction" (1950, 181).

Aside from FDR's own rhetorical efforts a number of events helped shift the codes and narratives used to understand Germany and Japan. The Spanish Civil War saw many on the Left move away from the understanding that neutrality in general and the Neutrality Act in particular were viable options in the face of a Fascist menace. Writers, intellectuals, and fellow travelers started to defect from pacifism. Whereas in 1935 Ernest Hemmingway had called for America to stay away from the "hell broth that is brewing in Europe," he could be found shortly afterward writing enthusiastically from the front lines about the heroic struggle for freedom in Iberia. *The Nation* and the *New Republic* became increasingly pro-Spanish Republic rather than proneutrality (Ekirch 1969). Japanese expansion into Manchuria encouraged the view that it was militaristic and imperialistic (Wray 1990). By the late 1930s public sentiment in America was falling out strongly against Japan, with public pressure over air attacks on Chinese civilians contributing to the decision to implement a "moral embargo" on the export of aircraft in 1938 (Utley 1990). Anti-Nazi feelings became stronger, sustained by stories of atrocities in Germany and testimony from Jewish refugees and prestigious intellectuals such as Thomas Mann. Feature articles in major news magazines turned against the Nazis and polls indicated strong support for a movement to boycott German goods. German agents reported concern at the level of hatred for Hitler and National Socialism in America. By 1941, conspiracy theories, rumors of Fifth Column activity, and documents and maps purporting to demonstrate German designs on the Western Hemisphere were helping Roosevelt fuel a sense of fear and anxiety and generate the impression that Germany was not merely bad, but also dangerous. These fell on fertile soil. As early as 1938 many panicking in response to the celebrated radio broadcast of *War of the Worlds* by Orson Welles and the Mercury Theatre reported that they had thought it was a German attack. Films such as Alfred Hitchcock's *Foreign Correspondent* and Henry Luce's *The Ramparts We Watch* spelled out Germany's imperialist designs in no uncertain terms (Herzstein 1989), while Edward R. Murrow's broadcasts from London during the blitz created a sense of urgency and solidarity. Support for American rearmament grew alongside sympathy for the beleaguered British and the desire to help them materially in their hour of need. Conscription was introduced for the first time with hardly a protest, there was a "destroyers for bases" deal with Britain and the Lend-Lease Act of early 1941. In a situation where anti-fascism could be described as a "cult" by even a liberal like Alfred A. Bingham (Ekirch 1969, 233), America did everything it could short of war to confront the Nazis, to be as un-neutral as possible without violating its neutrality and entering the conflict.

Pearl Harbor is often considered a crucial event or turning point. It did not however generate a tire-smoking U-turn in American attitudes by itself. Rather it was pivotal in that it finally discredited American isolationism. Its event interpretation hinged upon prior cultural groundwork that had established apocalypticism as a genre possibility, even if this had reached its thematic apogee in treatments of Hitler and concerns over Europe rather than Japan. In a context where Japan and Germany were already polluted and known to have sinister designs the surprise attack was really just a final, decisive clue about the genre in which events were to be understood. The act had served to demonstrate once and for all the evil duplicity of fascism and Japanese imperialism, the dangers of "totalitarianism." Roosevelt's (1950, 522–31) fireside chat following the declaration of war with Japan maps out this apocalyptic scenario unambiguously: gangsters had "banded together to make war upon the whole human race" (522); the entire world was "one gigantic battlefield" (523); this was "the most tremendous undertaking of our American history" (524); the nation is "fighting for its existence and its future life" (527); American force was to be directed "toward ultimate good as well as against ultimate evil" (530). In this spirit the Los Angeles Times (editorial, December 8, 1941) could call for an end to "foolish if well-meant isolationist obstructions" and the New York Times could confidently declare that "this was never an intra-European war. It was intended from the beginning as a World War." This was to be against a "hydra-headed evil, a gigantic force which already has whole continents by the throat," a "rendezvous with destiny" (editorial, December 8, 1941). A new genre template had been institutionalized and remained plausible as a result of the diverse theaters of battle, the scale of the war, and the manifest military and industrial power of the adversaries. It was vindicated afterward by discovery of the Holocaust and Hitler's weapons programs, which had developed workable ballistic missiles and jet airplanes. In contrast to, say, the War in Iraq where no evidence of a credible military or terrorist threat was found or World War I where deaths just looked pointless, there were no quibbles after the event that this war had been avoidable. The struggle did not just look apocalyptic at the time—the reading has stood up over the decades. Hitler remains modernity's greatest villain, the Nazi party its most evil force, the years of struggle a true hinge of history.

Initiated as part of a cold war fight against the menace of communism, with the more precise strategic aim being to "contain" Chinese and Russian influence in Southeast Asia, the Vietnam "Conflict" involved an army of up to half a million American troops as well as extensive air and naval forces. At its peak the war cost $2,000 million every month. Yet for all this investment of money and material it was to become perhaps the least legitimate and most controversial war of recent times, creating wrenching divisions in civil society, desertion and draft dodging, street demonstrations and closed campuses, prayer vigils, and a vocal veterans movement opposed to the war. The scenario clearly indicates the political consequences of trying to engage in a conflict without a consistent or widely accepted legitimating narrative and the way that the popular will to fight or pay for such activity evaporates without a sustained and plausible apocalyptic message. In his memoir Colin Powell reports that he had arrived in Vietnam in 1962 standing on "a bedrock of principle and conviction" (1995, 145) "to stop the spread of Marxism; to help the South Vietnamese save their country from a communist takeover" (ibid., 80). This personal understanding was far from unique, in fact it was typical and was made possible by the widely shared discourse within which the war in Indochina was situated. This understood the communist insurgency to be not simply a local struggle but rather part of the slow-burning apocalyptic contest between freedom and tyranny that was the cold war. In this narrative communism assumed the mantle of totalitarian evil previously sported by Nazi Germany, and its containment became the central task of American foreign policy (Podhoretz 1989, 27). The much touted "domino theory"—itself a specification of the Truman Doctrine of 1947—understood each and every nation as part of a wider theater of conflict wherein world domination was the ultimate prize. As Secretary of State Dean Rusk put it in 1966, America's commitments in Vietnam were "absolutely essential to the preservation of peace rights around the globe" (quoted in Graebner 1989, 12) because communism had to be contained. Speaking at Johns Hopkins University on April 7, 1965, President Johnson tried to explain the need for the war to the American people, stating (just like Eden, Mollet, and the two George Bushes in other contexts familiar by now to readers of this book) that the fight was "for a world where every country can shape its own destiny"; urging that retreat from Vietnam would see the "battle renewed in one country and then another" for "the appetite of aggression is never satisfied"; and quoting the Bible: "Hitherto shalt thou come, but no further" (Johnson 1965).

Opinion polls suggest a steady decline in support for the war from 1965 onward (Braestrup 1989, 266). Colin Powell also reports that within a few years the soldiers fighting the war "lacked inspiration and a sense of purpose" (1995, 132). Desertion became a problem. This was a response born partly of the frustrations of combat experience, and partly from the failure of the apocalyptic genre to become dominant. Able critics of the Vietnam conflict attempted deflation and relentlessly narrated in the tragic genre. It was taken to be a pointless exercise in which young American lives were wasted, in which politicians were unable to provide leadership and Pentagon technocrats had lost contact with realities on the ground. The politics of the military draft were understood as an antidemocratic form of class discrimination. The binary rationale of the fight against communism was subject to critique and the complexities of a nationalist, anticolonial struggle were advanced as an alternate context. No longer a global fight, the war could better be seen as a local, internal struggle—a civil war where America did not belong. The abstractions of the domino theory seemed to require a leap of faith and did not hold up well when it came to identifying an immediate, concrete challenge to American survival. As the young John Kerry was to put it in his now famous testimony to the U.S. Senate Foreign Relations Committee in 1971 representing Vietnam Veterans against the War, "there is nothing in South Vietnam which could happen that realistically threatens the United States of America." There was anger that the troops had been told about a "mystical war against communism," when in truth this was a "civil war, an effort by people who had for years been seeking their liberation from any colonial influence whatsoever" (Kerry 1985, 454). The Vietcong were an enemy on the ground but increasingly the real foe came to be seen as the misguided American elites and politicians sending troops to their senseless death. American soldiers were interpreted as bogged down in a pointless regional struggle that had increasingly tenuous connections to any world-historical fight against communism. This was a "half-hearted half-war" (Powell 1995, 148) for which America's leaders struggled to find a convincingly apocalyptic justification. Indeed their failure to provide just such a story at crucial junctures was a major contributor to the rise of the tragic genre. When field reports from Walter Cronkite and others on the Tet offensive documented futility and chaos, President Johnson was unable to respond with a compelling alternative (Braestrup 1989, 266; Delli Carpini 1990).

These blunders and silences were all the more important because of the presence of talented and eloquent spokespersons for the opposing position such as Dr. Martin Luther King Jr., who in April 1967 broke his silence and delivered a sermon titled "Declaration of Independence from the War in Vietnam." He spoke of the "madness" of the destruction and suffering and the need to defeat communism not through war but through a positive commitment to peace and social justice (King 1985). Other intellectuals pushed the envelope. Figures such as Stokely Carmichael, Susan Sontag, Norman Mailer, Tom Hayden, and Conor Cruise O' Brien developed romantic stories that often inverted the moral coding of America and North Vietnam. These suggested that Ho Chi Minh ("Uncle Ho") was a heroic man of the people, that the North Vietnamese were nation-building, peace-loving freedom fighters, and "Amerika" was the imperialist power who would be inevitably defeated by this popular will. Now involvement in the war was not simply futile and pointless, it was also evil. As Paul Hollander (1989) points out, such critique of the war was fused with a broader indictment of "Amerikan" society as capitalist, bureaucratic, technocratic, sexist, etc. etc. to such as extent that its opponent was exempted from moral scrutiny. Fellow travelers turned a blind eye to atrocities, to "reeducation camps," and to human rights abuses, reading North Vietnam as a communist utopia of open and authentic human relationships. Reinforced by popular song, the alternative press and social movements (Franklin 1990; Storey 1990), this developed narrative underpinned grassroots opposition to violence on campuses and among the new class of intellectuals.

For a while President Nixon attempted to turn around this losing genre war and insisted on the need for continuing apocalyptic readings. If the United States acted like a "pitiful, helpless giant" he warned, then "the forces of totalitarianism and anarchy will threaten free nations and free institutions throughout the world" (Nixon 1985a, 451). In his November 1969 address announcing the "Vietnamization" policy, Nixon admitted that "Americans have lost confidence in what their Government has told them about our policy," but went on to remind the audience that the struggle was about confronting "great powers who have not yet abandoned their goals of world conquest," and that failure in Vietnam would "spark violence . . . in the Middle East, in Berlin, eventually in the Western Hemisphere" (Nixon 1985b, 432). Yet ironically it was the deflation to low mimesis for which his administration is now best remembered. Low mimesis empowers legalistic, technocratic, and managerialist solutions to crisis. Henry Kissinger's advocacy of détente held that dealings with the communist powers could be bureaucratically stabilized and professionally regulated due to shared commitments and interests and by making use of treaties, inspections, and diplomacy. Nixon could now put his efforts into thawing out relations with China and Russia. Apocalypticism could be abandoned at least for the time being as the operative genre for thinking about the cold war. South Vietnam could be surrendered to the North and the troops could come home.

STATES, WARS, AND CIVIL SOCIETIES

The fact that even in these major wars leaders and elites were beholden to and constrained by narration in the public sphere for motivational inputs, popular legitimacy, and what we might think of as simply "reasons to fight" brings us back to the question with which we started: Why War? The findings of this book suggest that we need to think again about the origins of international violence, and specifically to move beyond the realist, étatist paradigm that has dominated sociology and political science in thinking about this issue. The problem of how society regulates and controls the use of violence has been central to social theory since the time of Thomas Hobbes. Where Hobbes pointed to the purview of the sovereign, today we generally indicate the authority of the state. Max Weber's famous definition of the state as an organization with a monopoly on the legitimate use of force is emblematic of this move. This was mated to his historical account of the state accomplishing internal pacification and subordination through the progressive disarming of feudal and regional elites. Consequent research on war, revolution, and militarism as well as in international relations more broadly has overwhelmingly centered on the role of the state in controlling, initiating, and perpetuating violence within and outside its borders (e.g., Mann 1986, 1988; Morgenthau 1985; Shaw 1984, 1991; Skocpol 1979) and tends to understand such activity, as we saw in the first chapter of this book, as a rational action organized around its pursuit of security or domination.

From this theoretical blueprint of an active, rational, calculating, all-powerful state it is but a short step to arguments suggesting that the state apparatus calls the shots and that the broader public is impotent, its consent "manufactured," or its attitude overly indifferent or fatalistic. We need not have recourse to crude conspiracy theories or Frankfurt School visions of a mass society to substantiate this position. Consider a writer as sophisticated as Michael Mann (1987). Mann illustrates such a theme with his understanding of how the culture and organization of militarism has shifted over recent decades in the major powers. He identifies a "deterrence science militarism" held by elites and organized around themes of technological development, dispute management, and rational policy formation as the driving force in conflicts in the post–World War II era. In the Western powers the military is now said to be cut off from and peripheral to the wider society and is allegedly able to conduct its business largely without public interest or involvement. As for that wider public, Mann says it has lapsed into what he calls "spectator sport militarism"—a kind of armchair activity that involves heavy media dependence for information and the vicarious emotional rewards of participation at a distance but no personal risk or sacrifice. Watching wars today, he says, is "not qualitatively different from the Olympic Games" (1987, 48) as we cheer on our troops from the comfort of the sofa.

This kind of vision of wars as the monopoly property of states, with publics dependent and irrational, is challenged by empirical realities of the kind discussed in this book. We have seen that wars are actively contested within and outside the formal political apparatus with efforts toward reason pivotal to the life of civil society. We have seen that political leaders can be called to account more often than they would like and that public scrutiny and public opinion operates as a potent constraint on state actions. Importantly, we have also discovered that the relevant cultural matrix for interpreting war is not only that of militarism or national military history. In fact specifically martial themes are played out in and through a more general and encompassing civil discourse. All this suggests that we need to retrieve theories of civil society as an important counter to the étatist version of political philosophy and to bring the deliberative activity of the public sphere back into our understanding of wars, their initiation, conduct, and consequences. This entails thinking about the culture structures that inform societal decision making and the ways that civil discourses are mobilized to determine lines of action and pathways for moral accountability. In sum, theorizing the discursive switching points and semiotic armatures through which situations are interpreted and history executed. In so doing we come to understand collective violence as a cultural act underpinned to a greater or lesser extent by what Jean-Jacques Rousseau would have called the popular will and Durkheim the collective conscience.

This book has provided one set of answers to this question of how the culture of a civil society might regulate war. Yet it is not the first attempt at the task. The original philosophers of civil society were intrigued by societal shifts in norms about violence. We find Adam Smith writing in his *Theory of Moral Sentiments:*

Can there be greater barbarity, for example, than to hurt an infant? Its helplessness, its innocence, its amiableness, call forth the compassion, even of an enemy, and not to spare that tender age is regarded as the most furious effort of an enraged and cruel conqueror. What then should we imagine must be the heart of a parent who could injure that weakness which even a furious enemy is afraid to violate? Yet the exposition, that is, the murder of new-born infants, was a practice allowed of in almost all the states of Greece, even amongst the polite and civilized Athenians; and whenever the circumstances of the parent rendered it inconvenient to bring up the child, to abandon it to hunger, or to wild beasts, was regarded without blame or censure. (A. Smith 1976 [1759], 209–10)

Smith gives voice here to the position of the Scottish Enlightenment that evolving levels of civility and its adjunct of empathic moral sentiment had long operated to move the goalposts on acceptable and unacceptable violence. In this vision the internal pacification of the nation had come not so much from the enforcement of growing state control, as Weber was later to argue, but rather found its origins in incremental shifts in sensibility operating over the *longue durée* of civilization as we evolved from savagery to barbarism to civilization. Such transformations have been most famously and systematically traced by Norbert Elias (1994), whose major studies document the emergence of civilizing, violence-averse norms over the past several centuries. For all their utility such claims about empathy and ethos are rather diffuse and abstract and cannot take us very far if we are looking to support a structural model of culture of the kind that informs this study. The potential for such an understanding can, however, be found in the work of Smith's peer Adam Ferguson, who realized not only that war was about conquest, domination, and security, but also that it was regulated by culture and that moral sentiments were encoded in exemplary stories. He writes:

> The hero of the Greek fable, endued with superior force, courage, and address, takes ever advantage of an enemy, to kill with safety to himself; and actuated by a desire of spoil, or by a principle of revenge, is never stayed in his progress by interruptions of remorse or compassion. . . . Our modern fable, or romance, on the contrary, generally couples an object of admiration, brave, generous, and victorious; or sends the hero abroad in search of mere danger, and of occasions to prove his valor . . . indifferent to spoil, he contends only for renown, and employs his valor to rescue the distressed and to protect the innocent . . . professes a contempt of stratagem and unites in the same person, characters and dispositions seemingly opposite; ferocity with gentleness, and the love of blood with sentiments of tenderness and pity. (Ferguson 1966 [1767], 200–201)

For Ferguson, then, there has been a wholesale shift in the ways that we narrate acceptable violence and implicitly in the kinds of legitimate violent action that are possible. Stories about heroes, motives, and violence have determinate properties that influence our thinking. They have closed down certain violent options. This is helpful but there is also a need to move beyond his position. Ferguson's thesis is sketchy at best and does not really come to terms with the ways that civil society might use narrative as a resource in its deliberations or as a tool for understanding unfolding current affairs. Moreover, Ferguson, like Elias and Smith, assumes that civilization has operated largely as a constraint on violence and that civil society is the carrier of a culture of pacification. The result for social theory can be a schizophrenic vision—still current in some quarters of the peace studies field—where violence is understood as driven by *raison d'état* and peace by the endemic culture of democratic publics. The path opened up in this book has suggested that we do not live in a civil sphere dominated by a single pacific narrative. There are no grounds for optimism about the future. Rather we need to consider the interplay of contending narratives in the civil discourse—some conducive to violence and some resistant—and to investigate the ways that these unfold in complex real-time sequences as we deliberate on difficult choices.

Whatever the narrative details, it is clear that the Scottish Enlightenment thinkers were on the right track and that the specter of the rational state needs to be confronted with a more dialogic vision of state and civil society. By bringing in civil society in this way we can open up important normative agendas in thinking about war. The dominant étatist/rationalist paradigm has disturbing moral implications because it absolves from responsibility those outside the state/military apparatus. The argument that the civil sphere can make a difference frees us from the bad faith of this spectator subject position. In validating the situation-specific interpretive and dialogic activity of communicating citizens, for example, this book is consistent with intuitively and normatively appealing models of deliberative democracy and the moral autonomy of the subject. Yet it also calls for their reformulation in a more cultural direction. In the model of discourse ethics proposed by Jürgen Habermas (1984) great weight is given to the quest for a rationally achieved consensus organized by the search for "undistorted communication" and "good reasons." Power is understood as the principal source of distortion and danger for this communicative process, with procedural rules and good faith our best guarantee for communicatively rational outcomes. The story we have been telling in this book suggests that such genetically achieved rational communication and consensus may be impossible to attain even if such conditions are fulfilled. We can never be fully rational, truly objective, fully reflexive in thinking about the need for this or that war because our efforts toward rationality are constrained not only by power but also by the symbolic systems and culture structures we need to think with. The "good reasons" that are put forward about the need to enter or avoid a war, the diverse facts and items of evidence that are presented—these can make sense only when placed within an implicit genre that secretly loads the dice when it comes to action path selection. Moreover, the selection of this genre is one that involves a nonrational moment, the leap of faith that is the genre guess. This cannot be avoided if we are to be able to make any choice at all. When the impulse to rationality and the ineluctable symbolic are fused in this way, then decision making will always entail some cultural contamination, some furtive bias no matter how earnest our efforts to stick to the facts or be true to our discourse ethics.

If living in a harmonious world without wars is an impossibility, then the next best thing might be to live in a world where we could be assured that all our wars were necessary ones—a world in which the evidence could speak for itself and we could go to bed and sleep soundly knowing that the facts of the case had dictated our difficult but ultimately correct decision to send in the troops. The story told in this book has been a rather different one. It is of a world of choices and interpretations and moral visions as much as of reason, a world where deliberation is both enabled and constrained by culture-structures, a world where we must ultimately take responsibility for our genre guess. The fact that we cannot stand outside of culture and arrive with confidence at some true reading of each apparent crisis is bad news for critical theory with its utopian aspirations for the machinery of rational discourse ethics. Yet in acknowledging that culture-structures inform reason we attain greater potentials for reflexivity and auto-critique, and with this some slim chances of regaining provisional mastery over the narrative forms that through millennia of conflict have exerted a subtle tidal pull on our thoughts and actions. Understanding this gravity of deep culture-structure and figuring out just how genre choices shape the way that we make history is a small step toward a more deliberate and reasoned making of that history—military or otherwise.

POSTSCRIPT ON THE WAR IN IRAQ

As this book goes to press at the start of June 2005, the controversy over the War in Iraq continues. It seems useful to provide a very brief update on the ways that the genre politics reported in chapter 5 have played out since the completion of the manuscript in December 2004. The situation in Iraq has remained difficult and subject to two contending narrations.

By May 2005 the justification of the War in Iraq was finally starting to look like an issue that could be pushed to the back burner in the United States. President Bush, for his part, had shifted his rhetorical agenda away from the earlier apocalyptic treatments of Iraq in the context of WMD toward providing an explanation for a continuing U.S. military presence and its consequent troubles. His was a romantic narrative in which freedom and democracy were being built. Countering claims that this was a U.S. army of occupation and a puppet regime, he could point to an elected Iraqi government that was reaching out to the Sunni and had requested the UN that 140,000 American service personnel be allowed to remain in their country. Yet newspapers remained full with reports of the kidnapping and murder of foreigners (including aid workers from neutral nations), the violent actions of the elusive militant Abu Masab Zarquawi, a complex armed insurgency, and allegations against U.S. military personnel of prisoner abuse. The interpretive question remained whether this mess was an inevitable and temporary consequence of the tough love that was bringing freedom to Iraq (romance) or an unnecessary product of ongoing American mismanagement (tragedy). Now around 38% of Americans approved of Bush's handling of Iraq and 57% disapproved (CBS News Poll, May 20–24, available at www.pollingreport.com); some 47% thought America did the right thing in invading Iraq and 49% thought that it should have stayed out. This was an ambivalent legacy indeed.

Unlike Bush, Tony Blair continued to be dogged by his role in advocating the War in Iraq in 2002 and 2003. In the general election of May 2005 he scraped back into power, but was punished by the electorate, his majority dropping by more than half and his party getting the votes of only 21% of adult Britons. Commentators attributed much of the swing not only to his apocalyptic stance on Iraq, which many had not shared and that had not been vindicated by WMD finds, but also to Blair's muddled, sneaky-looking handling of the case for war. These had proven soft targets for Labour's opponents as they applied the Discourse of Repression during campaigning. Just days before the election it was revealed that back in March 2003 attorney general Lord Goldsmith had advised Blair on the legality of invading Iraq. He had initially suggested seeking a further UN resolution in support of the war, but this opinion had not been passed on to the cabinet. For the first time Blair began to look like a liability and talk set in about him standing down to make way for chancellor Gordon Brown. It was said this would enable Labour to put a line under Iraq and move forward. By contrast the war's vocal opponent George Galloway (see pp. 185–86) triumphantly ousted New Labour's high profile Oona King in the inner city Bethnal Green constituency and the war sceptical Liberal Democrats made substantial gains in seats with large Muslim populations.

In France antagonism toward the United States and its unilateral action remained. Unfortunately for Jacques Chirac the War in Iraq was not a front-burner issue in his nation, so although popular, his stance from 2003 carried little weight. The French had not been involved in the invasion, their troops were not dying, they were not really responsible. Through 2004 and 2005 Chirac's fate became increasingly tied to domestic concerns such as unemployment, taxation, fuel costs, and immigration and the diffuse genre-inflated anxieties that surrounded these. In May 2005 the French people rejected a European Union Constitution in a referendum. This was widely understood as a rebuke for Chirac's domestic rather than foreign policy. As for Spain, in April 2004 Prime Minister Zapatero cited his election pledges to the people and announced that he was pulling Spanish troops out of Iraq. Consistent with the genre politics we reviewed in chapter 5 he continued to advocate a greater role for the UN in Iraqi reconstruction and to commit substantial numbers of Spanish troops to peace-keeping efforts around the globe.

These outcomes should be regarded as provisional. In the first chapter I indicated the ways in which the interpretation of unfolding events was a high-risk activity, noting "the rug might be pulled from under our feet at any moment by a new revelation or twist in emergent circumstances" (p. 31). The War on Terror is currently ongoing—arguably so is the War in Iraq. Contingencies such as terrorist attacks, evidentiary discoveries on WMD, the trial of Saddam Hussein, the capture, death, or continuing disappearance of Osama bin Laden, the success or failure of rebuilding in Iraq—all these will have decisive impacts on the plausibility of the diverse genre guesses that are currently doing battle. For want of a time machine I am unable to write about what the future has in store. That said, readers who have taken on board the lessons of this book will have all the tools they need for making sense of these yet to be fought genre wars.

New Haven
June 1, 2005

NOTES

CHAPTER 1

1. The model described here outlining a structuralist approach to the culture of the public sphere was largely developed by Jeffrey Alexander, Steven Sherwood, and the author at UCLA in the period from 1987 to 1992. As this has subsequently become modestly influential it is worth recounting the history of this innovation. Our background inspiration came from a cultural (i.e., not structural or functionalist) reading of Durkheim's *Elementary Forms of Religious Life*. Here was an account of society that seemingly put drama and symbolism, binary classifications and myths, emotions and beliefs at the center of the analytic agenda for sociology. In this spirit, by the late 1980s Alexander had "discovered" the sacred and profane codes of civil society through his neo-Durkheimian investigations of Watergate and readings in the American Studies field of authors like Bernard Bailyn. In his writings from this period we also find the widespread invocation of narrative as a feature of civil discourse, but usually in the more idiographic sense of stories built up from historical experiences. In effect these stories were local, emergent specifications of broader and more universal themes such as salvation, damnation, and evil. During the late 1980s we continued to make empirical investigations applying the binary codes (these first appeared in the early 1990s, e.g., Alexander 1992; Alexander and Smith 1993; P. Smith 1991) but were becoming more excited by narrative's potential to capture the color and texture of the collective conscience. Three further factors prompted the shift toward the model underpinning this book. (1) Sherwood and I observed a small theoretical disconnect between Alexander's approach to narrative and the more systematic cultural logic of the codes. The uncomfortable divide between hermeneutics and structuralism seemed to be repeated here. (2) Our belief in a more structural, typological approach to public sphere narrative as a possibility was confirmed by our scattered ongoing empirical investigations of 1980s public sphere controversies (on Reagan, Gorbachev, Oliver North and Irangate, General Noriega). Here we saw rather cartoonish stereotyping and the eternal return of the same tropes. (3) A reading of Kenneth Burke was also instrumental.

Whereas Clifford Geertz had used Burke to flag the local, particular, and proliferating, we saw Burke (for example in *A Grammar of Motives*) arguing in the constructivist vein but simultaneously insisting that rhetorical forms closed down possibilities for narration and often operated by means of binary switches. Next a chance reading of a Robert Scholes primer (*Structuralism in Literature*) and an encounter with the work of Hayden White pointed us toward Northrop Frye's *Anatomy of Criticism*. It was instantly apparent that this text answered our theoretical needs. We could talk about narrativity but in a way that was consistent with the principles of structuralist semiotics and therefore amenable to the construction of generalizable cultural theory. In Steve Sherwood's phrase we now had a systematic way to understand the process of "narrating the social." The imaginative faculty of Durkheim's "collective conscience" could be seen as shaped by the genre conventions of the kind that Frye identified and not simply as the telling of this or that unique story. The earliest publications in this mode appeared in the *Journal of Narrative and Life History* (Sherwood 1994; P. Smith 1994), although Sherwood, Alexander, and I circulated typescripts using the model as early as 1989/1990. These generally explored the narration of the personalities of the day: Ronald Reagan, Oliver North, George Bush, Saddam Hussein, Mikhail Gorbachev, Manuel Noriega. My PhD thesis from 1993 was the prototype for this book. Steve Sherwood's thesis on the narration of John Lennon as artistic hero was completed in 2003.The first monograph length applications of the theory to be published were by Agnes Ku (1999) and Ronald Jacobs (2000).

2. Durkheim's influence runs deep in this book although in the text he has been displaced by semiotics and structuralist hermeneutics. I did not want this to become another book of Durkheim critique, application, or interpretation. Let it be said that the model elaborated in these pages takes as its point of origin Durkheim's claims that social life is sometimes ritualized and is lived in part through collective representations, that society is animated by a moralized collective conscience and that the classification of the world into the sacred and profane provides a wellspring for action. Ideas about the public sphere, the theories of structuralist poetics and understandings of dialogic exchange are really just a way of elaborating upon these fundamental insights and thinking through what they might mean in an account of contemporary political life.

3. Please note that the claim is neither made that these codes are universal in social life, nor that they are the only form of culture that can be at play in public debate (see Battani et al. 1997; Alexander and Smith 1999). Clearly other spheres such as the military or the arts or the family will have different understandings of the sacred and profane. For example, to treat one's own children without some measure of favoritism would be deviant; to disregard hierarchy in the army would lead to a court martial. I have already demonstrated that fascism and communism as political cultures have distinctive regulatory codes (P. Smith 1998). In fascism, for example, emotion is valued over reason and violence over law. The claim, to repeat, is simply that these codes are pivotal, perhaps dominant, in *public sphere debate in liberal democratic contexts*.

4. The model I have been developing here is derived loosely from Frye but does not slavishly follow his template. Some of the criteria for narrative inflation and deflation are mentioned in his work in only an implicit way and have been reconstructed, others are my own innovation. Moreover, Frye's systems of fictional modes and mythoi seem overly complex. They are perhaps more suited to the study of literature or folklore than public sphere narration and it is no surprise that even commentators sympathetic to him seem compelled to simplify or to develop contending taxonomies (see Denham 1978). Hayden White, for example, speaks of comedic, ironic, tragic, and romantic narrations. Yet for Frye irony is a component of both comedy and tragedy, and the distinction between comedy and heroic romance is acknowledged as

problematic because they share common structural features. Like Hayden White's approach, the model presented here with its limited pool of four genres can be thought of as a simplification and clarification that makes Frye workable for the practical purposes at hand. We are more interested in plot, for example, than the ways that this might intersect with the uses and forms of poetic metaphor or meter. By the same logic, insofar as civil discourse on war is a serious matter comedy drops out of the frame although it clearly has potential applications to events such as sex scandals.

5. Fredric Jameson (1982: 107–8) is more than a little disingenuous in positioning Frye in the category of a "semantic" genre critic. Frye's Aristotelian leanings clearly give him a foot in both camps. He is interested not only in the spirit or sensibility of each mode, but also in the formal or structural foundations for these. Jameson's move, of course, is designed to reserve for neo-Marxist literary criticism the role of the dialectical hero who is able to reconcile the two approaches in a movement toward "totality."

6. The position taken here on the relationship between facts and stories has been developed analogically from the work the philosopher of perception Edmond Wright (1990, 1999). The position of "new representationalism" (in effect a materialist constructivism) that he has developed argues that a distinction needs to be made between non-epistemic sensing and motivated perception and that an evolutionary advantage has accrued to humans from their ability to exchange and update perceptions-of-entity that are derived from the clues thrown out by a continuum or flux. Perception in this sense is social. By loose analogy civil discourse can be understood as a practical collective mechanism for assembling clues into usable and exchangeable information. There are fascinating and yet to be explored connections between Wright's "viscous realism" and Hirsch's theory of interpretation in that both involve the creative assembly of less-meaningful elements into more-meaningful wholes and the possibility for adaptive upgrading of mistaken interpretation through dialogue.

CHAPTER 2

1. This said, the Internet did play some part in the research strategies of this book and a note on this is in order. For the final empirical chapter on the War in Iraq I made use of the Internet in addition to hard copy, but primarily as a research tool for collecting conventional forms of public sphere discourse. I did look at some quasi-magazine, lobbying sites run by diverse interest groups such as moveon.org and antiwar.com that seemed to be becoming more influential. In chapter five some of this material is quoted. For the most part the Internet was used in this chapter to retrieve online versions of mainstream press and to visit official sites such as the White House or H.M. Stationery Office whence speeches and reports could be downloaded. I also made use of online search engines and databases such as LexisNexis. The major benefit of the Internet here was convenience—I could cover a lot of ground very quickly from the comfort of my office. However, I found no real net information gain compared to a trip to the newspaper or microform room of the research library—at least for this kind of project. Even in fringe group and lobbying Web sites the arguments were bolstered by the same code and genre characteristics that I had already located in the mainstream press. For reasons of transparency I have not reported on chat rooms or web logs (blogs) here. Although there is currently much talk about these it is unclear whether their material has archival status or influence and their relationship to the public sphere needs to be more adequately theorized. Rather than introduce a new complexity into the final chapter I opted for the most part to

stick with the same print media sources used in the Suez and Gulf War investigations and to maximize the comparability of data over the cases.

A brief word is also in order about the citation system for primary sources. The system of in-text citation adopted provides readers with quick visual clues as to where material comes from as they read and does not require repeated reference to endnotes. However, this choice also required that the names of authors and article titles not be included so as to maintain continuity and flow. For the most part page numbers are omitted. Newspapers have long been published in various editions and with diverse supplements complicating these in inscrutable ways. Moreover, newspaper material retrieved online does not generally provide a page number cross-reference to the hard copy. I have indicated the date of publication and (in the citation or the text) if the quotation is from an editorial, op-ed, or letter—otherwise, it is an article of reportage. This should be sufficient for interested readers to locate the material for themselves. For the most part the names of journalists and writers in the media are excluded from the citation as irrelevant. I made exceptions where I judged the author to be a public sphere intellectual or commentator of repute. This was most often the case with op-ed items. The selection of exhibits for presentation in this text was nonrandom. I favor material from the more influential organs rather than from those that are simply popular or merely peripheral. Hence, in the case of the United States a lot of "evidence" comes from the *New York Times* and *Time;* in the United Kingdom from *The Times* and *The Guardian;* in France from *Le Monde,* and in Spain from *El País* and *Cambio 16.* However, data from other sources (e.g., *The Nation, El Sol, La Croix, The Listener*) is also included to add depth to the account and to demonstrate the breadth of the research effort underlying this project.

CHAPTER 3

1. Note the ambiguity of this action. Had Saddam Hussein chosen the same target for his sharp-shooting the Coke bottles would almost certainly have been transformed into symbols of the America he wished to smash rather than into evidence of an all-American disposition. This is a nice example of the totalizing effect of narrative, the way that details and clues are assimilated to a wider pattern that closes off alternative interpretations.

2. In another publication (P. Smith 1991) I note that disputes between Latin American nations were seen by the British as pointless "squabbles" in contrast to the reasoned and serious nature of its war with Argentina over the Falklands/Malvinas in 1982. The "squabble" is a signifier that downgrades conflicts and minimizes their portentousness. It is a good "tell" that the speaker does not have an apocalyptic vision of the issues in hand.

3. The language game of the blunder or mistake was also used to effect cultural repair in the case of the Amiriya bunker. See the discussion of the Gulf War, p. 120.

4. In his autobiography, *Full Circle,* Eden (e.g., 1960, 430–32) devotes some extraordinary passages to Egypt and its leader. These provide strong evidence that his genuine feelings toward Nasser were of fear and hatred, shaped by an apocalypticism in *excess* of that of in his public language at the time. While these writings can no doubt be interpreted as an attempt at post-facto justification, the overwhelming impression obtained from reading them is to the contrary. Indeed, if Eden's intention is to clear his own name he fails, appearing bitter, obsessive, and irrational. This being the case we have fairly strong evidence here that Eden actually meant what he said.

CHAPTER 4

1. Local standards, as we will see, also provided a resource for the classification for Kuwait as worth saving during the Gulf crisis itself.

2. The ability of culture to inflate and distort objective conditions is nicely demonstrated by the gross over-estimation of Iraq's military capabilities. Of all the media I looked at printed during the Desert Shield phase of the crisis (before the disparity of American and Iraqi strength became apparent in the empirical test) only *Soldier of Fortune* (November 1990) seems to have realistically assessed the comparative merits of the forces of the two sides. *Soldier of Fortune* also provided a remarkably accurate forecast of the strategy and costs of the war.

3. For a more extensive discussion of the repair of the dominant U.S. narrative during the Gulf war see P. Smith 1997.

4. The similarity of this statement with those of the British during Suez is remarkable— although it becomes less so once we understand how genre politics works.

5. The truth value of this statement becomes problematic when we consider that around 100,000 Iraqis died in one of the most one-sided wars in history. This disparity between reality and representation highlights the totalizing power of narrative.

6. In their studies of the Tiv economy of Nigeria the Bohannans discovered a hierarchy between two classes of goods. Slaves, gold, and horses were exchangeable for each other, but not for lesser commodities such as maize or pots. Generalizing from this argument we see that media of exchange between subsystems are not always as exchangeable as functionalists imagine, for cultural codes constrain such activity. Consider for example the words of the well-known Beatles song expressing how money could not buy love.

7. For extra data, see also the statistics presented in the discussion of the war's legitimacy in France, p. 140.

REFERENCES

MEDIA SOURCES

UNITED STATES

American Conservative, American Enterprise, Chicago Tribune, Congressional Record, Dissent, Harpers, International Herald Tribune, Los Angeles Times, The Nation, The New Republic, Newsweek, New York Times, New Yorker, Policy Review, Time, Soldier of Fortune, U.S. News and World Report, Vanity Fair, Washington Post.

BRITAIN

Daily Telegraph, Economist, Guardian/Manchester Guardian, Hansard, The Independent, The Listener, Manchester Guardian, Observer, Spectator, Sunday Times, Times.

FRANCE

La Croix, L'Express, Le Figaro, Le Monde, Le Monde Diplomatique, Liberation, Paris-Match, Point, Nouvelle Observateur.

SPAIN

ABC, Cambio 16, El Independiente, Leviathan, El Mundo, El País, El Sol, La Vanguardia Española.

OTHER REFERENCES

Abbott, Andrew. 2001. *Time Matters*. Chicago: University of Chicago Press.

Albright, Madeleine. 2003. *Madame Secretary*. New York: Miramax Books.

Alexander, Jeffrey. 1988. *Action and Its Environments*. New York: Columbia University Press.

———. 1992. "Citizen and Enemy as Symbolic Classification." In *Cultivating Differences*, ed. Michele Lamont and Marcel Fournier, 289–308. Chicago: University of Chicago Press.

————. 2004a. "From the Depths of Despair: Performance, Counterperformance and September 11." *Sociological Theory* 22, no. 1: 88–105.

————. 2004b. "Social Pragmatics." *Sociological Theory* 22, no. 4: 527–73.

Alexander, Jeffrey, and Philip Smith. 1993. "The Discourse of American Civil Society: A New Proposal for Cultural Studies." *Theory and Society* 22, no. 2: 151–207.

————. 1999. "Cultural Structures, Social Action and the Discourses of American Civil Society." *Theory and Society* 28, no. 3: 455–61.

————. 2001. "The Strong Program in Cultural Theory: Elements of a Structural Hermeneutics." In *Handbook of Sociological Theory*, ed. Jonathan Turner, 135–50. New York: Kluwer Academic/Plenum Publishers.

Amsel, Georges, Jean-Pierre Pharabod, and Raymond Sene. 1981. "Osirak et la proliferation des armes atomiques." *Les Temps Modernes* 422: 375–424.

Andreski, Stanislav. 1971. "Evolution and War." *Science Journal* January: 89–92.

Apter, David. 1967. *The Politics of Modernization*. Chicago: University of Chicago Press.

Aristotle. 1987. *Poetics*. Indianapolis: Hackett Publishing Company.

Atkinson, Rick. 1993. *Crusade: The Untold Story of the Persian Gulf War*. Boston: Houghton Mifflin.

Aubrey, Crispin. 1982. *Nukespeak: The Media and the Bomb*. London: Comedia.

Axelrod, Robert, and Robert O. Keohane. 1985. "Achieving Cooperation under Anarchy: Strategies and Institutions." *World Politics* 38: 226–54.

Bailyn, Bernard. 1967. *The Ideological Origins of the American Revolution*. Cambridge, MA: Belknap Press.

Bakhtin, Mikhail. 1981. *The Dialogic Imagination*. Austin: University of Texas Press.

Barthes, Roland. 1970. *Mythologies*. Paris: Editions du Seuil.

————. 1975. *S/Z*. London: Cape.

————. 1977. "Rhetoric of the Image." In *Image/Music/Text*. London: Fontana.

Battani, Marshall, David R. Hall, and Rosemary Powers. 1997. "Cultures' Structures: Making Meaning in the Public Sphere." *Theory and Society* 26, no. 6: 781–812.

Becker, Howard. 1982. *Art Worlds*. Berkeley: University of California Press.

Begg, Clive. 2003. "The Third Way in Action." PhD thesis, University of Queensland. Australia.

Bendix, Reinhardt. 1964. *Nation-Building and Citizenship*. Berkeley: University of California Press.

Billings, Victoria. 1986. "Culture by the Millions: Audience as Innovator." In *Media, Audience, and Social Structure*, ed. Sandra J. Ball-Rokeach and Muriel G. Cantor, 200–213. Beverly Hills, CA: Sage.

Blainey, Geoffrey. 1988. "Death Watch and Scapegoat Wars." In *The Causes of War*, 68–86. New York: Free Press.

Blake, R. 1978. "Anthony Eden." In *British Prime Ministers in the Twentieth Century*, ed. J. P. Mackintosh. London: Weidenfeld and Nicholson.

Bloch, Ruth. 1985. *Visionary Republic*. Cambridge: Cambridge University Press.

Bohannan, Paul, and Laura Bohannan. 1968. *Tiv Economy*. Evanston, IL: Northwestern University Press.

Bourdache, Colette, and Pierre Miquel. 1980. *Les années cinquante*. Paris: Fayard.

Bourdieu, Pierre. 1977. *Outline of a Theory of Practice*. Cambridge: Cambridge University Press.

Braestrup, Peter. 1989. "A Look Back at Tet 1968." In *The Vietnam Debate: A Fresh Look at the Arguments*, ed. John Norton Moore, 265–74. Lanham, MD: University Press of America.

Braithwaite, John. 1989. *Crime, Shame, and Reintegration.* Cambridge: Cambridge University Press.

Brenner, Robert. 1991. "Why Is the United States at War with Iraq?" *New Left Review* 185: 122–37.

British Government. 2002. *Iraq's Weapons of Mass Destruction.* London: The Stationery Office.

Bush, George W. 2003. *We Will Prevail.* New York: Continuum International Publishing Group.

Campbell, John. 1987. "Legitimation Meltdown." *Political Power and Social Theory* 6: 133–58.

Cantor, Muriel G., and Joel M. Cantor. 1986. "Audience Composition and Television Content: The Mass Audience Revisited." In *Media, Audience, and Social Structure,* ed. Sandra J. Ball-Rokeach and Muriel G. Cantor, 214–25. Beverly Hills, CA: Sage.

Carnegie Endowment for International Peace. 2003. *WMD in Iraq.* Washington, DC: Carnegie Endowment for International Peace.

Clarke, Richard A. 2004. *Against All Enemies.* New York: Free Press.

Clausewitz, Carl von. 1968. *On War.* New York: Barnes and Noble.

Clinton, Bill. 2004. *My Life.* New York: Alfred Knopf.

Cohen, Jean L., and Andrew Arato. 1992. *Civil Society and Political Theory.* Cambridge, MA: MIT Press.

Cohn, Norman. 1961. *The Pursuit of the Millennium.* New York: Harper.

Commission on Presidential Debates. 2004. *The 2004 Presidential Debates.* Available online at www.debates.org. Accessed December 17, 2004.

Courtier, Paul. 1983. *La Quatrième République.* Paris: Presses Universitaires de France.

De Fleur, Melvin L., and Sandra J. Ball-Rokeach. 1966. *Theories of Mass Communication.* New York: Longman.

Delli Carpini, Michael X. 1990. "US Media Coverage of the Vietnam Conflict in 1968." In *The Vietnam Era: Media and Popular Culture in the US and Vietnam,* ed. Michael Klein, 38–64. London: Pluto Press.

Denham, Robert D. 1978. *Northrop Frye and Critical Method.* University Park: Pennsylvania State University Press.

Dennis, Everette E., George Gerbner, and Yassen N. Zassoursky. 1991. *Beyond the Cold War: Soviet and American Media Images.* Newbury Park, CA: Sage.

Dilthey, Wilhelm. 1989. *Introduction to the Human Sciences.* Princeton, NJ: Princeton University Press.

Dower, John W. 1986. *War without Mercy: Race and Power in the Pacific War.* New York: Pantheon.

Doyle, William. 1999. *Inside the Oval Office.* New York: Kodansha International.

Durkheim, Émile. 1965 [1912]. *The Elementary Forms of Religious Life.* New York. Free Press.

Durkheim, Émile, and Marcel Mauss. 1963 [1903]. *Primitive Classification.* Chicago: University of Chicago Press.

Duroselle, Jean-Baptiste. 1982. "Changes in French Foreign Policy since 1945." In *France: Change and Tradition,* ed. Stanley Hoffman, 305–58. London: Gollancz.

Eckstein, Harry. 1975. "Case Study and Theory in Political Science." In *Handbook of Political Science,* ed. F. I. Greenstein and N. W. Polsby, 79–137. Reading, MA: Addison Wesley.

Eden, Anthony. 1960. *Full Circle.* London: Cassell.

Edles, Laura. 1998. *Symbol and Ritual in the New Spain.* Cambridge: Cambridge University Press.

Einstein, Albert, and Sigmund Freud. 1939. *Why War?* London: Peace Pledge Union.

Ekirch, Arthur A. 1969. *Ideologies and Utopias: The Impact of the New Deal on American Thought.* Chicago: Quadrangle Books.

Elias, Norbert. 1994. *The Civilizing Process.* Cambridge, MA: Blackwell.

Elster, Jon. 1985. *Making Sense of Marx.* Cambridge: Cambridge University Press.

Elton, Geoffrey. 1953. *The Tudor Revolution in Government.* Cambridge: Cambridge University Press.

Evans-Pritchard, E. E. 1937. *Witchcraft, Oracles and Magic among the Azande.* Oxford: Clarendon Press.

Eyerman, Ron. 2001. *Cultural Trauma: Slavery and the Formation of African American Identity.* New York: Cambridge University Press.

Ferguson, Adam. 1966 [1767]. *An Essay on the History of Civil Society.* Edinburgh: Edinburgh University Press.

Fonvieille-Alquier, François. 1976. *Plaidoyer pour la IVe République.* Paris: Editions Robert Laffont.

Foot, Michael, and Mervyn Jones. 1957. *Guilty Men, 1957: Suez and Cyprus.* London: Gollancz.

Foucault, Michel. 1975. *Discipline and Punish.* Harmondsworth, UK: Penguin.

Franklin, H. Bruce. 1990. "1968: The Vision of the Movement and the Alternative Press." In *The Vietnam Era: Media and Popular Culture in the US and Vietnam,* ed. Michael Klein, 65–81. London: Pluto Press.

Frye, Northrop. 1957. *The Anatomy of Criticism.* Princeton, NJ: Princeton University Press.

———. 1976. *The Secular Scripture.* Cambridge, MA: Harvard University Press.

Fullick, Roy, and Geoffrey Powell. 1979. *Suez: The Double War.* London: Hamish Hamilton.

Fussell, Paul. 1975. *The Great War in Modern Memory.* New York: Oxford University Press.

Gallo, Max. 1973. *Spain under Franco: A History.* London: Allen and Unwin.

Gallup Poll. 1976. *The Gallup International Opinion Polls: France 1939, 1944–1975.* New York: Random House.

Gans, Herbert, J. 1979. *Deciding What's News.* New York: Pantheon Books.

Garfinkel, Harold. 1967. *Studies in Ethnomethodology.* Englewood Cliffs, NJ: Prentice Hall.

Geertz, Clifford. 1973. *The Interpretation of Cultures.* New York: Basic Books.

Gibson, James William. 1986. *The Perfect War: Technowar in Vietnam.* Boston: Atlantic Monthly Press.

Gitlin, Todd. 1980. *The Whole World Is Watching.* Berkeley: University of California Press.

Goffman, Erving. 1963. *Behavior in Public Places.* New York: Free Press.

———. 1967. *Interaction Rituals.* New York: Anchor.

Goulding, Peter. 1977. "Media Professionalism in the Third World: The Transfer of an Ideology." In *Mass Communication and Society,* ed. James Curran, Michael Gurevitch, and Janet Woollacott. London: Edward Arnold.

Graebner, Norman. 1979. *The Age of Global Power: The United States since 1939.* New York: John Wiley.

———. 1989. "The Question of Ends and Means: American Policy in Vietnam." In *The Vietnam Debate: A Fresh Look at the Arguments,* ed. John Norton Moore, 9–21. Lanham, MD: University Press of America.

———. 1990. "Nomura in Washington." In *Pearl Harbor Reexamined,* ed. Hilary Conroy and Harry Wray, 107–18. Honolulu: University of Hawai'i Press.

Gramsci, Antonio. 1992. *Prison Notebooks: Volume 1.* New York: Columbia University Press.

Greene, John Robert. 2000. *The Presidency of George Bush.* Lawrence: University Press of Kansas.

Greimas, Algirdas. 1990. *The Social Sciences: A Semiotic View.* Minneapolis: University of Minnesota Press.

Griswold, Wendy. 1983. "The Devil's Techniques: Cultural Legitimation and Social Change." *American Sociological Review* 48: 668–80.

Grosser, Alfred. 1961. *La IVe République et sa politique extérieure.* Paris: Librairie Armand Colin.

Grugel, Jean, and Tim Rees. 1997. *Franco's Spain.* London: Arnold.

Habermas, Jürgen. 1984. *The Theory of Communicative Action.* Boston: Beacon Press.

———. 1989. *The Structural Transformation of the Public Sphere.* Cambridge, MA: MIT Press.

Hall, John R. 1999. *Cultures of Inquiry.* Cambridge: Cambridge University Press.

Hall, Stuart. 1973. "The Determinations of New Photographs." In *The Manufacture of News,* ed. Stanley Cohen and Jock Young, 176–90. London: Constable.

———. 1983. "The Great Moving Right Show." In *The Politics of Thatcherism,* ed. Stuart Hall and Martin Jaques, 19–39. London: Lawrence and Wishart.

Hanley, D. L., A. P Kerr, and N. H. Waites. 1984. *Contemporary France: Politics and Society since 1945.* London: Routledge and Kegan Paul.

Hastings, Elizabeth, and Philip Hastings. 1992. *Index to International Public Opinion, 1990–91.* Westport, CT: Greenwood Press.

Held, David. 1989. *Political Theory and the Modern State.* Stanford, CA: Stanford University Press.

Herzstein, Robert E. 1989. *Roosevelt and Hitler: Prelude to War.* New York: Paragon House.

Hirsch, E. D., Jr. 1967. *Validity in Interpretation.* New Haven, CT: Yale University Press.

———. 1976. *The Aims of Interpretation.* Chicago: University of Chicago Press.

Hirschman, Albert O. 1991. *The Rhetoric of Reaction.* Cambridge, MA: Belknap Press.

Hitchens, Christopher. 1991. "Realpolitik in the Gulf." *New Left Review* 186: 89–101.

Hollander, Paul. 1989. "Alienation and Judgments about the United States and Its Adversaries." In *The Vietnam Debate: A Fresh Look at the Arguments,* ed. John Norton Moore, 289–98. Lanham, MD: University Press of America.

Horkheimer, Max, and Theodor Adorno. 1972 [1944]. *The Dialectic of Enlightenment.* New York: Herder and Herder.

House of Commons Foreign Affairs Committee. 2003. *The Decision to Go to War in Iraq.* London: The Stationery Office.

Hunt, Lynn. 1986. *Politics, Culture, and Class in the French Revolution.* London: Methuen.

Husserl, Edmund. 1973. *The Idea of Phenomenology.* The Hague, Netherlands: M. Nijhoff.

Isoart, Paul. 1978. "Rapport: La Guerre D'Algerie." In *La Quatrième République,* ed. Paul Isoart. Paris: Librairie Generale de Droit et de Jurisprudence.

Jacobs, Ronald. 2000. *Race, Media, and the Crisis of Civil Society.* Cambridge: Cambridge University Press.

Jacobs, Ronald, and Philip Smith. 1996. "Romance, Irony, and Solidarity." *Sociological Theory* 15, no. 1: 60–80.

James, Robert Rhodes. 1986. *Anthony Eden.* London: Weidenfeld and Nicolson.

James, William. 1910. *The Moral Equivalent of War.* New York: American Association for International Conciliation.

Jameson, Fredric. 1981. *The Political Unconscious.* Ithaca, NY: Cornell University Press.

Johnson, Lyndon B. 1965. "Speech at Johns Hopkins University, April 7, 1965." In *Public Papers of the Presidents of the United States: Lyndon B. Johnson,* 394–97.

Kane, Anne. 1991. "Cultural Analysis in Historical Sociology: The Analytical and Concrete Forms of the Autonomy of Culture." *Sociological Theory* 9, no. 1: 53–69.

Kant, Immanuel. 1965. *Critique of Pure Reason.* New York: St. Martin's Press.

Keane, John. 1988. *Civil Society and the State: New European Perspectives.* London: Verso.

Keohane, Robert O. 1984. *After Hegemony.* Princeton, NJ: Princeton University Press.

Kerry, John. 1985 [1971]. "Vietnam Veterans against the War: Testimony to the U.S. Senate Foreign Relations Committee, April 22, 1971." In *Vietnam and America: A Documented History,* ed. Marvin E. Gettleman, Jane Franklin, Marilyn Young, and H. Bruce Franklin, 451–58. New York: Grove Press.

King, Martin Luther, Jr. 1985 [1967]. "Declaration of Independence from the War in Vietnam." In *Vietnam and America: A Documented History,* ed. Marvin E. Gettleman, Jane Franklin, Marilyn Young, and H. Bruce Franklin, 306–16. New York: Grove Press.

Ku, Agnes. 1999. *Narratives, Politics, and the Public Sphere: Struggles over Political Reform in the Final Transitional Years in Hong Kong (1992–1994).* Aldershot, UK: Ashgate.

Kuhn, Thomas S. 1962. *The Structure of Scientific Revolutions.* Chicago: University of Chicago Press.

La Gorce, Paul Marie de. 1979. *Apogée et mort de la IVe République.* Paris: Bernard Grasset.

Lazarsfeld, Paul, B. Berelson, and H. Gaudet. 1944. *The People's Choice.* New York: Columbia University Press.

Leach, Edmund. 1969. *Genesis as Myth and Other Essays.* London: Cape.

Lévi-Strauss, Claude. 1964. *Mythologiques.* Paris: Plon.

———. 1968. *The Savage Mind.* Chicago: University of Chicago Press.

———. 1969. *The Elementary Structures of Kinship.* Boston: Beacon Press.

Lincoln, Bruce. 2002. *Holy Terrors: Thinking about Religion after September 11.* Chicago: University of Chicago Press.

Lippmann, Walter. 1934. *Public Opinion.* New York: Macmillan.

Lipset, Seymour. 1963. *The First New Nation.* New York: Basic Books.

Luhmann, Niklas. 1982. *The Differentiation of Society.* New York: Columbia University Press.

Lyons, Michael. 1994. *World War I: A Short History.* Englewood Cliffs, NJ: Prentice Hall.

Malinowski, Bronislaw. 1964. "An Anthropological Analysis of War." In *War: Studies from Psychology, Sociology, and Anthropology,* ed. Leon Bramson and George W. Goethals, 245–68. New York: Basic Books.

Mann, Michael. 1986. *The Sources of Social Power.* Cambridge: Cambridge University Press.

———. 1987. "The Roots and Contradictions of Modern Militarism." *New Left Review* 162: 35–50.

———. 1988. *States, War, and Capitalism.* Oxford: Basil Blackwell.

Mannheim, Karl. 1972. *Ideology and Utopia.* London: Routledge and Kegan Paul.

Marcuse, Herbert. 1964. *One Dimensional Man.* Boston: Beacon Press.

Marwick, Arthur. 1965. *The Deluge: British Society and the First World War.* London: Macmillan.

Marx, Karl, and Friedrich Engels. 1970. *The German Ideology.* New York: International Publishers.

McCormack, Thelma. 1986. "Reflections on the Lost Vision of Communication Theory." In *Media, Audience, and Social Structure,* ed. Sandra J. Ball-Rokeach and Muriel G. Cantor, 34–42. Beverly Hills, CA: Sage.

McGrath, Jim, ed. 2001. *Heartbeat: George Bush in His Own Words.* New York: Scribner.

McQuail, Denis. 1985. "Sociology of Mass Communication." *Annual Review of Sociology* 11: 93–111.

Mead, Margaret. 1964. "Warfare Is Only an Invention—Not a Biological Necessity." In *War:*

Studies from Psychology, Sociology, Anthropology, ed. Leon Bramson and George W. Goethals, 269–74. New York: Basic Books.

Medhurst, Martin J. 1990. *Cold War Rhetoric: Strategy, Metaphor, and Ideology.* New York: Greenwood Press.

Melville, Herman. 1948. *Billy Budd.* Cambridge, MA: Harvard University Press.

Mendès-France, Pierre. 1987. *Oeuvres complètes, vol. 4, "Pour une république moderne, 1955–1962."* Paris: Gallimard.

Mill, John Stuart. 1967 [1843]. *A System of Logic.* Toronto: University of Toronto Press.

Mills, C. Wright. 1978. "Situated Actions and Vocabularies of Motives." In *Symbolic Interaction,* ed. Jerome G. Manis and Bernard N. Meltzer, 301–8. Boston: Allyn and Bacon.

Morgenthau, Hans. 1985. *Politics among Nations: The Struggle for Power and Peace.* New York: Knopf.

Musil, Robert. 1953. *The Man without Qualities.* London: Secker and Warburg.

Namier, Lewis B. 1930. *England in the Age of the American Revolution.* London: Macmillan.

Needham, Rodney. 1962. *Structure and Sentiment.* Chicago: University of Chicago Press.

Negrine, Ralph. 1989. *Politics and the Mass Media in Britain.* London: Routledge.

Newcomb, Horace M., and Paul M. Hirsch. 1984. "Television as a Cultural Forum." In *Interpreting Television,* ed. Willard Roland and Bruce Watkins. Beverly Hills, CA: Sage.

Nixon, Richard. 1985a [1970]. "Rationale for the Invasion of Cambodia." In *Vietnam and America: A Documented History,* ed. Marvin E. Gettleman, Jane Franklin, Marilyn Young, and H. Bruce Franklin, 447–51. New York: Grove Press.

———. 1985b [1969]. "Vietnamization." In *Vietnam and America: A Documented History,* ed. Marvin E. Gettleman, Jane Franklin, Marilyn Young, and H. Bruce Franklin, 428–41. New York: Grove Press.

Noelle-Neumann, Elisabeth. 1973. "Return to the Concept of Powerful Mass Media." *Studies of Broadcasting* 9: 67–112.

Offe, Klaus. 1984. *Contradictions of the Welfare State.* London: Hutchinson.

Palmer, Bruce, Jr. 1984. *The 25-Year War: America's Military Role in Vietnam.* Lexington: University Press of Kentucky.

Parsons, Talcott. 1964. *The Social System.* New York: Free Press.

———. 1968. *The Structure of Social Action.* New York: Free Press.

Payne, Stanley G. 1967. *Franco's Spain.* New York: Crowell.

Podhoretz, Norman. 1989. "Questions and Errors of Fact: The Myths and Realities of Vietnam." In *The Vietnam Debate: A Fresh Look at the Arguments,* ed. John Norton Moore, 23–29. Lanham, MD: University Press of America.

Pollack, Kenneth. 2002. *The Threatening Storm: The Case for Invading Iraq.* New York: Random House.

Powell, Colin. 1995. *My American Journey.* New York: Random House.

Preston, Paul. 1993. *Franco: A Biography.* New York: HarperCollins.

Propp, Vladimir. 1968. *Morphology of the Folktale.* Austin: University of Texas Press.

Przeworski, Adam. 1985. *Capitalism and Social Democracy.* Cambridge: Cambridge University Press.

Ragin, Charles. 1987. *The Comparative Method.* Berkeley: University of California Press.

Rambo, Eric, and Elaine Chan. 1990. "Text, Structure, and Action in Cultural Sociology." *Theory and Society* 19: 635–48.

Reissman, Catherine Kohler. 1993. *Narrative Analysis.* Newbury Park, CA: Sage.

Ricoeur, Paul. 1967. *The Symbolism of Evil.* New York: Harper and Row.

———. 1970. *Freedom and Nature.* Evanston, IL: Northwestern University Press.

———. 1981. *Hermeneutics and the Human Sciences: Essays on Language, Action, and Interpretation.* New York: Cambridge University Press.

———. 1984. "Myth as the Bearer of Possible Worlds." In *Dialogues with Contemporary Continental Thinkers,* ed. Richard Kearney. Manchester: Manchester University Press.

Rioux, Jean-Pierre. 1983. *La France de la IVe République, vol. 2, L'expansion et l'impuissance.* Paris: Editions du Seuil.

Roosevelt, Franklin D. 1950. *Public Papers and Addresses of Franklin D. Roosevelt: Volume 10.* New York: Russell and Russell.

Rouse, A. L. 1961. *Appeasement: A Study in Political Decline, 1933–1939.* New York: Norton.

Runciman, W. G. 1983. *A Treatise on Social Theory.* Cambridge: Cambridge University Press.

Sahlins, Marshall. 1976. *Culture and Practical Reason.* Chicago: University of Chicago Press.

Said, Edward. 1979. *Orientalism.* New York: Vintage Books.

Salmon, Trevor. 1992. "The Nature of International Security." In *International Security in the Modern World,* ed. Roger Carey and Trevor C. Salmon, 1–19. New York: St Martin's Press.

Saussure, Ferdinand de. 1960. *Cours de linguistique générale.* Paris: Payot.

Schulzinger, Robert. 1990. *American Diplomacy in the Twentieth Century.* Oxford: Oxford University Press.

Schumpeter, Joseph A. 1950. *Capitalism, Socialism, and Democracy.* New York: Harper and Row.

Scott, Marvin B., and Stanford M. Lyman. 1968. "Accounts." *American Sociological Review* 33, no. 1: 46–61.

Shaw, Martin. 1991. *Post-Military Society.* Oxford: Polity Press.

———. 1984. *War, the State, and Society.* London: Macmillan.

Shawcross, William. 2003. *Allies: The U.S., Britain, Europe and the War in Iraq.* New York: Public Affairs.

Sherwood, Steven Jay. 1994. "Narrating the Social." *Journal of Narrative and Life History* 4, no. 1–2: 69–88.

Shils, Edward. 1975. *Center and Periphery: Essays in Macrosociology.* Chicago: University of Chicago Press.

Skidelsky, Robert. 1970. "Lessons of Suez." In *The Age of Affluence,* ed. Vernon Bogdanor and Robert Skidelsky. London: Macmillan.

Skinner, Quentin. 1988. *Meaning and Moral Order.* Oxford: Polity Press.

Skocpol, Theda. 1979. *The State and Social Revolutions.* Cambridge: Cambridge University Press.

———. 1985. "Cultural Idioms and Political Ideologies in the Revolutionary Reconstruction of State Power: A Rejoinder to Sewell." *Journal of Modern History* 57, no. 1: 86–96.

Skocpol, Theda, and Margaret Somers. 1980. "The Uses of Comparative History in Macrosocial Inquiry." *Comparative Studies in Society and History* 22: 174–97.

Slotkin, Richard. 1973. *Regeneration through Violence.* Middletown, CT: Wesleyan University Press.

———. 2001. "Our Myths of Choice." *Chronicle of Higher Education,* September 28, 2001.

Smelser, Neil. 1976. *Comparative Methods in the Social Sciences.* Englewood Cliffs, NJ: Prentice Hall.

Smith, Adam. 1976 [1759]. *The Theory of Moral Sentiments.* Oxford: Oxford University Press.

Smith, Dorothy. 1978. "K Is Mentally Ill." *Sociology* 12: 23–53.

Smith, Philip. 1991. "Codes and Conflict: Towards a Theory of War as Ritual." *Theory and Society* 21: 103–38.

———. 1994. "The Semiotic Foundations of Media Narratives: Saddam and Nasser in the American Mass Media." *Journal of Narrative and Life History* 4, no. 1–2: 89–118.

———. 1997. "Civil Society and Violence." In *The Web of Violence*, ed. Jennifer Turpin and Lester Kurtz, 91–116. Urbana: University of Illinois Press.

———. 1998. "Barbarism and Civility in the Discourses of Fascism, Communism, and Democracy: Variations on a Set of Themes." In *Real Civil Societies*, ed. Jeffrey Alexander, 115–37. London: Sage.

———. 2000. "Culture and Charisma: Outline of a Theory." *Acta Sociologica* 43, no. 2: 101–11.

———. 2004. "Marcel Proust and Successor and Precursor to Pierre Bourdieu: A Fragment." *Thesis Eleven* 79: 112–23.

Somers, Margaret R. 1992. "Narrativity, Narrative Identity, and Social Action: Rethinking English Working-Class Formation." *Social Science History* 16, no 4: 591–630.

Souriau, Etienne. 1950. *Les deux cent mille situations dramatiques*. Paris: Flammarion.

Spanier, John. 1977. *American Foreign Policy since World War II*. New York: Praeger.

Speier, Hans. 1980. "The Rise of Public Opinion." In *Propaganda and Communication in World History, vol. 2, The Emergence of Public Opinion in the West*, ed. Harold Lasswell, Daniel Lerner, Hans Speier, 147–67. Honolulu: Published for the East-West Center by the University Press of Hawaii.

Stephens, Robert H. 1971. *Nasser: A Political Biography*. London: Penguin Press.

Stinchcombe, Arthur. 1978. *Theoretical Methods in Social History*. New York: Academic Press.

Stoessinger, John. 1979. *Crusaders and Pragmatists: Movers of Modern American Foreign Policy*. New York: Norton.

Storey, John. 1990. "Bringing It All Back Home: American Popular Song and the War in Vietnam." In *The Vietnam Era: Media and Popular Culture in the US and Vietnam*, ed. Michael Klein, 82–106. London: Pluto Press.

Storr, Anthony. 1968. *Human Aggression*. Harmondsworth, UK: Penguin.

Swidler, Ann. 1986. "Culture in Action: Symbols and Strategies." *American Sociological Review* 51, no. 3: 273–86.

Tiger, Lionel. 1984. *Men in Groups*. New York: Marion Moyars.

Tiryakian, Edward. 2005. "Durkheim, Solidarity, and September 11." In *The Cambridge Companion to Durkheim*, ed. Jeffrey Alexander and Philip Smith, 305–21. Cambridge: Cambridge University Press.

Trythall, John W. D. 1970. *Franco: A Biography*. London: Hart-Davis.

Turner, Jonathan. 1989. "Introduction: Can Sociology Be a Cumulative Science?" In *Theory Building in Sociology*, ed. Jonathan Turner, 8–18. Newbury Park, CA: Sage.

Turner, Victor. 1969. *The Ritual Process*. London: Routledge and Kegan Paul.

Utley, Jonathan. 1990. "Cordell Hull and the Diplomacy of Inflexibility." In *Pearl Harbor Reexamined*, ed. Hilary Conroy and Harry Wray, 75–84. Honolulu: University of Hawai'i Press.

Wagner-Pacifici, Robin. 1986. *The Moro Morality Play*. Chicago: Chicago University Press.

Waltz, Kenneth. 1979. *Theory of International Politics*. Reading, MA: Addison Wesley.

Walzer, Michael. 1985. *Exodus and Revolution*. New York: Basic Books.

———. 1991. "The Idea of Civil Society." *Dissent* Spring: 293–304.

Warburg, James. 1966. *The United States in the Postwar World*. New York: Atheneum.

Weber, Max. 1991. *From Max Weber*, ed. H. H. Gerth and C. Wright Mills. New York: Routledge.

————. 1978. *Economy and Society.* Berkeley: University of California Press.

Wendt, Alexander. 1992. "Anarchy Is What States Make of It: The Social Construction of Power Politics." *International Organization* 46, no. 2: 391–425.

————. 1999. *Social Theory of International Politics.* Cambridge: Cambridge University Press.

White, Hayden V. 1987. *The Content of the Form.* Baltimore: Johns Hopkins University Press.

Wilford, Timothy. 2001. *Pearl Harbor Redefined.* Lanham, MD: University Press of America.

Winoch, Michel. 1978. *La République se meurt: Chronique 1956–1958.* Paris: Editions du Seuil.

Woodward, Bob. 1991. *The Commanders.* New York: Simon and Schuster.

————. 2003. *Bush at War.* New York: Simon and Schuster.

Wray, Harry. 1990. "Japanese-American Relations and Perceptions, 1900–1940." In *Pearl Harbor Reexamined,* ed. Hilary Conroy and Harry Wray, 1–15, Honolulu: University of Hawai'i Press.

Wright, Edmond. 1990. "New Representationalism." *Journal for the Theory of Social Behavior* 20, no. 1: 65–92.

————. 1999. "The Game of Reference." *Acta Analytica* 14, no. 22: 179–96.

Wright, Quincy. 1942. *A Study of War.* Chicago: University of Chicago Press.

Yoder, Amos. 1986. *The Conduct of American Foreign Policy since World War II.* New York: Pergamon Press.

INDEX